QUE DES BONS LÉGUMES!
WHAT LOVELY VEGETABLES!

MEUHH, BÊÊHH, GROINK,
MOO, BAA, OINK

PO

FRENCH FEASTS

For the four I love: Isa, Jean, Zoé, Basile.

A big thank you to Marie-Pierre who survived a horde of surfers and an invasion
of gremlins to take all of the photos… Hey, I'm still missing a *knak*…
A big thank you to José who survived gallons of red and mountains of food
to draw, munch, scribble and, above all, get me "cooking"… A godsend for a cook…
Thanks to my spiritual guide Jacky Dulou and also to his brothers: Jacky Cotivet in Lyon,
Jacky Itxaqiss in the Basque Country, Jacky Lamazou in Brittany, Jacky Hans in Alsace,
Jacky Marsouille in Provence… Hmm, they've all got something in common!
Thanks to *M'sieur Pignon* for his tripely presence.
Thanks to GG for his scallops, that's cunning for a journalist.
Thanks to all of you who posed without smiling… Photos are a serious business!
Thanks to Emmanuel and Amaryllis for their patience,
allô, it's Madame Ciminninininni… on the line.

First published by Marabout (Hachette Livre) 2007
Published in 2008 by Murdoch Books PTY LIMITED
Published in 2009 by Stewart, Tabori & Chang
An imprint of ABRAMS

Text copyright © 2009 by Stéphane Reynaud
Photographs copyright © 2009 by Marie-Pierre Morel
Illustrations copyright © 2009 by José Reis de Matos

Library of Congress Cataloging-in-Publication Data

Reynaud, Stéphane.
  French feasts : 299 traditional recipes for family meals and gatherings /
Stéphane Reynaud.
    p. cm.
  Includes indexes.
  ISBN 978-1-58479-794-4
  1. Cookery, French. I. Title.
  TX719.R437 2009
  641.5944—dc22

                              2008052599

The text of this book was composed in Batarde Coulée, Bodoni SeventyTwo, Eraser Dust,
Gill Sans Std, ITC Garamond Std, Judy Finckel, and P22 Garamouche.

Printed and bound in China
10 9 8 7 6 5 4 3 2 1

ABRAMS
THE ART OF BOOKS SINCE 1949

115 West 18th Street
New York, NY 10011
www.abramsbooks.com

STÉPHANE REYNAUD

FRENCH FEASTS

299 Traditional Recipes for Family Meals & Gatherings

PHOTOGRAPHS BY MARIE-PIERRE MOREL
ILLUSTRATIONS BY JOSÉ REIS DE MATOS

Stewart, Tabori & Chang | New York

SOMMAIRE/CONTENTS

le poids de la ripaille
M'sieur Reymond

78866

au sa villa 93   Montreuil

I remember the Sundays of my childhood (just one a week was never enough), when, once everyone was seated around the table, we seemed to put down roots so that the moment became frozen in time. Everything came to a stop; benevolence reigned. We needed solid constitutions to withstand the advancing tide of entrées, brave the bounty of meats with all the trimmings, find a residue of appetite when faced with the groaning cheese board, and finally close our meal with creams and cakes. The meals lingered on for hours—there was a lot to be eaten! "You'll have some more gratin, won't you, *mon p'tit?* You're shooting up, at your age you need to eat," my grandmother would say to me, wrapped in her flowered apron, after having already served me two helpings.

There was something noble about eating; it was a true privilege of the strong of body. To be well-built you need a good appetite; and appetite, believe me, was something everyone had. The smell of strong coffee hung in the air and escargot-scented burps rang out the feast's end. We were blissfully content, slumped over the table that looked like a victorious battlefield, our bellies filled with memories of good food. With the benefit of hindsight I suspect that was also due to the effect of the *eaux-de-vie* (spirits) taken at the end of the meal: the product of many fruits distilled by a family friend, they encouraged a mood of congeniality and a shared lethargy.

Songs punctuated the day, old classics at the beginning of the meal, turning X-rated once the *Vieille Prune* (a plum brandy) got the upper hand. In short, the Sunday meal had a perpetually festive air, and the reddened faces bore witness to it. The late-afternoon walk, a gentle excuse to digest, allowed the 6 o'clock champagne to chill in peace. We kids got sponge cake to dunk in flutes filled to the brim. A Sunday that begins well must end well. Out come the *boules,* the crowd is reassembled, hunting and fishing memories turn into epic tales, football matches into World Cup finals. It's a *ripaille*—a rip-roaring French feast—and it's good. It's late, the leftovers are gone, the bottle's dregs have dried up, the yawns are contagious, the time has come to say goodbye. *Bring on next Sunday!*

La Charcuterie
de **COLETTE SIBILIA**
COLETTE SIBILIA's Charcuterie

La ferme au gras
de **BERNADETTE**
BERNADETTE'S Duck Farm

LE JAMBON CRU

LE BEAUJOLAIS

Faire ses conserves
à la maison
Make your own preserves

CHARCUTERIE,
tout est permis!

Anything goes!

Canard gras en kit
The fattened duck kit

FOIE GRAS MI-CUIT
EN CONSERVE AU NATUREL
Preserved semi-cooked foie gras

La charcuterie de Colette Sibilia

Colette Sibilia is the living memory of all that charcuterie from Lyon can offer our fickle palates. Queen of the *cervelas* (a Lyonnais pork sausage), champion of the *graton* (chitterling), expert in the *sabodet* (pig's head sausage), Colette tends to sausage meat like others tend their roses, allowing her sausages to acquire a natural bloom.

As a worthy representative of the history of all things porcine, Colette has passed on her passion for porky products to a whole generation of gourmands. She has been able to elevate this excellent animal to the rank of international star, so that it shines under the floodlights of all self-respecting kitchens.

LEFT
rabbit pâté
with rosemary

RIGHT
chicken liver
parfait

pâté de lapin au romarin

RABBIT PÂTÉ WITH ROSEMARY
FOR 1 GOOD-SIZED TERRINE - PREPARATION TIME: 45 MINUTES
COOKING TIME: 1 HOUR + 48 HOURS RESTING TIME

Rabbit ....1 pound 5 ounce
Chicken livers ....7 ounces
Pork loin ....7 ounces
Heavy cream ....¾ cup
Eggs 2
Soft white sandwich bread ....1 slice
Shallots 2
Rosemary ....2 sprigs
White port ....2½ tablespoons
White wine ....½ cup
Grated fresh ginger ....1 teaspoon
Quatre-épices (spice mix) ....1 teaspoon
Salt, pepper

1. Debone the rabbit, and dice the chicken livers and the pork loin. Marinate for 12 hours in the port, wine, diced shallots, and one sprig of rosemary. Add the spices (*quatre-épices*, a blend of ground pepper, cloves, nutmeg, ginger or cinnamon).
2. Soak the bread in the cream. Chop up the bread and add the eggs, then the chopped marinated meats. Mix together and season with salt and pepper. Place in a terrine dish with the other sprig of rosemary on top.
3. Cook in a water bath in a 350°F oven for 1 hour. Chill for 48 hours before serving.

WINE: CONDRIEUX

parfait de foies de volaille

CHICKEN LIVER PARFAIT
FOR FOUR 7-OUNCE PARFAITS - PREPARATION TIME: 30 MINUTES
COOKING TIME: 15 MINUTES

Chicken livers .... 1 pound 2 ounces
Bacon ....3½-ounce slab
Onion 1
Garlic .... 2 cloves
Juniper berries 5
Ground cinnamon ....1 pinch
Butter ....7 ounces
Walnut oil .... 1 tablespoon
Piment d'Espelette (hot paprika) ....1 pinch
Port ....⅓ to ½ cup
Salt

1. Fry the onion and garlic in the walnut oil until golden. Add the chicken livers, along with the chopped bacon and juniper berries. Sear the livers and remove from the pan.
2. Deglaze the pan with the port, scraping up all the bits on the bottom, and cook until syrupy. Return the livers to the pan and mix well.
3. Process the mixture with three-quarters of the butter, then add the cinnamon and season with salt.

4. Mold the parfait into small terrine dishes. Melt the remaining butter, drizzle it over the parfaits, then sprinkle with the *piment d'Espelette* (hot paprika). Chill well. Eat within 4 days.

WINE: WHITE PORT

galantine de volaille

CHICKEN GALANTINE
FOR 1 GALANTINE - PREPARATION TIME: 60 MINUTES
COOKING TIME: 2 HOURS + 1 HOUR 30 MINUTES +
24 HOURS RESTING TIME

Bresse chicken (or the best-quality chicken you can get) 1
Veal meat ....7 ounces
Pork loin ....7 ounces
Ham ....3½ ounces
Bacon ....3½-ounce slab
Sheets of pork fat (bards) 3
Cognac ....2½ tablespoons
Eggs 3
Heavy cream ....⅓ to ½ cup
Pistachio nuts (shelled) ....⅓ cup
Shallots 2
Paprika ....1 pinch
Carrots 3
Leek 1
Onion studded with cloves 1
Bouquet garni 1
Salt, pepper

1. Have the butcher bone and flatten the chicken. Reserve the carcass, and remove and set aside the thigh meat.
2. Simmer the carcass with the carrots, onion, leek, and bouquet garni in a large volume of water for 2 hours.
3. Cut the ham into strips, then sauté with shallots and flambé with the cognac.
4. Finely chop the veal, chicken thigh, bacon, and pork loin. Combine with the eggs, cream, pistachio nuts, paprika, along with the sautéed ham and shallot mixture and season.
5. Place sheets of pork fat side by side on a piece of plastic wrap. Lay the boned chicken on top, flesh side up, and cover with the meat mixture. Wrap the chicken tightly in the pork fat—this is called "barding". The *galantine*, pâté wrapped in chicken, must be hermetically sealed in the plastic wrap.
6. Remove the chicken carcasses and condiments, and strain the stock. Roll up the chicken galantine in a cloth and tie with string. Poach in the stock for 1 hour 30 minutes.
7. Carefully remove the cloth and the plastic wrap, then shape the galantine into a terrine dish, pressing down to draw out the liquid. Chill for 24 hours before eating.

WINE: MEURSAULT

LEFT
pork
rillettes

RIGHT
game
terrine

16

rillettes de cochon

PORK RILLETTES
FOR SIX 7-OUNCE POTS - PREPARATION TIME: 20 MINUTES
COOKING TIME: 5 HOURS + 48 HOURS RESTING TIME

Pork loin	1 pound 2 ounces
Pork hock or shank	1
Bacon	3½-ounce slab
Pork belly	3½ ounces
Thyme	3 sprigs
Onions	2
Lard	2⅓ cups
White wine	4 cups

Salt, pepper

1. Chop all of the meat into 1-inch cubes.
2. Melt 2 cups of the lard over low heat. Add the chopped onions, all the meat, and thyme leaves. Cook, covered, very gently for 5 to 6 hours, adding the wine at regular intervals and stirring frequently; the longer and more gently the mixture is cooked, the better the pork spread will be. Season once the meat has cooked down and the mixture has a uniform texture.
3. Spoon into six small pots, pressing down well, and cover with remaining rendered lard. Chill for 48 hours before serving.

WINE: MORGON

terrine de gibier

GAME TERRINE
FOR 1 GOOD-SIZED TERRINE - PREPARATION: 30 MINUTES
COOKING TIME: 1 HOUR 30 MINUTES + 24 HOURS MARINATING
TIME + 4 TO 5 DAYS RESTING TIME

Game meat	1 pound 2 ounces
Bacon	7-ounce slab
Pork loin	14 ounces
Pork belly	5½ ounces
Chicken livers	5½ ounces
Red wine	1 cup
Onions	2
Shallots	2
Garlic	3 cloves
Carrots	2
Quatre-épices	1 teaspoon
Paprika	1 teaspoon
Juniper berries	1 teaspoon
Bay leaves	3

Salt, pepper

1. Chop the game meat and bacon into small cubes. Let the meat marinate for 24 hours in the wine, along with the chopped carrots, thinly sliced onions, spices, and crushed juniper.
2. The next day, chop the rest of the meats with the garlic and shallots. Combine all ingredients and season.
3. Mold the mixture into a terrine dish and arrange the bay leaves on top. Cook in a water bath in a 350°F oven for 1 hour 30 minutes. Chill for 4 to 5 days before serving.

WINE: PINOT NOIR D'ALSACE

terrine de campagne

COUNTRY TERRINE
FOR A 2 LB. 4 OZ. TERRINE - PREPARATION TIME: 30 MINUTES
COOKING TIME: 1 HOUR 30 MINUTES + 24 HOURS MARINATING
TIME + SEVERAL DAYS RESTING TIME

Pork loin	10½ ounces
Pork liver	7 ounces
Pork fat	1
Pork fatback	7 ounces
Smoked bacon	3½-ounce slab
Garlic	6 cloves
Shallots	3
Rum	2½ tablespoons
Red wine	¾ cup
Coarsely ground black pepper	1 teaspoon
Quatre-épices	1 teaspoon
Parsley	1 bunch
Eggs	3
Heavy cream	⅔ cup

Salt, pepper

1. Chop up the pork loin, pork liver, pork fat back, bacon, garlic, and shallots. Place in a bowl and add the minced parsley, rum, wine, and spices. Season, cover with plastic wrap, and chill for 24 hours.
2. Slice the sheets of pork fat into very long strips. Lay them in a lattice pattern at the base of a terrine, letting the strips overhang its sides. Whisk the eggs with the cream, and then combine with the meat mixture. Pile into a terrine, and cover with overlapping strips of pork fat. Cook in a water bath in a 350°F oven for 1 hour 30 minutes.
3. Chill for several days before eating; the flavor of the terrine improves as it matures.

WINE: BROUILLY

La ferme au gras de Bernadette

The southwest is a corner of France abundant in happiness. What luck to come from a part of the country where it's a good thing to be a duck. This animal is king here. No more large animals with manes. Hurray for the feathered beast! It's a far cry from the abandoned ugly duckling that gets mocked with such enthusiasm. Today the duck is proud of its status, head held high like a lighthouse in the middle of a storm, feet a shade of orange that would make any lover of the '70s jealous, feathers shining like a disco ball.

The duck nevertheless retains that awkward quality, with its bottom in the air when setting out on an impromptu stroll, hopping from foot to foot. But that's just another reason why we love him. He's an animal as comfortable in the water as in the air—just try and compete with him as a swimmer! Not to mention fly beside him! He'll have the last laugh.

We call duck "fattened" (*gras*) when it is force-fed with corn and its liver becomes enlarged and loaded with reserves as if preparing for a long voyage without stopovers. It has the pig as a distant cousin; everything in the duck is good. From the neck down to the feet, from the liver to the gizzard, it knows how to make itself appreciated in its entirety. Still, a duck's peaceful farm life and daily feasting comes at a cost: it ends up on our plates!

With a gentle touch, Bernadette transforms the animal into *magrets* (breasts) and terrines, *cou farci* (stuffed duck neck) and foie gras. She puts as much passion into raising her ducks—with an incredible respect for their environment—as she does into cooking them. Every part of the duck has its own recipe, every recipe has its own pleasures, and God knows that's a good thing.

OIE OU CANARD, IL FAUT CHOISIR !

GOOSE OR DUCK, YOU HAVE TO CHOOSE!

PLEASURE OR PLEASURE?

This is a dilemma that is relatively easy to resolve. But believe me, whether you choose goose or duck, the answer doesn't matter much since you have already decided to indulge your appetite.

Foie gras dates back to ancient Egypt when it came from the geese of the Nile. The gourmands of the time noticed that halfway through the goose migration season the livers of the geese were abnormally large, filled with the energy reserves required for their long journey. The gustatory curiosity of the Egyptians gave rise to the first consumption of foie gras and, consequently, the first force-feeding (*gavages*).

Goose foie gras is often considered by purists to be the more delicate variety of the two, with a more subtle finesse in the mouth. Duck foie gras, for its part, has a more pronounced and rustic flavor.

WHOLE? *EN BLOC*? MOUSSE? PÂTÉ?

Be aware when buying foie gras that you need to distinguish between *foie gras entier* (whole foie gras), made up of one or two lobes from the same animal, and *bloc de foie gras avec morceaux* ("block" of foie gras with pieces), made from 50 percent foie gras pieces in the case of goose foie gras and 35 percent foie gras pieces in the case of duck foie gras. As for *mousse de foie* (foie gras mousse), it contains 50 percent emulsified foie gras; *pâté de foie gras* (foie gras pâté), 50 percent foie gras; and *parfait de foie gras* (foie gras parfait), 75 percent foie gras.

KIT DE CANARD GRAS
FATTENED-DUCK KIT

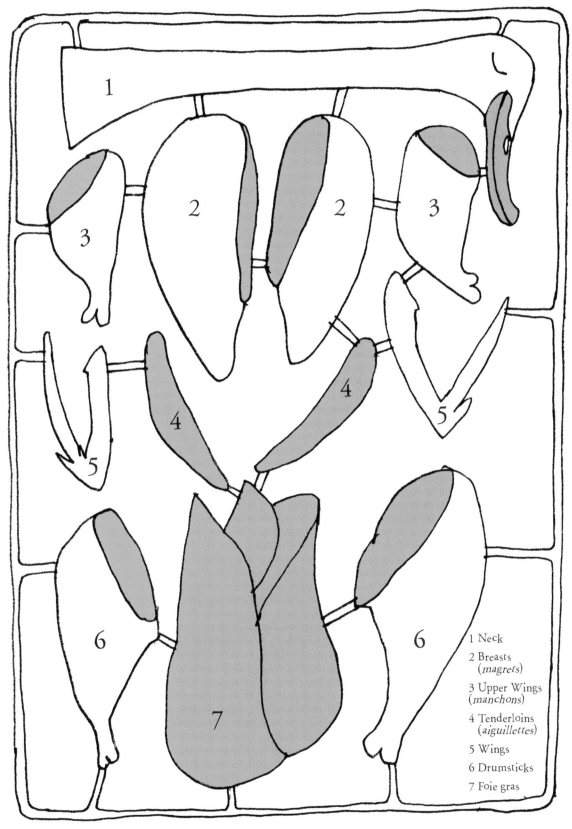

1 Neck

2 Breasts
(*magrets*)

3 Upper Wings
(*manchons*)

4 Tenderloins
(*aiguillettes*)

5 Wings

6 Drumsticks

7 Foie gras

LEFT
semi-cooked
foie gras
terrine for
Sunday

RIGHT
canned
foie gras

24

foie gras en terrine mi-cuit pour dimanche

SEMI-COOKED FOIE GRAS TERRINE FOR SUNDAY
FOR A 2 LB. 4 OZ. TERRINE - PREPARATION TIME: 30 MINUTES
COOKING TIME: 30 MINUTES + 12 HOURS RESTING TIME

Foies gras .... 2 (2 pounds 4 ounces in total)
Quatre-épices .... 1 teaspoon
White port .... ¼ cup
Pain d'épice ....2 slices
Salt, pepper

1. Brown the slices of *pain d'épice* (a spice bread) slices in a 200°F oven, and then process into breadcrumbs.
2. Remove the veins from the foies gras as delicately as possible. Marinate the foies gras in the port and *quatre-épices* for 10 minutes and season.
3. In a terrine, arrange one layer of foie gras and sprinkle with the *pain d'épice* crumbs. Add another layer of foie gras, and sprinkle with more *pain d'épice*. Finish with a final layer of foie gras and press it down. Cover the terrine and chill for 2 hours.
4. Place the terrine in a cold water bath and bake in a low-temperature (200°F) oven for 30 minutes. Chill overnight and enjoy the following day.

WINE: A "VENDANGE TARDIVE" TOKAY

foie gras en conserve pour plus tard

PRESERVED FOIE GRAS FOR LATER
FOR FOUR 9 OUNCE JARS - PREPARATION TIME: 30 MINUTES
COOKING TIME: 45 MINUTES

Foies gras .... 2 (2 pounds 4 ounces in total)
Armagnac .... 2½ tablespoons
Salt, pepper

1. Devein the two foies gras by separating the lobes and removing the veins, keeping the lobes as intact as possible.
2. Rinse your jars with the Armagnac.
3. Season the lobes of foies gras, and gently pack them into the jars without damaging them.
4. Fill a large saucepan with water and bring to a boil. Immerse the jars, keeping them under the water (using a weight) for 45 minutes. Monitor the water temperature, which must stay between 195°F and 200°F. Store chilled.

WINE: MUSCAT DE RIVESALTES

foie gras cru au sauternes pour tout de suite

FRESH FOIE GRAS WITH SAUTERNES FOR EATING IMMEDIATELY
FOR 6 - PREPARATION TIME: 10 MINUTES

Lobe of fresh foie gras 1
Sauternes wine .... ½ cup
Toasted baguette ....6 slices
Red berries (red currants, for example)
Sea salt, coarsely ground black pepper

1. Use a vegetable peeler to create shavings of fresh foie gras. Remove the veins and nerves as you go.
2. Arrange the shavings on toasted baguette slices.
3. Using a brush, daub the shavings with Sauternes. Season with sea salt, coarsely ground black pepper, and some red berries—and if you find a nice truffle at the back of the fridge, top the shavings of foie gras with a few slices!

WINE: SAUTERNES

FAIRE SES CONSERVES
MAKE YOUR OWN PRESERVES

Jars with a
metal screw-
top lid.

Seal

Jars with
a glass lid.

1 Filling the jars

2 Sealing the jars

3 Sterilization

Place the jars in a large
pot, properly wedged
apart, and cover with
boiling water.

Let the filled jar
simmer gently fo
1 hour 30 minute

4 Seal and
label the jars

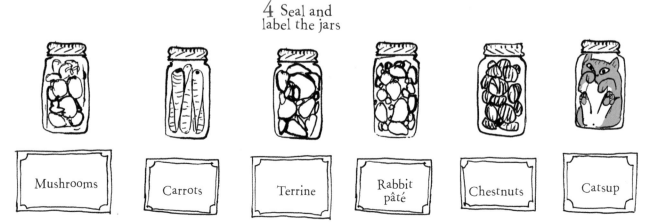

Mushrooms

Carrots

Terrine

Rabbit
pâté

Chestnuts

Catsup

FOIE GRAS MI-CUIT
EN CONSERVE AU NATUREL
PRESERVED SEMI-COOKED FOIE GRAS

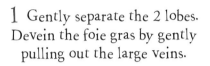

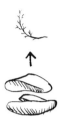

1 Gently separate the 2 lobes. Devein the foie gras by gently pulling out the large veins.

2 Sprinkle the foie gras with salt and pepper.

3 Roll up the foie gras, and place in the jar.

4 Put the duck fat on top

5 Close the jar, not forgetting the rubber seal.

6 Process for 30 minutes in a large pot filled with boiling water.

7 Allow to cool.

And keep 2 to 3 months in a cool place.

LEFT
whole
foie gras
poached with
spices

RIGHT
pan-fried
foie gras
with prunes

30

foie gras entier poché aux épices

WHOLE FOIE GRAS POACHED WITH SPICES
FOR 6 - PREPARATION TIME: 40 MINUTES
COOKING TIME: 15 MINUTES + 12 HOURS MARINATING TIME

Whole fresh foie gras 1
Red wine ....8 cups
Ground cinnamon .... 1 teaspoon
Quatre-épices... 1 teaspoon
Ground ginger .... 1 teaspoon
Cloves 3
Star anise .... 3 pods
Crème de cassis liqueur..½ cup
Light brown sugar ....2 tablespoons
Sea salt

1. Gently caramelize the sugar in a pan, then stir in the wine. Add all the spices, along with the liqueur, and allow to reduce by half.
2. Immerse the foie gras in the simmering wine. Then remove from the heat. leaving the foie gras to poach in the wine. Turn it over regularly until it is cooked through, then allow to cool completely.
3. Refrigerate overnight in the spiced wine.
4. The next day, degrease the foie gras. Serve it with sea salt.

WINE: PEDRO XIMENEZ

foie gras poêlé aux pruneaux

PAN-FRIED FOIE GRAS WITH PRUNES
FOR 6 - PREPARATION TIME: 30 MINUTES
COOKING TIME: 10 MINUTES + 12 HOURS MARINATING TIME

Escalopes of fresh foie gras ....6 (about 4 ounces each)
Pitted prunes..18
Red wine .... 1 cup
Ground cinnamon .... 1 teaspoon
Quatre-épices.. 1 teaspoon
Star anise .... 2 pods
Light brown sugar ....2 tablespoons
Butter, chilled..2½ tablespoons
Sea salt

1. Boil the prunes for 5 minutes with the wine, spices, and sugar. Then cover and leave overnight at room temperature.
2. Remove the prunes and reduce the spiced wine until it has a syrupy consistency. Whisk in the butter to make a sauce; then return the prunes to the mixture.
3. Cook the escalopes in a hot pan for about 3 minutes on each side, until golden brown and tender—it all depends on how thick they are. Season with sea salt.
4. Arrange each escallop on a plate, surrounded by the prunes and sauce.

WINE: RED PORT

foie entier poché aux p'tits légumes

WHOLE FOIE GRAS POACHED WITH BABY VEGETABLES
FOR 6 - PREPARATION TIME: 45 MINUTES
COOKING TIME: 1 HOUR 40 MINUTES + 30 MINUTES RESTING TIME

Whole fresh foie gras 1
Bouquet garni 1
Leeks 3
Onions..4
Celeriac (celery root)..½
Baby carrots 6
Scallions (or bulb green onions, if available) 6
Fennel ....1 bulb
Celery .... 3 stalks
Anise seeds .... 1 teaspoon
Sea salt, coarsely ground black pepper

1. Slice and carefully wash the leeks. Peel and chop the onions and celeriac.
2. Bring 8 cups of salted water to the boil, and add the leeks, onion, celeriac, bouquet garni, and anise seeds. Cook for 1 hour; then remove the vegetables.
3. Add the peeled carrots, the fennel bulb cut into 6 pieces, the finely sliced celery, and the spring onions to the stock. Cook for an additional 30 minutes
4. Add the whole foie gras and bring to a boil. Then remove it from the heat and let it rest for 30 minutes.
5. Serve the slices of foie gras like a *pot-au-feu*, topped with the vegetables and seasoned to taste with sea salt and coarsely ground black pepper.

WINE: BRUT CHAMPAGNE

LEFT
foie gras with
pain d'épice
crumble

RIGHT
foie gras
crème brûlée

crumble de pain d'épice et foie gras

FOIE GRAS WITH PAIN D'ÉPICE CRUMBLE
FOR 6 - PREPARATION TIME: 45 MINUTES
COOKING TIME: 30 MINUTES

Escalopes of fresh foie gras	6 (about 4 ounces each)
Pain d'épice	2 slices
Butter	⅓ cup
Flour	½ cup
Light brown sugar	⅓ cup
Balsamic vinegar	¾ cup
Cornmeal	⅔ cup
Raisins	½ cup
Milk	2 cups

Salt, pepper

1. In a pan, reduce the balsamic vinegar by half with a tablespoon of the light brown sugar.
2. Toast the rounds of *pain d'épice* in the oven before grinding them to a powder. Blend in the melted butter, flour, and sugar. Spread mixture on a sheet of parchment paper and bake in a 350°F oven until golden brown.
3. Meanwhile, bring the milk to the boil with the raisins, and stir in the cornmeal in a steady stream. Cook for 10 minutes and season.
4. Cook the foie gras escalopes in a hot pan for about 3 minutes on each side, until golden brown and tender; it will depend on how thick they are. Season.
5. Arrange each foie gras escallop on a mound of cornmeal, topped by the crumble and drizzled with caramelized vinegar.

WINE: A CHEWY JURANÇON

crème brûlée au foie gras

FOIE GRAS CRÈME BRÛLÉE
FOR 6 - PREPARATION TIME: 15 MINUTES
COOKING TIME: 35 MINUTES

Fresh foie gras	10 ounces
Heavy cream	2 cups
Egg yolks	5
Nutmeg	1 pinch

Salt, pepper
Light brown sugar

1. Devein the foie gras and process until smooth.
2. Whisk the cream with the egg yolks, add nutmeg, and season. Combine the mixture with the foie gras mousse and pass through a fine sieve, known as a *chinois*.
3. Pour the foie gras cream into six ramekins and place in a water bath in a 235°F oven for 30 minutes. Check for doneness with the tip of a knife: it should come out clean.
4. Sprinkle with a bit of brown sugar; then caramelize quickly under a hot broiler.

WINE: CHABLIS

cou de canard farci

STUFFED DUCK NECK
FOR 1 NECK - PREPARATION TIME: 30 MINUTES
COOKING TIME: 45 MINUTES

Skin from a duck neck	1
Duck meat (with skin)	10 ounces
Foie gras	3½ ounces
Duck fat	⅓ cup

Salt, pepper

1. Chop the duck, leaving on its skin, and season well.
2. Stuff the duck neck skin with the chopped duck mixture, placing the foie gras in the middle, and close up the long neck skin like a sock. Place the neck in a preserving jar, covered with melted duck fat, and seal the jar.
3. Fill a saucepan with water and bring to a boil. Submerge the jar, keeping it underwater (using a weight) for 45 minutes. Monitor the water temperature, which must remain between 195°F and 200°F.
4. Remove from the water bath with tongs and allow to cool, then slice and serve.

WINE: IROULÉGUY

pâté ∂e tête

HEAD CHEESE
FOR 1 GOOD-SIZED TERRINE - PREPARATION TIME: 60 MINUTES
COOKING TIME: 4 HOURS + 24 HOURS RESTING TIME

Pig's ears 2
Pig snout 1
Pork cheeks 4
Pork tongue 1
Pig's trotters (pig's feet)
(pigs are said to be "as silly as their feet," hence
the use of the trotters rather than brains.)..........................2
Carrots...2
Shallots..2
Tarragon..1 bunch
Parsley...4 sprigs
Leek..1
Onions...3
Fennel ....1 bulb
Garlic..3 cloves
Bouquet garni...1
Salt, pepper

1. In a large pot of water, cook the pig's ears, snout, cheeks, tongue, and trotters, along with diced carrots, leek, onions, fennel, shallots, and bouquet garni, for 3 hours.
2. Remove the meats, debone the trotters, and roughly chop the meat.
3. Finely chop the shallots, tarragon, and parsley. Then combine with the meat and season.
4. Let the cooking liquid reduce. Remove the vegetables and blend with the meat mixture. Pile the mixture into a terrine, but don't pack it down too much. Then pour in the reduced stock to cover. Allow the mixture to set in the refrigerator for 24 hours.

WINE: SAINT-AMOUR

chou farci

STUFFED CABBAGE

FOR 6 - PREPARATION TIME: 45 MINUTES
COOKING TIME: 50 MINUTES

Savoy cabbage 1
Sausage meat .... 1 pound 5 ounces
Chorizo sausage...1
Shallot 1
Garlic... 2 cloves
Heavy cream...½ cup
Egg 1
Dried porcini mushrooms.......................................¾ ounce
White wine.. 1 cup
Coarse salt
Salt, pepper

1. Soak the dried mushrooms in hot water for 20 minutes.
Drain and reserve the mushrooms.
2. Select six good cabbage leaves. Boil some water, adding
some coarse salt. Blanch the cabbage leaves to soften them,
and refresh them immediately under cold water. Remove the
central rib without damaging the cabbage leaf.
3. Sauté 1⅔ cups shredded cabbage with the chopped shallot
and garlic. Add the diced chorizo sausage, then the soaked
mushrooms. Stir in the cream and simmer gently.
4. Combine the cabbage mixture with the sausage meat and
egg, and season. Divide into six portions; then neatly roll
each portion in a blanched cabbage leaf.
5. Pack the leaves tightly in a gratin dish, pour on the wine,
and cook in a 350°F oven for 45 minutes. Enjoy hot or cold.

WINE: MADRIAN

JAMBON CRU

An indispensable party item for any spontaneous entertainer. *Jambon cru* (cured ham) is a veritable savior of the impromptu drinks, the perfect opener to any meal, the silencer of sudden cravings. But on the journey from a pig's thigh to the cellar hook there's a whole art involved in creating *jambon cru*. This art is completely bound up in the know-how and *terroir* of our Masters of Ham. The breed of the pig, where it is reared, and the quality of the maturation process are all primordial elements that contribute to the quality of the *jambon*.

Most important, to attain the status of a *jambon*, it must be:
• a good pig from a quality breed, well raised
• dry-salted by an expert hand endowed with know-how and a few herbs and spices
• matured in rooms with specific criteria for ventilation, temperature, and humidity.

MATURATION TIME

JAMBON CRU
less than 130 days

JAMBON SEC
130 days minimum

JAMBON SEC SUPÉRIEUR
210 days minimum

Under the right circumstances, the ham will be transformed; it will ripen, bringing out all of its flavors. The flesh will redden, the flavors will become concentrated, at which point it will be time to debone the ham. Only a seasoned hand has the skill to do this properly, but it can also be enjoyed on the bone, a pleasure in its own right when the time comes to carve and scrape.

There are so many different *jambons* on the market today at such widely varying prices that a familiarity with the quality European labels is essential.

A.O.P.

APPELLATION D'ORIGINE PROTÉGÉE
(PROTECTED DESIGNATION OF ORIGIN)
The *jambon* is produced, matured, and cured in a specific geographic zone using protected traditional methods.

I.G.P.

INDICATION GÉOGRAPHIQUE PROTÉGÉE
(PROTECTED GEOGRAPHICAL DESIGNATION)
The *jambon* is linked to a specific *terroir* during the production, maturation, or curing stages (*jambon de Bayonne, jambon des Ardennes, jambon d'Ardèche*).

S.T.G.

SPÉCIALITÉ TRADITIONNELLE GARANTIE
(TRADITIONAL SPECIALITY GUARANTEED)
The *jambon* is produced according to a traditional method during the maturation or rearing stages.

Cured sausage is the natural ally of *jambon*: Both can cheerfully share the same hook since the sausages meet the same set of expectations as *jambon*, which is be eaten at any given moment. Cured sausage is a mixture of fat and lean pork that has undergone a fermentation process inside a natural casing, concentrating the flavors and cultivating a "bloom" that gives it its final appearance. And don't forget: good charcuterie deserves good cutlery!

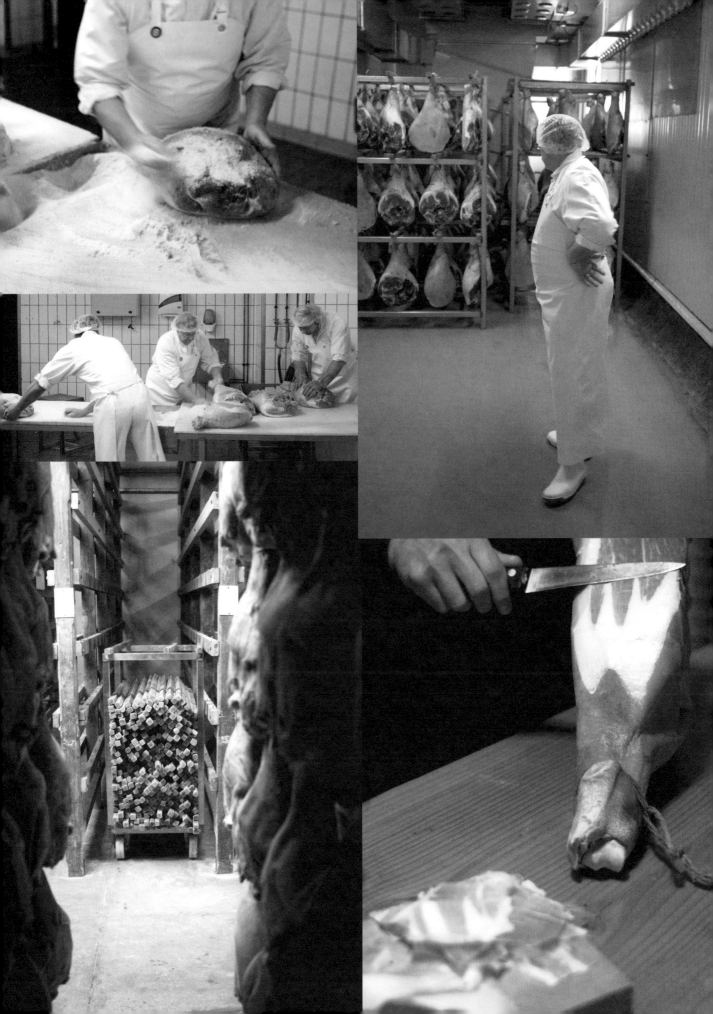

LE BEAUJOLAIS

NESTLED BETWEEN BURGUNDY AND THE RHÔNE VALLEY, BEAUJOLAIS ENJOYS A WORLDWIDE REPUTATION. THIS REPUTATION IS DUE TO THE ANCESTRAL SAVOIR-FAIRE THAT TRANSFORMS THE GAMAY GRAPE INTO WINE.

IO VINTAGES BEAR THE BEAUJOLAIS NAME:

BROUILLY I 200 HA
*When you drink Brouilly, everything smiles at you,
the Mrs. included!*

CHÉNAS 260 HA
Chénas for lunch, Chénas for dinner!

CHIROUBLES 350 HA
Chiroubles in August, pâté in a crust!

CÔTE-DE-BROUILLY 290 HA
*From the slopes of Mont Brouilly,
down the Côte-de-Brouilly!*

FLEURIE 800 HA
*When the hill is like the wine,
then all is well; when your face is like the wine
then all is very well!*

JULIÉNAS 580 HA
A full bottle is an unopened bottle!

MORGON I 100 HA
Everything goes well with Morgon, even Morgon!

MOULIN À VENT 650 HA
Moulin à vent, a windmill for all weather!

RÉGNIÉ 650 HA
A glass of Régnier, a prince among Beaujolais!

SAINT-AMOUR 280 HA
*We should always be devoted to our saints…
especially when thirsty!*

Jean Foillard

WHO SAYS BEAUJOLAIS IS NOTHING SPECIAL?

This is one of those preconceived ideas that is shattered under the collective weight of several tasting sessions. Beaujolais is good. You just need to find the right vintner!

Thank you, Monsieur Jean, for championing the Gamay, for the frissons of pleasure we get with the first mouthful of your wine.

Thank you, Monsieur Jean, for having turned a pig into sausages; they should be mandatory with your wine.

Thank you, Monsieur Jean, for silencing all those silly nay-sayers who have obviously never broken the wax seal on one of your bottles.

Thank you, Monsieur Jean, for being a winemaker!

La trilogie du gras-double
the tripe trilogy

Les pieds et paquets
chez Jean-Yves et Louis
Trotters and parcels with Jean-Yves and Louis

la trilogie
du gras-double
the tripe trilogy

comment faire
des andouillettes
tirées à la ficelle ?
how do you make traditional string-tied andouillettes?

Le café des fédérations
The Café des Fédérations

VIVE LA TRIPAILLE!

LONG LIVE OFFAL!

FAIRE UNE PELOTE DE CHAUSSETTES
FAÇON «ANDOUILLETTES TIRÉES À LA FICELLE»
POUR FÉDOR

MAKE A TRADITIONAL STRING-TIED-ANDOUILLETTE
SOCK TOY FOR FIDO

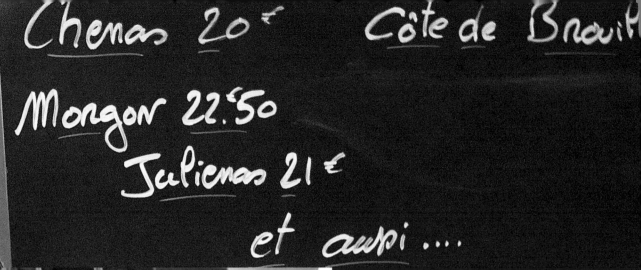

Chenas 20€   Côte de Brouilly

Morgon 22.50

Julienas 21€

et aussi ....

The 'bouchons' of Lyon

The term *bouchon* goes back to the days when thirsty horsemen would stop at taverns to guzzle a glass of Beaujolais. These taverns were marked by a bundle of straw—a *bouchon de paille*—attached to their door. These days, *bouchons* serve typical Lyonnaise dishes such as *quenelles* (oval-shaped meat or fish dumplings poached in liquid), *gras-double* (tripe), *andouillettes* (chitterling sausages), and *cervelle des canuts* (soft white cheese spread, flavored with herbs and vinegar)—all in a warm and friendly atmosphere. Conviviality is de rigeur: the sharp accent and frank opinions help to totally immerse you in this culture. *Fouilla!* (Woo-hoo!)

A little vocabulary à la lyonnaise

So there I was, after I'd *màchonné* (eaten up big), my *embuni* (belly) ready to explode with *gratons* (pork cracklings), on the slopes of the *Croix-Rousse* (a hill in Lyon), starting to *japiller* (yap away) like a *gone* (big kid). Not like a *galapiat* (boor) only good for giving people the *embiernes* (shits), but like a real *d'Yon* (Lyon native), all *flapi* (loose) after having *corgnolé* (downed) a good *barreille* (large barrel) of Beaujolais. *Nom d'un rat* (swear to God), my *clavettes* (joints) are completely *détrancanées* (unhinged), ready to *tomber en faïence* (fall apart).

Once I'm *remis sur mes fumerons* (back on my feet), I'll take a *riron* (stroll) around the *Terreaux* (city center of Lyon), a matter of *barsaquer* (getting it on) with the first *pourpeuse* (curvy girl) who comes along. You've been warned: once the spirit of the *bouchon* takes hold, anything

MOULES' MARINIÈRE

BREAD
fiber and vitamins
(also useful for spreading butter on)

CHARCUTERIE
a little animal protein, some fatty acids
(very fatty indeed), iron

CHEESE
high in calcium

GRATIN OF CARDOON WITH MARROW
vitamins for a rosy glow

RED WINE
guaranteed antioxidant!

Yves

AND THE CAFÉ DES FÉDÉRATIONS

At the Café des Fédérations, Yves upholds a grand tradition of hospitality. With a name like that (*Fédération* = labor union), you could hardly expect any less. He is the noble descendant of the local silk worker of Croix-Rousse hill fame who, by dint of spinning miles of silk from dawn to dusk for just a few *sous*, rose up one day in 1831 to declare loudly and clearly to his French employer that he'd had enough of being underpaid. From the slopes of Croix-Rousse to the heart of Lyon, the silk worker marched behind the black flag to organize a large part of the Lyonnaise population around his claims.

This workers' revolt sounded the alarm from deep within French territory, sparking conflict that reached even to Paris.

The silk workers were well organized and, every morning, in a solemn ritual, shared bread and wine to give themselves courage. This tradition of "breaking bread" together lives on, and Yves, as a well-intentioned nutritionist, can attest to the beneficial character of the meal. There he stands, a noble guardian of the temple, his knife never very far away, a dishcloth flung over his shoulder, a smile that says it all.

sabodets au vin rouge

PIG'S HEAD SAUSAGE IN RED WINE
FOR 6 - PREPARATION TIME: 20 MINUTES
COOKING TIME: 1 HOUR

Sabodet (rustic pig's head sausage)	2
Onions	2
Onion studded with 2 cloves	1
Carrots	2
Leek	1
Boiling potatoes	12
Veal stock	2 cups
Red wine	1 cup
Salt, pepper	

1. Chop the onions and sweat them in a large heavy saucepan along with the thinly sliced leeks. Add the peeled carrots, cut into chunks.
2. Arrange the sausages and clove-studded onion on top of the vegetables, add the wine, and bring to the boil. Pour in the stock: the sausages need to be covered with liquid.
3. Simmer very gently for 30 minutes. Then add the peeled and halved potatoes and cook for an additional 20 minutes.
4. Serve in the cooking pot.

WINE: SAINT-JOSEPH ROUGE

tête roulée

ROLLED PIG'S HEAD
For a good *tête roulée*, find a good butcher!

cervelas pistaché

PORK SAUSAGE WITH PISTACHIO NUTS
FOR 6 - PREPARATION TIME: 15 MINUTES
COOKING TIME: 30 MINUTES

Truffled *cervelas* sausage with pistachio nuts	1
Vitelotte (sweet-tasting, purple) potatoes	1 pound 5 ounces
Mesclun greens	7 ounces
Shallot	1
Crème fraîche	⅓ cup
Truffle oil	1 teaspoon
Olive oil	
Balsamic vinegar	
Salt, pepper	

1. Poach the sausage with the peeled potatoes for 30 minutes.
2. Slice the shallot very thinly and mix it with the crème fraîche. Season and add the truffle oil.
3. Make a vinaigrette of three-quarters olive oil and one-quarter balsamic vinegar.
4. Slice the sausage and potatoes into rounds and arrange on plates. Top the potatoes with the truffled crème fraîche.
5. Dress the salad greens with the vinaigrette and scatter on the plate. Serve lukewarm.

WINE: CROZES-HERMITAGES

LEFT
pig's head
salad

RIGHT
marrow bones,
pure and
simple

54

salade de museau

PIG'S HEAD SALAD
FOR 6 - PREPARATION TIME: 20 MINUTES
COOKING TIME: 3 HOURS

Pig's head, deboned and ready to cook ....½
Pig tongues 2
Bouquet garni 1
Leeks 3
Onions...3
Scallions (bulb green onions if available).............................3
Peanut oil...5 fluid ounces
Walnut oil...2½ tablespoons
Cider vinegar ....2½ tablespoons
Dijon mustard .... 1 tablespoon
Salt, pepper

1. Cook the pig's head and tongues for 3 hours in a large volume of water, along with the bouquet garni, the leeks, and the onions; the meat must be very tender. Peel the tongues and allow the whole mixture to cool.
2. Make a vinaigrette by mixing together the mustard, vinegar, and the oils. Slice the head and tongues as thinly as possible; chop the green onions.
3. Mix everything together and season. Serve with a green salad.

WINE: BEAUJOLAIS BLANC

os à moelle tout simplement

MARROW BONES, PURE AND SIMPLE
FOR 6 - PREPARATION TIME: 5 MINUTES
COOKING TIME: 30 MINUTES

Good marrow bones 12
Bouquet garni 1
Onion studded with 4 cloves...1
Country-style bread...12 slices
Chives..12 blades
Sea salt .... 1 pinch
Dog..1 (if possible)

1. Boil a large quantity of water, adding the bouquet garni and the onion. Plunge the marrow bones into the water and cook for about 30 minutes—they are ready when the tip of a knife can pierce the marrow.
2. Toast the slices of bread and snip the chives.
3. Spread the bread with the hot marrow, add some sea salt and chives, and give the empty bones to the dog!

WINE: BROUILLY

saucisses de Morteau

MORTEAU SAUSAGE
FOR 6 - PREPARATION TIME: 20 MINUTES
COOKING TIME: 45 MINUTES

Morteau sausages...2
Potatoes...3
Carrots...3
Scallions (or bulb green onions) 3
Olive oil
Salt, pepper

1. Peel the potatoes and carrots; then cut them into rounds.
2. Poach the sausages in rapidly simmering water. After 20 minutes, add the potatoes and the carrots and cook for another 20 minutes.
3. Cut the scallions into long strips, chopping the green ends.
4. Once the vegetables are cooked, drain, mix in some olive oil, and season. Serve them with a chunk of sausage on top, and sprinkle with the minced scallions.

WINE: ARBOIS

LEFT
sausage
Lyonnaise

RIGHT
crispy pig's
trotters

saucisson à la lyonnaise

SAUSAGE LYONNAISE
FOR 6 - PREPARATION TIME: 20 MINUTES
COOKING TIME: 45 MINUTES

Lyonnaise sausages (or good pork sausages)........................2
Boiling potatoes..12
Onion studded with cloves...1
Mild white onions..3
Mustard ....1 tablespoon
Wine vinegar..1 tablespoon
Olive oil ....¾ cup
Salt, pepper

1. Drop the sausages in simmering water and cook with
a clove-studded onion. After 15 minutes, add the peeled
potatoes and cook until tender in the sausage water.
2. Peel the white onions and slice them thinly. Make a thick
vinaigrette by blending the mustard, vinegar, and olive oil;
season and pour the mixture over the sliced onions.
3. Drain and carve the sausages and potatoes into thick
slices. Dress with the onion vinaigrette.

WINE: CÔTE-DU-RHÔNE

pieds de cochon qui croustillent

CRISPY PIG'S TROTTERS
FOR 6 - PREPARATION TIME: 45 MINUTES
COOKING TIME: 3 HOURS + 15 MINUTES + 20 MINUTES REFRIGE-
RATION TIME

Pig's trotters 6
Bouquet garni...1
Onions..5
Spinach..4 cups
Whole hazelnuts ....⅓ cup
Shallots..2
Phyllo pastry sheets...6
Butter...1 tablespoon
Egg 1
Salt, pepper

1. Simmer the pig's trotters in a large volume of water for
3 hours, along with the peeled onions and bouquet garni:
the meat must be completely falling off the bones.
2. Remove the onions from the water and coarsely chop
them. Fully debone the trotters, and combine the trotter
meat and onions.
3. Quickly wilt the spinach in the butter.
4. Process the trotter mixture and spinach, adding the
hazelnuts and chopped shallots; season generously.
5. Fashion the trotter mixture into a large roll using plastic
wrap and chill. Unwrap and cut the roll into 6 equal portions.
Wrap each one in a sheet of pastry and seal the edges with
beaten egg.
6. Bake in a 315°F oven for 15 minutes. Serve immediately.

WINE: HERMITAGE ROUGE

foie de veau au citron

CALF'S LIVER WITH LEMON
FOR 6 - PREPARATION TIME: 45 MINUTES
COOKING TIME: 15 MINUTES + 20 MINUTES REFRIGERATION TIME

Thick slices of calf's liver 6
Chives...6 sprigs
Tarragon...1 bunch
Chervil..1 bunch
Shallot ....½
Garlic...1 clove
Lemon 1
Salted butter..⅓ cup
Unsalted butter ....1½ tablespoons
Dry bread...3 slices
Fried croutons..30

1. Make an herb crust by processing together the chives,
tarragon, chervil, shallot, salted butter, and bread. Spread the
mixture to a thickness of ¼ inch between two sheets of
parchment paper. Chill for 20 minutes. Divide the herb crust
into six portions.
2. Extract the segments from the lemon, being careful to
discard the bitter white pith. Set aside.
3. Chop the garlic and sauté gently in the unsalted butter.
Add the liver slices and pan-fry, keeping them nice and
pink.
4. Place a portion of herb crust on each liver slice and bake
in a 350°F, or moderate, oven for 5 minutes. Add the lemon
segments and croutons, and serve.

WINE: CHINON

Making genuine
andouillette sausage
"tirée à la ficelle"
(string-tied)

Bobosse junior
STURDY AS FIFTEEN ANDOUILLETTES!

He was led to the trade by the sweetest path: that of love. He married the beautiful girl, he married the *charcuterie*, and he almost married Bobosse, his father-in-law. Bobosse junior has an anvil-lifting physique, sturdy as fifteen *andouillettes*. Following in Bobosse's footsteps, he's always ready for a day of charcuterie, his delivery vans filled to the brim with good things.

King of the *andouillette tirée à la ficelle* (string-tied chitterling sausages), Bobosse had the misfortune one day to note the presence of mad cow disease, so mad that he was absolutely forbidden to use any calf's caul in the manufacture of his *andouillettes*. What

to do? Devil take the mad cow—bring on the savoir-faire. Pig's tripe replaced the calf's caul and the recipe was changed somewhat, but the technique that's so essential to making *andouillettes* remained the same. What magic to see these piles of mustard-sweating chitterlings, rolled around expert fingers, disappear into an intestinal sock to finally reveal themselves as genuine *andouillettes*. A nice bath to relax in, a few hours to soak, and they are ready to inspire your cooking. Grilled or cooked with mustard, with a little cream or white wine, the *andouillette* has what it takes to satisfy your desires—all of them!

Chez Hugon

It's not a joke: this happens to be Lyon's gastronomical Mecca, the temple of *la cochonnaille* (pork cuisine), the palace of the *andouillette* (chitterling sausage). And Hugon is the ruler of all. Be careful, though: once you cross the threshold of this place, no one can be held responsible for what happens inside. You could happily lose yourself, buried under a pile of tripe, drowned by gallons of chilled Mâcon, knocked out by tarts and pralines. And faced with Huguette's benevolent smile, one cannot help but say *encore*: lead the charge against gout and cholesterol—the only *goutte* (nip) you can get at Hugon is behind the bar and 46° proof. Away with "beanpole" figures and waters too still to be honest. Hurray for bellies as cushioned as a *baba*!

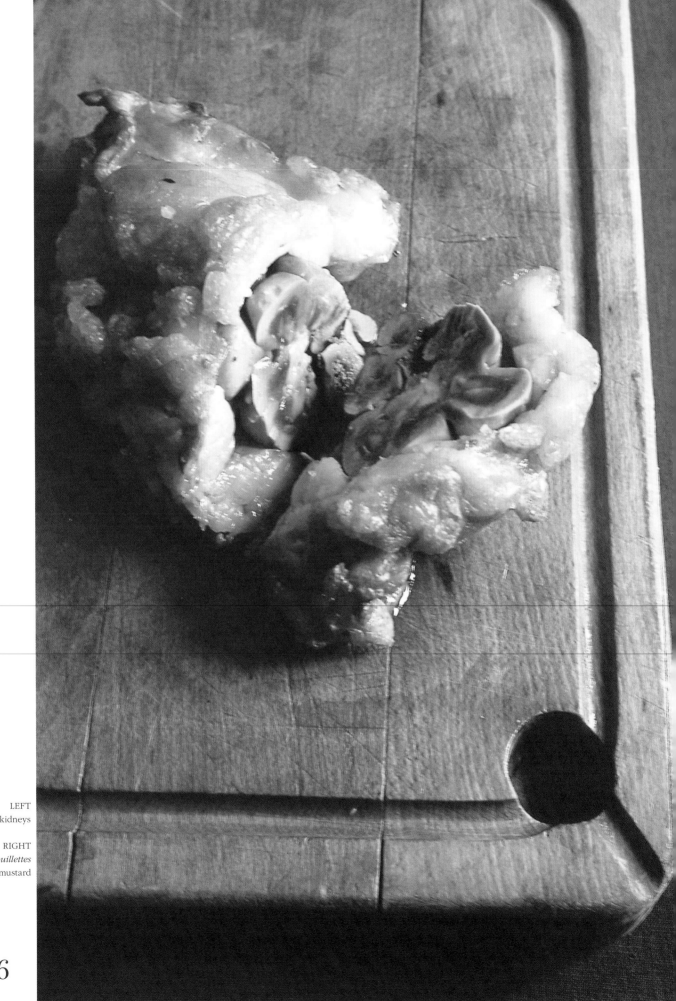

rognons de veau

VEAL KIDNEYS
FOR 6 - PREPARATION TIME: 30 MINUTES
COOKING TIME: 15 MINUTES

Veal kidneys in their fat 3
Salt, pepper
String

1. Carefully separate the kidneys from their coating of fat, reserving the fat. Remove the fine membrane of the kidneys as well as the fatty center. Season, encase the kidneys in their fat, and tie up each kidney like a roast.
2. Bake in a 425°F oven for 15 minutes. Allow them to rest for 5 minutes before serving, so they are juicy; they should still be a little bloody.

WINE: CORNAS

andouillettes à la moutarde

ANDOUILLETTES WITH MUSTARD
FOR 6 - PREPARATION TIME: 15 MINUTES
COOKING TIME: 20 MINUTES

Andouillettes tirées à la ficelle (chitterling sausages).........................6
White wine...1 cup
Shallots...3
Heavy cream..¾ cup
Dijon mustard ....1 tablespoon
Salt, pepper

1. Prick the sausages. Peel and dice the shallots.
2. Gently sauté the sausages and shallots in a frying pan. Once the shallots have cooked down, deglaze the pan with the wine, scraping up the bits on the bottom, and allow the liquid to reduce by half.
3. Arrange the sausages in a gratin dish.
4. Add the cream to the wine mixture and again allow it to reduce. Mix the mustard into this reduction. Then season, and pour over the sausages. Cook in a 200°F oven for 5 minutes; the sauce mustn't boil. Serve immediately.

WINE: CHENAS

boudin aux pommes

BLOOD SAUSAGE WITH APPLES
FOR 6 - PREPARATION TIME: 30 MINUTES -
COOKING TIME: 15 MINUTES

Boudin noir (blood sausage or blood pudding)... 2 pounds 4 ounces
Granny Smith apples..3
Shallots...3
Rutabagas...3
Honey...1 tablespoon
Butter...1 tablespoon
White port...⅓ to ½ cup
Oil, for the pan

1. Cook the chopped rutabagas in rapidly simmering water. Cut each apple into six wedges and remove the core. Peel the shallots and cut them in half.
2. Melt the butter in a pan, and saute the apples and shallots until nicely browned. Add the honey and deglaze with the port, scraping up all the bits on the bottom. Add the rutabaga to the pan and heat through.
3. Cut the sausage into six portions and brown them gently in oil (just to heat through). Dress sausages with the port-flavored *jus,* and serve with the apples, shallots, and rutabaga.

WINE: SANCERRE BLANC

LES GUIGNOLS
FONT RIPAILLE
THE GUIGNOLS HAVE A GOOD TIME

Guignol

Madelon

Gnafron

Flageolet

FAIRE UNE PELOTE DE CHAUSSETTES
FAÇON « ANDOUILLETTES TIRÉES À LA FICELLE » POUR FÉDOR
MAKE A "SAUSAGE" SOCK TOY FOR FIDO

1

Take a beige
men's sock

2

Take five mustard-
colored nylon stockings.

3

Cut the sock
like this.

4 Roll the stockings
this way.

5

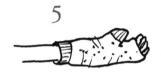

Put your hand
inside the sock.

6

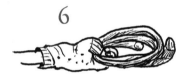

Grab the stocking
wreath.

8

Close the other
end as shown.

7

Turn the sock
inside out.

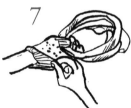

Here Fido, go play!

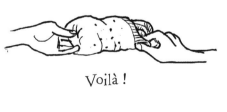

Voilà !

LEFT
beef tongue in
Madeira sauce

RIGHT
breaded
rolled calf's
head with
almonds

72

tête de veau classique

CLASSIC CALF'S HEAD
FOR 6 - PREPARATION TIME: 45 MINUTES
COOKING TIME: 3 HOURS

Rolled calf's head with tongue	1
Calf's brain	1
Onions	3
Bouquet garni	1
Celery stalk	1
Potatoes	6
Snow peas	2 cups
Carrots	6
Tomatoes	2
Scallions (bulb green onions if available)	2
Chives	4 sprigs
Olive oil	3½ fluid ounces

SAUCE GRIBICHE

Egg yolk	1
Hard-boiled egg	1
Peanut oil	¾ cup
Wine vinegar	1 teaspoon
Mustard	1 teaspoon
Capers	1 teaspoon
Cornichons	1 teaspoon
Salt, pepper	

1. Peel all of the vegetables. Place the calf's head in a large saucepan with the bouquet garni, celery, and onions. Cover with water and cook for 2 hours 30 minutes. Add the carrots, diced potatoes, and the calf's brain. Cook for another 20 minutes, and add the snow peas. Cook for 1 more minute, then turn off the heat.
2. Plunge the tomatoes into boiling water for 10 seconds. After removing the skin and seeds, chop the flesh into small cubes. Chop the scallions and snip the chives. Combine the tomato, green onion, and chives together with the olive oil.
3. Make a sauce gribiche by whisking the egg yolk, mustard, and vinegar, slowly adding the oil to make a mayonnaise. Stir in the chopped boiled egg, chopped cornichons, and capers.
4. Arrange the simmered vegetables in a shallow bowl. Add the tomato mixture and season. Place a slice of calf's head on top, add some of the calf's brain, and top with a spoonful of sauce gribiche. Eat within 4 days.

WINE: SAUMUR

langue de bœuf sauce madère

BEEF TONGUE IN MADEIRA SAUCE
FOR 6 - PREPARATION TIME: 45 MINUTES
COOKING TIME: 3 HOURS 30 MINUTES

Beef tongue	1
Bouquet garni	1
Carrots	3
Onions	3
Celery stalks	3
Shallots	2
White wine	½ cup
Madeira wine	⅓ to ½ cup
Heavy cream	¾ cup
Flour	1 pinch
Cornichons	12
Capers	1 tablespoon
Tarragon	1 bunch
Olive oil	
Salt, pepper	

1. Peel the carrots and onions and slice them thinly. Drop the tongue in a saucepan filled with water, bring to a boil, and cook for 5 minutes. Rinse the meat and repeat the process, this time adding the carrots, onions, bouquet garni, and celery. Cook for 3 hours, or until the meat is very tender.
2. Once the tongue is cooked, remove the skin, and thinly slice the tongue lengthwise. Keep it warm in the stock.
3. Peel the shallots and chop them finely. Sauté in olive oil, add flour, and deglaze the pan with the wine, scraping up the bits on the bottom. Allow the liquid to reduce by half, add a ladle of the cooking stock, then the Madeira and cream. Allow to barely simmer until the sauce coats the back of a spoon, and season.
4. Julienne the cornichons and add them to the sauce with the capers. Cover the tongue slices with this sauce and sprinkle with tarragon leaves.

WINE: BOURGUEIL

tête de veau panée aux amandes

BREADED ROLLED CALF'S HEAD WITH ALMONDS
FOR 6 - PREPARATION TIME: 30 MINUTES
COOKING TIME: 3 HOURS + 20 MINUTES

Rolled calf's head with tongue	1
Onions	3
Bouquet garni	1
Celery stalk	1
Eggs	2
Ground almonds	1 cup
Breadcrumbs	1 cup
Unsalted butter	¼ cup
Sundried tomatoes in oil	⅔ cup
Arugula leaves	3½ ounces
Young beet greens	3½ ounces
Oil for deep-frying	
Sea salt, pepper	

1. Peel the onions. Place the calf's head in a large saucepan with the bouquet garni, celery, and onions. Cover with water and simmer for 3 hours. Allow the calf's head to cool.
2. Mix the breadcrumbs and ground almonds. Season.
3. Pat the calf's head dry and cut into six slices, each ¾-inch thick. Beat the eggs, dip the calf's-head slices in the egg, and then into the crumbs.
4. Melt the butter in a sauté pan, add the calf's-head slices, and cook until browned.
5. Briefly deep-fry the arugula and beet greens. Serve over the calf's-head slices on a bed of simmered vegetables and sliced sun-dried tomatoes, sprinkled with sea salt.

WINE: SAINT-NICOLAS DE BOURGUEIL

la trilogie du *gras-double*

TRIPE TRILOGY

If the tripe we call *gras-double* is absolutely not *gras* (fatty), why the name, you ask? So much nonsense has been spoken on this subject that it is time to establish the truth once and for all—or add yet more nonsense! The story is a bit long but worth the time.

It will be noted, to our advantage, that if Lugdunum (Lyon) was the capital of the Gauls, this was not owing to chance but rather to the simple fact that Caesar, a great lover of tripe, wanted to honor the town in which he had discovered two new ways of preparing it: one with butter (breaded tripe) and the other with oil (tripe with onions)! Said Caesar: "It's true they're a little fatty, but it's so different from the tripe we usually eat, it absolutely must be called something else!"[1]

Two slightly fatty recipes, and suddenly "tripe boiled for hours before being made into a dish" becomes "*gras-double*" (double fat) for posterity.

When Julius Caesar decided to write up his exploits in a book, he was a bit stuck on the title. On the one hand, he wanted to pay homage to his soldiers, who effectively "de-triped" their adversaries in a stiff game of one-upmanship, and thus to all those guts scattered on the battlefield. On the other hand, since he had eaten two excellent tripe dishes in Lyon, a conquered Gallo-Roman town, he wanted this fact to be known. Make no mistake: Caesar wanted to "talk tripe"! He thought of a promising title,

La Guerre du gras-double[2] (*The Tripe War*). But his personal communications adviser, one Johannes Lupus Rapinus (a very famous comic playright of the time), told him: "With that title, Caesar, believe me, you won't get very far!" Caesar listened to him and the work became famous under the name *The Gallic War*.

> "WHEN GEORGE LUCAS CREATED THE *STAR WARS* TRILOGY, HE WAS TO A LARGE EXTENT INSPIRED BY THE *GRAS-DOUBLE* TRILOGY AND THE 'MICHELIN STAR' WARS."

Many years passed, until in the 1930s the *gras-double* war re-emerged, in a form as brutal as it was unexpected, between *la Mère* Fillioux, partisan of the *tablier de sapeur* (breaded tripe), and *la Mère* Brazier defending, on her part, the *gras-double à la lyonnaise* (tripe with onions).

In his *Trois étoiles au Michelin*, Jean-François Mesplède only hints at this terrible quarrel with these famous words of Mère Fillioux's on the subject of Mère Brazier: "How can she cook? In my kitchen she washed the dishes!"[3]

The battle between the two *mères* was an Homeric one. Jean Giraudoux, who witnessed the scene, said to them: "*Mesdames*, such *salades* (dramas) over *gras-double*, it's too much! The *gras-double* war will not take place!"[4] Then he added: "I should make it into a play!" A wise man, by the name of Daniel Bouchet, pointed out: "Jean! With *gras-double* in the title, believe me, you won't get very far!"[5] Giraudoux kept only the Homeric aspect of this Lyon-based psychodrama and created, in 1935, *The Trojan War Will Not Take Place*. For her part, Mère Fillioux said to herself, "Tripe *en salade*, there's an idea! I'll have a go at it."[6]

And so it is that in Lyon, the *gras-double* was, from then on, *triple*. And one could treat oneself to a tripe trilogy, even if it's fairly rare for all three recipes to be served in the same meal.

To put an end to the matter, let us nevertheless point out that when George Lucas created the *Star Wars* trilogy, he was to a large extent inspired by the *gras-double* trilogy and the (Michelin!) "Star Wars" indulged in by the famous *mères lyonnaises* before the Second World War.

Alert observers will notice, moreover, that, in the film the huge spaceship bears a remarkable resemblance to a pile of tripe!

Let us finally note that if Steven Spielberg hadn't said to Lucas, "George, with *gras-double* in the title, believe me, you won't get very far!", *Star Wars* would have been called *Gras-Double's War.*[7] *Voilá!* An injustice rectified at long last!

---

[1] As quoted by Johannes Lupus Rapinus, *In Vino Veritas*, Codex 13, Vatican Library.

[2] *Ibid.* (Ibid. means that it's the same book as cited in the footnote above. It's just to annoy the reader and be all "I'm writing a thesis on tripe and everything in it is true!")

[3] Jean-François Mesplède, *Trois étoiles au Michelin* (Éditions Gründ, 2004), p. 69.

[4] Quoted by Daniel Bouchet, *Je suis témoin, j'y étais!* (I'm a witness, I was there!), 180° Éditions, p. 51.

[5] *Ibid.* (See note 2).

[6] These footnotes are really a pain!

[7] This also explains the strange translation of *Star Wars* in French as *La Guerre des Etoiles* (The War of the Stars)! English speakers will confirm this fact: *Star Wars* should normally be translated as *Les guerres de l'Étoile* (The Wars of the Star), namely Mère Brazier's famous third star in the Michelin Guide, and not *La Guerre des Etoiles,* which in English would be "stars' war." Yes, indeed!

Daniel Tardy

ALIAS MONSIEUR PIGNON

Doctorate in *gras-double*, valedictorian with honors from ESG Lyon (*École Supérieure du Gras-double*), with a major in "I'll just add a little more fat."

Tell us, Monsieur Pignon, why don't you open a restaurant, you cook really well? Since you're an honors graduate of the *École Supérieure du Gras-double*, you can't blame us for asking!
What Monsieur Pignon likes is the tripe seller at the market.
What Monsieur Pignon likes is to see people eat without making them pay.
What Monsieur Pignon likes is to see people eat and make it his treat.
What Monsieur Pignon likes is to savor and share.
What Monsieur Pignon likes is to film and tell stories!
So don't go bothering him about a restaurant!

GRAS-DOUBLE
BOILED TRIPE

mode d'emploi

USER'S GUIDE

For those interested in the technical side, *gras-double* is the name given to beef tripe that has been washed and cooked for several hours. If it is not prepared according to a recipe with butter or oil, *gras-double* is simply protein and a natural dieter's dish—but as such it loses a great deal of its appeal!

BUYING

When you buy it from your butcher or tripe specialist, *gras-double* is ready to be seasoned. It must not be yellowish, but a beautiful pearly white, a sign of freshness. There are three different categories of tripe: the *reticulum*, with a honeycomb-like texture; the *omasum*, with little hanging leaves; and the *rumen*, which is flat and relatively smooth.

BEFORE USING

Boil the *gras-double* in a stewing pot filled with water to which a large spoonful of vinegar and a handful of coarse salt has been added.

Blanch for 3 to 5 minutes and drain in a colander.

Generously splash the drained *gras-double* with vinegar and allow to cool.

WINE: A GLASS OF CÔTES-DU-RHÔNE

gras-double à la lyonnaise

TRIPE LYONNAISE (WITH ONIONS)

1. Cut 1 pound 5 ounces prepared tripe into strips. Blanch and drain, and dress with vinegar while still warm.
2. Slice 3 onions. In a pan, sauté the onions in 2 tablespoons of sunflower or peanut oil. Cook uncovered, stirring regularly with a wooden spoon until the onions brown slightly.
3. Add the tripe. Continue cooking over high heat for 5 minutes. The tripe should be infused with the oil.
4. As soon as the onions and tripe begin to caramelize, serve them very hot on a salad of lettuce or, better still, lamb's lettuce salad (*mâche*) or dandelion greens. Deglaze the pan with wine vinegar, scraping up the bits on the bottom, and pour over the tripe and salad.

WINE: A GLASS OF CÔTES-DU-RHÔNE

salade de gras-double

TRIPE SALAD

1. Cut 1 pound 5 ounces prepared tripe into strips. Blanch and drain, and dress with vinegar while still warm.
2. In a salad bowl, make a generous dressing using 3 tablespoons of mustard to 6 tablespoons of sunflower or peanut oil. Whisk to make a thick mayonnaise-like sauce.
3. Place a third of this sauce in another salad bowl to dress some cooked sliced red beets.
4. Add the still-warm tripe to the salad bowl containing the remaining two-thirds of the mustard sauce. Mix so that the dressing is well absorbed. Add the juice of half a lemon and three turns of the pepper mill. That's all! No garlic, shallot, or chives, which would mask the subtle and very fine flavor of the tripe in delicate harmony with the sweet-tasting beet.
5. Serve with the beet salad and as much undressed lamb's lettuce (*mâche*) as you like. We leave the lamb's lettuce undressed so it doesn't spoil: statistics show that there is often some left over at the end of the meal, unlike the other two salad bowls of *gras-double* and beet!

WINE: A GLASS OF CÔTES-DU-RHÔNE

tablier de sapeur

BREADED TRIPE SQUARES ("FIREMAN'S APRON")

1. Make breadcrumbs by crushing some biscuits or toasted bread.
2. Cut rectangles of about 3 x 4 inches from the smooth parts of the tripe or the honeycomb. Blanch and drain them, and dress with vinegar while they are still warm.
3. In a shallow bowl, whisk together 2 whole eggs with one spoonful of sunflower or peanut oil. Add salt and pepper.
4. Heat a pan with a bit of good butter—be nice and generous with the butter!
5. Dry the rectangles of tripe well on paper towel.
6. Dip them into the egg, then into the breadcrumbs (as if preparing schnitzel), and cook until golden on both sides (about 3 minutes).
7. Serve very hot with a béarnaise sauce and steamed potatoes.

WINE: A GLASS OF CÔTES-DU-RHÔNE

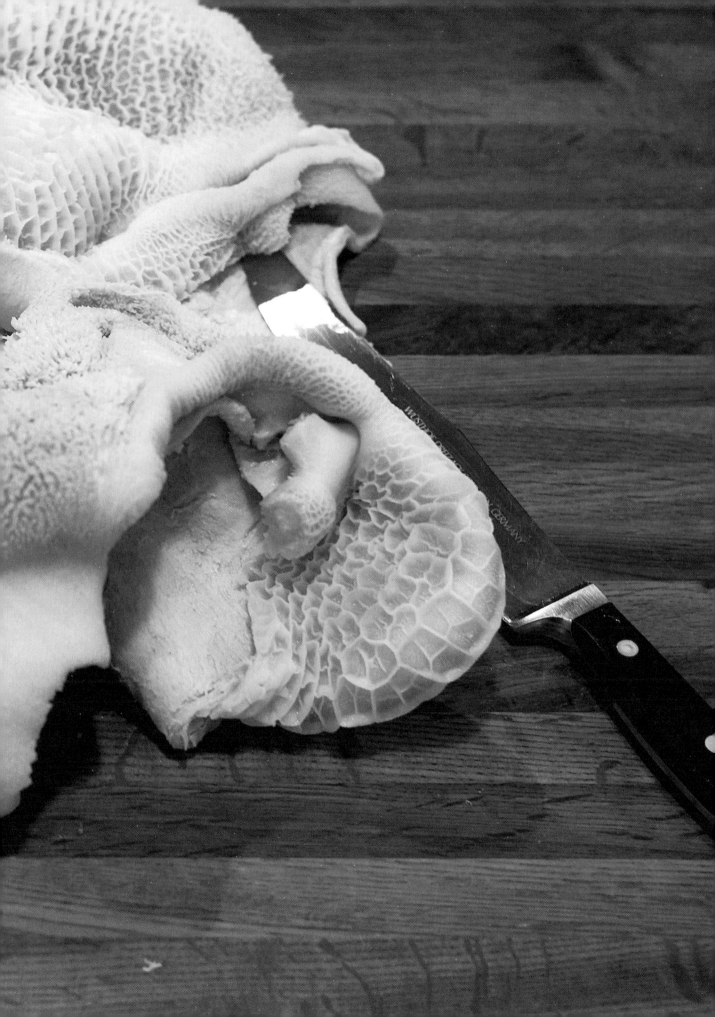

TRIPES À LA MODE DE CAEN

tripes à la mode de Caen

CAEN-STYLE TRIPE (IN CASSEROLE)
FOR 6 - PREPARATION TIME: 30 MINUTES
COOKING TIME: 6 HOURS

Prepared beef tripe	4 pounds 8 ounces
Calf's feet	2
Pork rind	1 pound 2 ounces
Bouquet garni	1
Onions	6
Carrots	6
Tomatoes	6
Hard cider	4 cups
Calvados	2½ tablespoons

Salt, pepper

1. Peel the vegetables. Mince the onions, and slice the carrots into rounds and the tomatoes into quarters. Cut the tripe into squares.
2. In a casserole dish, arrange layers of onions, tripe, pork rind, calf's feet, tomato, and carrot. Season, cover with cider and Calvados, and top with water so that the liquid is 2 inches above the tripe. Add the bouquet garni and cover.
3. Cook in a 300°F oven for 6 hours, regularly checking the amount of cooking liquid and adding more as necessary.

WINE: DRY ALCOHOLIC CIDER

tripes au vin blanc

TRIPE IN WHITE WINE
FOR 6 - PREPARATION TIME: 30 MINUTES
COOKING TIME: 6 HOURS

Prepared beef tripe	4 pounds 8 ounces
Calf's feet	2
Pork rind	1 pound 2 ounces
Bay leaves	3
Rosemary	1 large sprig
Cloves	4
Bouquet garni	1
Onions	6
Potatoes	6
White wine	8 cups

Salt, pepper

Use the same method as in tripe *à la mode de Caen* above—except for the potatoes, which are added to the casserole 20 minutes before the end of the cooking time.

WINE: MENETOU-SALON

pieds et paquets

TROTTERS AND PARCELS (CASSEROLE OF SHEEP'S TROTTERS AND TRIPE PARCELS)
FOR 6 - PREPARATION TIME: 20 MINUTES
COOKING TIME: 6 HOURS 15 MINUTES

Sheep's trotters	12
Parcels (rectangles of lamb's tripe stuffed with a parsley-flavored mince stuffing)	18
Bacon	7-ounce slab
Ripe tomatoes	6
Carrots	6
Red peppers	2
Garlic	6 cloves
Onions	2
Bay leaves	2
White wine	8 cups

Olive oil

1. Peel and chop the onions and garlic. Peel the carrots, and then slice into rounds. Cut the tomatoes into quarters and the peppers into strips.
2. In a flameproof casserole dish, sauté the diced bacon; then add the onions and garlic.
3. Arrange the trotters and parcels on top, adding the tomatoes, peppers, and carrot rounds. Cover with the wine (and extra water if necessary). Add the bay leaves and cover the casserole.
4. Cook in a 300°F oven for 6 hours, regularly checking the amount of cooking liquid and adding more as necessary. Serve with potatoes.

WINE: BANDOL ROUGE

Louis et Jean-Yves

PSYCHOPATHICALLY GENEROUS!

If you're talking *pieds et paquets* you're obviously talking about a large table. Don't think you can make one *pied* (trotter) and one *paquet* (parcel): in the first place, a lamb has four trotters, you can't waste three of them, and one parcel—please! You need to have a big group—high in number, certainly, but, above all, high in quality. There's no room for silliness: the *pieds and paquets* won't stand for it.

You need a congenial setting—a campsite or a restaurant, for example; fine weather is preferable but not indispensable; and, above all, the lilting accent of the south. When these ingredients are brought together, when Louis snickers with relish at his neighbor's antics and drags you into his giggling fits; when Jean-Yves trumpets tomorrow's breakfast-with-truffles—smile: anything goes. *Carpe diem!*

These two worthy representatives of the "only pleasure is giving pleasure" fraternity of Saint Martin de Crau are just the tip of the iceberg: the submerged part is just as endearing. THANK YOU!

LEFT
sweetbreads
in puff pastry
tartlets

RIGHT
veal
sweetbreads
with baby
vegetables

bouchées à la reine

SWEETBREADS IN PUFF PASTRY TARTLETS
FOR 6 - PREPARATION TIME: 20 MINUTES
COOKING TIME: 25 MINUTES

Puff pastry (see page 408 or else ready-made)	1 pound 2 ounces
Chicken *quenelles*	3
Mushrooms	7 ounces
Veal sweetbreads	14 ounces
Chicken stock	10 fluid ounces
Crème fraîche	2 tablespoons
Bouquet garni	1
Egg yolks	1 + 3
Salt, pepper	

1. Roll out the puff pastry to a ¾-inch thickness. Use a pastry cutter to form circles 4 inches in diameter. Arrange these pastry rounds on a baking sheet covered with parchment paper. Using a fork, score the circles. Brush with a beaten egg yolk and bake in a preheated 400°F oven for 15 minutes.
2. Meanwhile, simmer the sweetbreads for 15 minutes in a pot of boiling water with the bouquet garni. Rinse the sweetbreads in cold water, remove the outer membrane, and chop them into small cubes.
3. Heat the stock and poach the mushrooms in it.
4. Mix the crème fraîche with 3 egg yolks, add to the stock, and blend carefully, keeping the sauce over a water bath—it mustn't boil. Add the diced sweetbreads, the quenelles sliced into rounds, and the mushrooms. Season.
5. Remove the heart of the puff pastry tartlets, fill with the sweetbread cream, and top with a pastry hat.

WINE: CÔTES-DE-BEAUNE BLANC

ris de veau aux petits légumes

VEAL SWEETBREADS WITH BABY VEGETABLES
FOR 6 - PREPARATION TIME: 20 MINUTES
COOKING TIME: 20 MINUTES

Veal sweetbreads	1 pound 9 ounces
Bouquet garni	1
Veal stock	5 fluid ounces
Seasonal baby vegetables	1 pound 9 ounces
Ground almonds	1 tablespoon
Butter	2 tablespoons
Salt, pepper	

1. Cook the sweetbreads in boiling water with the bouquet garni for 20 minutes. Rinse the sweetbreads in cold water and remove their outer membrane.
2. At the same time, blanch the baby vegetables (turnips, carrots, peas, garlic, etc.), and then shock them in cold water. Melt the butter and brown the baby vegetables, keeping them crisp. Add the sweetbreads and lightly brown them, then add the ground almonds and stock, and season. The contrast between the creaminess of the sweetbreads and the crispness of the vegetables—Mmmm!.

WINE: SAINT-VÉRAN

ris de veau à la chicorée

VEAL SWEETBREADS WITH CHICORY
FOR 6 - PREPARATION TIME: 20 MINUTES
COOKING TIME: 30 MINUTES

Veal sweetbreads	1 pound 9 ounces
Bouquet garni	1
Baby turnips	12
Red port	2½ tablespoons
Liquid chicory extract (optional)	1 teaspoon
Veal stock	3½ fluid ounces
Butter	2 tablespoons
Salt, pepper	

1. Cook the sweetbreads in boiling water with the bouquet garni for 20 minutes. Rinse the sweetbreads and remove their outer membrane.
2. Meanwhile, blanch the turnips. Melt the butter, sauté the sweetbreads together with the turnips, and deglaze the pan with the port, scraping up the bits on the bottom.
3. Allow the sauce to reduce, add the stock, and reduce again. Add the chicory extract, if using, and season.

WINE: MEURSAULT

Les œufs de canne, d'autruche, de caille...

Duck eggs, ostrich eggs, quail eggs...

MAIS COMMENT DIABLE CUIRE UN ŒUF ?

HOW THE DEVIL DO YOU COOK AN EGG?

Les œufs au plat

Fried eggs

Les mouillettes
Soldiers for dipping

UNE DOUZAINE
D'ŒUFS
A DOZEN EGGS

Les œufs mayo
Hard-boiled eggs with mayonnaise

les ustensiles des œufs
Egg tools

Les omelettes baveuses
Runny omelettes

LA TAILLE DES ŒUFS
EGG SIZES

OSTRICH EGGS

Weighing up to 3 pounds 5 ounces, the ostrich egg is the largest of the eggs, corresponding to 2 dozen chicken eggs. It is the ideal meal for a large family—a soft-boiled ostrich egg served in the style of a Savoyard fondue, for example.

DUCK EGGS

Weighing about 3½ ounces, the duck egg is characterized by its white color. It must be eaten cooked, as it contains bacteria. It has a more pronounced taste than in chicken egg. Its white color makes it visible at night… so much the worse for it!

CHICKEN EGGS (JUST PLAIN EGGS)

Weighing about 2½ ounces, these are the most widely consumed eggs. Shaded white to brown, they are very high in pure protein and cholesterol. One mustn't overindulge! But which came first, the chicken or the egg? It seems that a very long time ago, or even longer than that, a dinosaur gave birth to a chicken (just between you and me, that chicken must have had a really hard time at school); and this wasn't about some drunken night out between dinosaur buddies, it's quite simply the theory of evolution.

QUAIL EGGS

These are the smallest in the family. A greenish color, speckled with brown, they can be eaten raw or cooked. It is the sight of this tiny egg that led to the bird who laid it being called a "quail"… Extreme cold has never, in fact, favored our masculine attributes and when it's freezing (*il caille*), the association with *la caille* (the quail) is compelling! An amusing paradox, since quail eggs are recommended as a remedy for masculine "failings": the bird's sweet revenge!

LES USTENSILES DES ŒUFS
EGG TOOLS

The egg carton

Egg cup

Egg topper

For poaching
heart-shaped eggs

For poaching
egg-shaped eggs

Egg separator

The beaters

For cutting
into wedges

For cutting into slices

CUISSON DES ŒUFS
COOKING EGGS

SOFT-BOILED

Carefully lower the eggs into just-simmering water that has had a spoonful of vinegar and coarse salt added to it. Cook for 3 minutes. Run them under iced water and remove their shells.

MEDIUM-BOILED

Carefully lower the eggs into just-simmering water that has had a spoonful of vinegar and coarse salt added to it. Cook for 5 minutes. Run them under iced water and remove their shells.

HARD-BOILED

Carefully lower the eggs into just-simmering water that has had a spoonful of vinegar and coarse salt added to it. Cook for 10 minutes. Run them under iced water and remove their shells.

POACHED

Break an egg into a ramekin, and bring a saucepan of water to the boil that has had 2 spoonfuls of vinegar added to it. When the water is just at simmering point, slide the egg out of the ramekin around the edge of the saucepan. Simmer for 2 minutes, drop into cold water and trim off any white threads.

SCRAMBLED

Break 3 eggs into a bowl and whisk them with 3½ fluid ounces of heavy cream. Melt a knob of butter in a sauté pan, set up a double-boiler, and place the sauté pan on top. Add the eggs and stir until cooked but still creamy.

FRIED (SUNNY SIDE UP)

Melt a knob of butter in a nonstick frying pan. When the butter takes on a golden color, break the eggs into the pan, lower the heat, allow to cook for 2 minutes, and add a dash of vinegar.

OMELETTE

Break 3 eggs into a bowl, whisk them, and add whatever pleases you. Melt a knob of butter in a nonstick frying pan. When the butter takes on a golden color, pour in the omelette mixture, and move it around the pan until the desired consistency is reached.

ŒUFS SUR LE PLAT
FRIED EGGS

The simple perfect

Duo or civil partnership

The Birkin

Trio

The French

The Japanese

Star-shaped

The botch-up

Pinion

The desirable

The eccentric

The runaway

The suggestive

The clown

The forgotten

ŒUFS À LA COQUE
ET PLEIN D'ACCOMPAGNEMENTS
SOFT-BOILED EGGS WITH LOTS OF TRIMMINGS

FOR 6 BREAD FINGERS
PREPARATION TIME: 10 MINUTES - COOKING TIME: 3 MINUTES

beurre et jambon
BUTTER AND HAM

Butter..½ tablespoon
Shallot .... ½
Chives.................................... 2 blades
Coarsely ground black pepper ....1 pinch
Ham...1 slice
Tarragon...1 sprig
Toasted bread fingers
(baguette or country-style loaf)..................6

1. Chop the shallot with the chives, add pepper, and work this mixture into the butter.
2. Spread your toast fingers with the butter mixture and top with a *chiffonnade* of shredded ham and tarragon.

brousse et piment
SHEEP'S CHEESE AND CHILI PEPPER

Brousse de brebis
(fresh sheep's cheese)..................1¾ ounces
Piment d'Espelette
(hot paprika or chili powder)............1 pinch
Olive oil ....1 teaspoon
Jambon cru....................................1 slice
Bread fingers made from a
country-style loaf...6

1. Mix the sheep's cheese with the chili powder or hot paprika and add the olive oil.
2. Shred the ham finely, keeping the fat.
3. Spread the bread fingers with the cheese mixture, and top with the chiffonnade of ham.

œufs de saumon
SALMON ROE

Salmon roe..1 ounce
Crème fraîche ....1 tablespoon
Lime...1
Cilantro...1 sprig
Bread fingers made from a
country-style loaf...6

1. Mix the crème fraîche with zest of the lime.
2. Spread the bread fingers with this mixture, arrange the salmon roe on top, and add a few cilantro leaves.

boudin noir et ail
BLOOD SAUSAGE AND GARLIC

Boudin noir (blood sausage)........3½ ounces
Scallion (or bulb green onion) 1
Garlic.. 1 clove
Olive oil ....1 teaspoon
Bread fingers made from a
country-style loaf...6

1. Sauté the chopped garlic in the olive oil until golden; then brown the bread fingers in this oil.
2. Remove the sausage skin, crumble the meat into the pan, and let it brown.
3. Spread the bread fingers with the sausage meat and top with the thinly sliced scallion or bulb green onion.

saumon et raifort
SALMON AND HORSERADISH

Horseradish...................................1 teaspoon
Fromage blanc
(fresh cheese) ....1 tablespoon
Coarsely ground black pepper ....1 pinch
Smoked salmon ....1 slice
Bread fingers made from a
country-style loaf...6

1. Mix the quark with the horseradish and pepper.
2. Cut the smoked salmon into thin strips.
3. Spread the bread fingers with the quark mixture and add the smoked salmon strips.

oignons et comté
ONIONS AND COMTÉ CHEESE

Yellow onions...2
Olive oil ....1 tablespoon
Soft brown sugar ....1 teaspoon
Vieux comté
(aged *comté* cheese)....................1¾ ounces
Bread fingers made from a
country-style loaf...6

1. Slice the onions and sauté in olive oil until they have softened. Add the sugar and allow onions to caramelize.
2. Spread the bread fingers with the onion jam, and top with cheese shavings.

LEFT
poached eggs
in red wine
sauce

RIGHT
baked eggs
with
Roquefort

98

œufs meurette

POACHED EGGS IN RED WINE SAUCE
FOR 6 - PREPARATION TIME: 15 MINUTES
COOKING TIME: 30 MINUTES

Eggs..6
Red wine..1 cup
Wine vinegar..¾ cup
Bacon..7-ounce slab
Shallots...2
Scallions (or bulb green onions if available).....................6
Garlic..1 clove
Bay leaf...1
Butter...½ tablespoon
Flour...1 teaspoon
Flat-leaf parsley
Salt, pepper

1. Peel the shallots and quarter them lengthwise; cut the bacon into chunks; and peel and crush the garlic clove.
2. Sauté the bacon pieces and shallots in the butter, add flour, and gently brown for 5 minutes. Stir in the wine, bay leaf, and scallions, and simmer for 20 minutes to thicken the sauce.
3. Poach the eggs in simmering water and vinegar.
4. Place each egg into a shallow dish, pour on the red wine sauce, and sprinkle with parsley.

WINE: MERCUREY ROUGE

œuf cocotte au roquefort

BAKED EGGS WITH ROQUEFORT
FOR 6 - PREPARATION TIME: 10 MINUTES
COOKING TIME: 10 MINUTES

Eggs..6
Walnuts..1 cup
Roquefort cheese...3½ ounces
Heavy cream..2½ cups
Grated nutmeg...1 pinch
Butter
Salt, pepper

1. Season the heavy cream with nutmeg, salt, and pepper.
2. Butter six individual ramekins and break an egg into each one, taking care not to break the yolk. Add a few walnut kernels, and chunks of Roquefort cheese to each ramekin; then pour the cream to fill each ramekin.
3. Place the ramekins in a water bath, and bake in a 400°F oven for 10 minutes.

WINE: SAUTERNES

œufs brouillés au haddock

SCRAMBLED EGGS WITH SMOKED HADDOCK
FOR 6 - PREPARATION TIME: 15 MINUTES
COOKING TIME: 20 MINUTES

Eggs..12
Smoked haddock (or cod)......................................7 ounces
Milk..1¼ cup
Heavy cream...⅓ to ½ cup
Butter...1 tablespoon
Chives...4 sprigs
Salt, pepper

1. Whisk together the eggs and cream.
2. Pour the milk into a pan and add an equal amount of water. Poach the haddock in the milk for 10 minutes. Drain and flake the flesh, removing the bones.
3. Melt the butter in a small pan, add the egg and cream mixture, and stir regularly. When the eggs begin to set, add the flaked haddock and the roughly snipped chives. Serve while still creamy; but be careful with the seasoning, since the fish is already very salty.

WINE: JURANÇON MOELLEUX

OMELETTE BAVEUSE
ET PLEIN D'ACCOMPAGNEMENTS
RUNNY OMELETTE WITH LOTS OF TRIMMINGS

FOR 6 - PREPARATION TIME: 15 MINUTES - COOKING TIME: 10 MINUTES

poutargue et citronnelle

BOTTARGA AND LEMONGRASS

Eggs 12
Bottarga (pressed mullet roe) .... ¾ ounces
Shelled shrimp .... 3½ ounces
Shallot 1
Lemongrass .... 2 stems
Cilantro .... 3 sprigs
Heavy cream .... ⅓ to ½ cup
Butter .... ½ tablespoon
Olive oil
Salt, pepper

1. Chop the shallot and the inner white core of the lemongrass blades. Thinly slice the bottarga.
2. Break the eggs into a bowl, add cream, and whisk together. Add the cilantro leaves.
3. Sauté the shallot and lemongrass in butter. Pour in the beaten eggs, add the shrimp and bottarga, and stir. Season carefully—the bottarga is already salty!—and add a dash of olive oil. Stop the cooking process when the mixture reaches the desired texture (runny or otherwise).

piquillos et fines herbes

PIQUILLO PEPPERS AND HERBS

Eggs 12
Piquillo peppers 6
Chives .... 4 sprigs
Chervil .... 4 sprigs
Tarragon .... 4 sprigs
Butter .... ½ tablespoon
Oil
Salt, pepper

1. Slice the piquillo peppers into strips and chop together all the herbs.
2. Break the eggs into a bowl and whisk until pale and frothy. Season.
3. Melt the butter in a nonstick frying pan with a drop of oil. Pour in the eggs, then add the piquillo strips, and finally the herbs; season and stir. Stop the cooking process when the mixture reaches the desired texture (runny or otherwise).

châtaignes et champignons

CHESTNUTS AND MUSHROOMS

Eggs 12
Mushrooms .... 10½ ounces
Preserved chestnuts, *au naturel*... 3½ ounces
Shallot 1
Parsley .... 2 sprigs
Garlic .... 1 clove
Butter .... ½ tablespoon
Oil
Salt, pepper

1. Slice the shallots and mushrooms into thin slivers. Roughly crush the chestnuts, and chop the garlic together with parsley.
2. Break the eggs into a bowl and whisk until pale and frothy. Season.
3. Melt the butter in a nonstick frying pan with a drop of oil. Then sauté all ingredients except for the eggs, adding the chestnuts last.
4. Add the eggs and stir. Stop the cooking process when the mixture reaches the desired texture (runny or otherwise).

lard et confit de canard

BACON AND DUCK CONFIT

Eggs 12
Bacon .... 3½ ounces
Cold duck confit .... 3½ ounces
Duck fat .... ½ tablespoon
Shallot 1
Truffle oil
Sea salt

1. Sauté the diced bacon in duck fat along with the flaked duck confit and sliced shallot.
2. Break the eggs into a bowl and whisk until pale and frothy. Pour them over the bacon mixture and cook, making sure the omelette is runny. Add a dash of truffle oil, season with sea salt, and serve.

foies de volaille

CHICKEN LIVERS

Eggs 12
Chicken livers .... 7 ounces
Chopped hazelnuts .... 1 tablespoon
Onion .... ½
Chives .... 2 sprigs
Walnut oil
Salt, pepper

1. Slice the onion thinly. Sauté with the chicken livers in walnut oil, adding the hazelnuts. Sauté the mixture until golden brown.
2. Break the eggs into a bowl and whisk until pale and frothy. Season.
3. Pour the eggs over the livers. Stir, season, and add the snippets of chives. Stop the cooking process when the mixture reaches the desired texture (runny or otherwise).

saumon fumé et œufs de lump

SMOKED SALMON AND LUMPFISH ROE

Eggs 12
Smoked salmon .... 2 slices
Lumpfish roe .... 1 tablespoon
Heavy cream .... 3½ fluid ounces
Sundried tomatoes .... ¼ cup
Lime .... zest
Olive oil

1. Cut the salmon into strips.
2. Break the eggs into a bowl, add the cream, and whisk the eggs and cream together. Add the lumpfish roe.
3. Sauté the sun-dried tomatoes and add the lime zest. Pour in the eggs and stir.
4. Turn off the heat and add the salmon. Stop the cooking process when the mixture reaches the desired texture (runny or otherwise).

LEFT
hard-boiled
eggs with
mayonnaise

RIGHT
aspic from my
childhood

IO4

œuf mayo

HARD-BOILED EGGS WITH MAYONNAISE
FOR 6 - PREPARATION TIME: 10 MINUTES
COOKING TIME: 10 MINUTES

Eggs	9
Egg yolk	1
Peanut oil	¾ cup
Olive oil	2½ tablespoons
White wine vinegar	1 teaspoon
Mustard	1 teaspoon
Arugula	
Salt, pepper	

1. Cook the eggs in boiling water for 10 minutes. Run them under cold water, then remove their shells.
2. Make a mayonnaise by mixing together the egg yolk, mustard, and vinegar; then season. Slowly whisk in the peanut oil (the amount of oil depends on the desired consistency) and finish by adding the olive oil.
3. Serve the eggs halved, topped by the mayonnaise and a few arugula leaves.

WINE: BLANC DE LOIRE

aspic De mon enfance

ASPIC FROM MY CHILDHOOD
FOR 6 - PREPARATION TIME: 30 MINUTES
COOKING TIME: 15 MINUTES

Aspic molds	6
Eggs	6
Ham (sliced off the bone)	2 slices
Diced tomato	1 tablespoon
Chicken stock	2¼ cup
Gelatin leaves	4
Coarsely ground black pepper	
Chervil	

1. Cook the eggs in boiling water for 10 minutes. Run them under cold water, then remove their shells.
2. Soften the gelatin in cold water. Bring the stock to a boil, add the gelatin, and whisk.
3. Pour 1⁄16 inch of the stock into each aspic mold. Add the chervil leaves, diced tomato, and black pepper; then allow to set.
4. Cut strips of ham to the same width as the molds.
5. Place a boiled egg in each mold, surround it with a strip of ham, cover with the remaining stock, and let the aspic set in the refrigerator for at least 4 hours.

WINE: BLANC DE LOIRE

soufflé au fromage

CHEESE SOUFFLÉ
FOR 6 - PREPARATION TIME: 15 MINUTES
COOKING TIME: 20 MINUTES

Eggs	6
Butter	2 tablespoons
Flour	¼ cup
Grated *comté* cheese	1¼ cups
Milk	7 fluid ounces
Heavy cream	⅓ cup
Grated nutmeg	½ teaspoon
Salt, pepper	

1. Separate the egg whites from the yolks.
2. Make a roux by melting 1½ tablespoons of butter in a pan and stirring in the flour. Cook for 2 minutes without browning, then add the cream and milk, and continue to stir until the mixture thickens.
3. Off the heat, add the grated cheese, allow it to melt, and stir in the egg yolks and nutmeg. Season and pour the mixture into a cold dish.
4. Butter a soufflé mold from top to bottom. Whisk the egg whites into very firm, shiny peaks. Fold them delicately into the egg mixture. Then fill the soufflé mold with the mixture until it is a quarter or a third full.
5. Bake in a preheated oven at 400°F for 20 minutes. Serve immediately.

WINE: BLANC DE LOIRE

À CHAQUE SAISON SES LÉGUMES !

Something extra: A VEGETABLE FOR EVERY FRENCH SEASON!

Fruits and their seasons

	J	F	M	A	M	J	J	A	S	O	N	D
Almond						X						
Apricot						X	X	X				
Bilberry							X	X				
Blackberry							X	X				
Blackcurrant							X	X				
Cherry						X	X	X				
Chestnut										X	X	
Clementine	X	X										
Fig							X	X	X	X		
Gooseberry							X	X				
Grape								X	X	X	X	
Kiwi		X										X
Lemon	X	X										
Mandarin												
Melon						X	X	X	X			
Mirabelle plum								X	X			
Orange	X	X										
Peach						X						
Pear	X	X							X	X	X	X
Plum							X	X	X			
Quince										X	X	
Raspberry					X	X	X	X				
Strawberry					X	X						
Walnut	X									X		
Watermelon							X	X				

Vegetables and their seasons

	J	F	M	A	M	J	J	A	S	O	N	D
Artichoke				X	X	X	X	X	X			
Beans					X	X	X	X				
Beet	X	X	X	X	X	X	X	X	X	X	X	X
Broccoli						X	X	X	X	X		
Cabbage	X	X	X					X	X	X	X	X
Capsicum (pepper)						X	X	X	X			
Cardoon												X
Carrot	X	X	X	X	X	X	X	X	X	X	X	X
Celery	X	X							X	X	X	
Chard									X	X		
Cucumber			X		X	X	X	X	X			
Eggplant						X	X	X	X	X		
Endive	X	X								X	X	X
Fennel		X				X	X					
Herbs					X	X						
Jerusalem artichoke	X	X	X									X
Leek	X	X								X	X	X
Lettuce			X	X	X	X	X	X	X			
Mushroom									X	X	X	
Parsnip	X	X								X	X	X
Peas				X	X	X	X					
Potato	X						X	X	X	X		
Pumpkin (squash)	X	X	X								X	X
Radish			X	X	X	X						
Salsify	X	X	X							X	X	X
Spinach			X	X	X				X	X		
Tomato						X	X	X	X			
Turnip	X									X	X	X
Zucchini				X	X	X	X	X	X			

La tarte aux cèpes
Porcini mushroom tart

QUE DE BONS LÉGUMES!
WHAT LOVELY VEGETABLES!

Soup, Stew, and consommé

La salade comme à Nice
Salad Nice-style

Bons ou Méchampignons ?
Mushrooms savory and unsavory

PURÉE, EN VEUX-TU? EN VOILÀ!

WANT SOME MASH? HERE YOU GO!

courgettes

ZUCCHINI

FOR 6 - PREPARATION TIME: 20 MINUTES
COOKING TIME: 10 MINUTES

Zucchini 6
Onions... 2
Ground aniseed .... 1 teaspoon
Butter, melted .... 3 tablespoons
Olive oil
Salt, pepper

1. Peel and slice the onions. Slice the zucchini into rounds.
2. Sauté the vegetables in olive oil until the zucchini and onions are nicely browned.
3. Purée the whole mixture, incorporating the butter. Add the aniseed and season.

petits pois et menthe

PEAS AND MINT

FOR 6 - PREPARATION TIME: 20 MINUTES
COOKING TIME: 10 MINUTES

Frozen peas .... 6½ cups
Mint .... 1 bunch
Heavy cream .... ¾ cup
Coarse salt
Salt, pepper

1. Add some salt to a saucepan of water and bring to a boil. Add the peas and cook for 8 minutes.
2. Rinse the peas under iced water to preserve their green color.
3. Purée the peas and strain the purée through a fine sieve to remove the skin. Finely shred the mint, stirring it into the purée. Add the cream to the purée and season.

céleri cuit-cru

CELERIAC (RAW AND COOKED)

FOR 6 - PREPARATION TIME: 20 MINUTES
COOKING TIME: 45 MINUTES

Celeriac (celery root).................................... 2
Heavy cream .... ½ cup
Salted butter.................................... ⅓ cup
Lemon 1
Ground cumin .... 1 teaspoon

1. Peel the celeriac. Cut one and a half of them into small cubes and cook in salted water for 45 minutes.
2. Chop the remaining celeriac into ¼-inch cubes and toss them with the lemon juice.
3. Purée the cooked celeriac and butter; then stir in the cumin, cream, and raw celeriac.

châtaignes

CHESTNUTS

FOR 6 - PREPARATION TIME: 30 MINUTES
COOKING TIME: 30 MINUTES

Jar of chestnuts .... 1 pound 2 ounces
Potatoes... 2 medium
Butter... ⅓ cup
Heavy cream .... ¾ cup
Sweet chestnut purée .... 2 tablespoons
Sea salt

1. Peel the potatoes and cut them into cubes.
2. Add some salt to a saucepan of water and bring to a boil. Add the potatoes and chestnuts and cook for 30 minutes, then put them through a food mill.
3. Melt the butter with the cream and warm up this mixture in a saucepan.
4. Add the cream mixture to the puréed potatoes and chestnuts. Stir in the sweet chestnut purée, and season.

pommes de terre et olives noires

POTATOES AND BLACK OLIVES

FOR 6 - PREPARATION TIME: 20 MINUTES
COOKING TIME: 30 MINUTES

Potatoes........................... 2 pounds 4 ounces
Greek-style dry-cured olives .... ¾ cup
Olive oil .... ⅔ cup
Thyme .... 4 sprigs
Salt, pepper

1. Peel the potatoes and cut them into cubes.
2. Add some salt to a saucepan of water and bring to a boil. Add the potatoes and cook for 30 minutes, then put them through a food mill.
3. Pit the olives and chop them well.
4. Combine the olive oil, thyme leaves, and chopped olives with the potato purée, then season.

carrots, fenouil et reglisse

CARROTS, FENNEL, AND LICORICE

FOR 6 - PREPARATION TIME: 20 MINUTES
COOKING TIME: 30 MINUTES

Carrots... 8 medium
Fennel .... 3 bulbs
Licorice............................. 2 sticks (optional)
Onions... 2
Heavy cream .... ¾ cup
Salt, pepper

1. Peel and cut the carrots into rounds. Thinly slice the fennel and onions.
2. Bring a saucepan of water to a boil with the sticks of licorice. Add the carrots, fennel, and onions, and cook for 30 minutes.
3. Remove the vegetables and purée them; then strain through a *chinois* (fine sieve). Mix with the cream and season.

LEFT
tomato
soup

RIGHT
split-pea
soup

soupe de tomates

TOMATO SOUP
FOR 6 - PREPARATION TIME: 15 MINUTES
COOKING TIME: 25 MINUTES

Ripe tomatoes	6
Shallot	1
Carrots	2
Potato	1
Tomato ketchup	1 tablespoon
White wine	½ cup
Cumin	1 pinch
Olive oil	
Salt, pepper	

1. Plunge the tomatoes into boiling water for 10 seconds. Remove their skins and reserve them.
2. Sauté the sliced shallot in some olive oil and add the peeled carrots, cut into rounds. Pour in the wine, add the tomatoes as well as the peeled potato, diced into cubes. Cover with water and simmer until the vegetables start to fall apart.
3. Process the whole mixture, and strain the soup through a *chinois* (fine sieve). Stir in the tomato ketchup and cumin, then season.
4. Fry the tomato skins in olive oil.
5. Serve the soup in bowls topped with the fried tomato skins.

WINE: SANCERRE BLANC

soupe de pois cassés

SPLIT-PEA SOUP
FOR 6 - PREPARATION TIME: 15 MINUTES
COOKING TIME: 50 MINUTES + 12 HOURS SOAKING TIME

Dried split peas	1 cup
Shallots	2
Carrot	1
Bay leaf	1
Thyme	1 large sprig
Ham hock	1
Smoked bacon	6 slices
White port	2½ tablespoons
Heavy cream	½ cup
Olive oil	
Salt, pepper	

1. Soak the split peas for 12 hours.
2. Sauté the sliced shallots in some olive oil. Add the ham hock and split peas to the pot, along with twice their volume in water. Cut the carrot into small cubes and add to the pot with the bay leaf and thyme.
3. Cook for 45 minutes, adding water if necessary to reach the desired consistency.
4. Remove the thyme, bay leaf, and ham hock. Purée half the lentil mixture with the cream and port, then mix back into the soup, and season.
5. Fry the bacon slices in olive oil and serve on top of the soup.

WINE: CORNAS

soupe à l'oignon pour digérer

ONION SOUP FOR DIGESTION
FOR 6 - PREPARATION TIME: 20 MINUTES
COOKING TIME: 30 MINUTES

Yellow onions	8
White wine	1 cup
Rounds of toasted baguette	6
Grated Gruyère cheese	
Olive oil	
Salt, pepper	

1. Slice the onions thinly and sauté them in the olive oil until they brown. Add the wine, allow to reduce by one-third, and add 8 cups of water.
2. Cook for 20 minutes—the onions must be meltingly tender and the soup a lovely brown color. Season and ladle into shallow heat-proof bowls.
3. To serve, cover the baguette croutons with grated Gruyère, arrange them on top of the soup bowls and place under a hot broiler to melt the cheese.

WINE: A GOOD MINERAL WATER WOULD BE PERFECT.

LEFT
cabbage
soup

RIGHT
pumpkin soup
with roasted
pumpkin
seeds

116

soupe au chou

CABBAGE SOUP
FOR 6 - PREPARATION TIME: 30 MINUTES
COOKING TIME: 45 MINUTES

Round green cabbage	1
Shallots	2
Potatoes	3
Heavy cream	2 cups
Bacon	10½-ounce slab
Olive oil	
Canola oil	
Salt, pepper	

1. Slice the cabbage very thinly, dice the shallots, and sauté both in olive oil without browning. Cover with 4 cups of water, then add the peeled and cubed potatoes, and cook for 20 minutes.
2. Purée the mixture, stirring in the cream and bacon. Cook for an additional 20 minutes, then season, and add a dash of canola oil before serving.

WINE: A GOOD DROP OF *BOUDIOU* (FOR HEAVEN'S SAKE!)

soupe de courge et ses graines grillées

PUMPKIN SOUP WITH ROASTED PUMPKIN SEEDS
FOR 6 - PREPARATION TIME: 15 MINUTES
COOKING TIME: 35 MINUTES

Cheese or sugar pumpkin	1 pound 12 ounces
Heavy cream	¾ cup
Grated nutmeg	1 teaspoon
Ground ginger	1 teaspoon
Light brown sugar	1 tablespoon
Olive oil	
Salt, pepper	

1. Peel the pumpkin and cut into large chunks.
2. Remove the pumpkin seeds and roast them in a 350°F oven with a little olive oil: they should be crunchy when done.
3. Cook the pumpkin chunks in a covered saucepan with a small quantity of water until tender.
4. Purée the soup, and add the cream, spices, and sugar. Cook an additional 5 minutes.
5. Garnish and serve with roasted pumpkin seeds.

WINE: BOURGOGNE BLANC

soupe au pistou

SOUP WITH PISTOU
FOR 6 - PREPARATION TIME: 30 MINUTES
COOKING TIME: 1 HOUR 20 MINUTES

Fresh white beans (navy, cannellini)	1½ cups
Green beans	3 cups
Snow peas	1½ cups
Potatoes	2
Carrots	2
Onions	3
Spaghetti	3½ ounces
Salt, pepper	

PISTOU SAUCE

Basil	1 bunch
Garlic	3 cloves
Pine nuts	⅓ cup
Finely grated parmesan cheese	⅓ cup
Olive oil	¾ cup

1. Rinse the white beans and trim the green beans. Peel the potatoes, carrots, and onions. Cut all the vegetables into a small dice and place in a pot. Cover them with twice their volume of water, bring to a boil, and cook gently for an hour.
2. Break up the spaghetti, add to the soup, and cook for an additional 15 minutes.
3. Meanwhile, make the pistou sauce. Combine the basil, garlic, pine nuts, and parmesan and crush with a mortar and pestle until the mixture forms a paste. Then gradually pour in the olive oil. (You can add the flesh of two blanched and peeled tomatoes to this mixture if you like.)
4. Season the soup and serve with the pistou sauce.

WINE: ROSÉ DE PROVENCE

LEFT
vegetable
soup, pure
and simple

RIGHT
emulsion of
creamed
cauliflower

soupe de légumes tout simplement

VEGETABLE SOUP, PURE AND SIMPLE
FOR 6 - PREPARATION TIME: 30 MINUTES
COOKING TIME: 45 MINUTES

Potatoes	4
Carrots	4
Sweet potato	1
Turnips	2
Leek	1
Onion	1
Celery stalks	2
Salted butter	⅓ cup
Cumin	1 teaspoon
Crème fraîche	⅓ cup
Chives	6 blades

Salt, pepper

1. Peel and dice all the vegetables. Place them in a pot, cover with twice their volume of water, and simmer slowly for 40 minutes.
2. Purée the soup mixture, either in a blender, food processor, or through a sieve, before adding the cumin. Add the butter and process again to emulsify the mixture. Season.
3. Combine the finely chopped chives and crème fraîche. Season and serve with a spoonful of crème fraîche on top.

WINE: AN INFUSION OF THYME LEAVES

crème de chou-fleur en émulsion

EMULSION OF CREAMED CAULIFLOWER
FOR 6 - PREPARATION TIME: 20 MINUTES
COOKING TIME: 40 MINUTES

Cauliflower	1
Potatoes	2
Shallots	2
White wine	½ cup
Heavy cream	¾ cup
Milk	½ cup
Piment d'Espelette (hot paprika)	1 pinch
White cardamom	1 pinch

Salt

1. Peel and chop the potatoes. Chop four-fifths of the cauliflower into chunks.
2. Slice the shallots and cook in the wine until the liquid has completely evaporated. Add the cauliflower and potato, cover with twice their volume of water, and simmer for 30 minutes. Add the cream and spices; then purée the mixture and season.
3. Grate the remaining cauliflower.
4. Heat the milk, stirring in the cauliflower cream. Process until light and moussey.
5. Serve the soup topped with a spoonful of mousse and grated cauliflower.

WINE: ANJOU BLANC

potage cultivateur

FARMER'S VEGETABLE SOUP
FOR 6 - PREPARATION TIME: 45 MINUTES
COOKING TIME: 30 MINUTES

Potatoes	6
Carrots	6
Leeks	2
Turnips	2
Olive oil	2 tablespoons

Salt, pepper

1. Peel all the vegetables and cut them into ½ x ¾-inch dice.
2. In a pot, bring enough water to a boil to cover the vegetables. Add the leeks and cook for 10 minutes before adding the other vegetables. Cook for an additional 15 minutes.
3. Add the olive oil, season, and serve.

WINE: A 'PELURE D'OIGNON' ROSÉ (PERFECT WITH THE SOUP!)

LEFT
thick onion
soup

RIGHT
beef
consommé

124

tourin

THICK ONION SOUP
FOR 6 - PREPARATION TIME: 20 MINUTES
COOKING TIME: 55 MINUTES

Onions..6
Parsley..1 bunch
White wine...½ cup
Egg yolks..4
Country-style bread....................................... 3 slices
Olive oil
Salt, pepper

1. Peel and slice the onions. In a large saucepan, soften them in olive oil until they are lightly browned. Add the wine, then 6 cups of water, and simmer for 45 minutes.
2. Finely chop the parsley and add to the soup.
3. Remove the soup from the heat and allow to cool slightly. Gently stir the egg yolks into the soup: be careful that the soup temperature doesn't exceed 175°F or the eggs may scramble.
4. Crumble the bread on top before serving.

WINE: WHITE WINE FROM TOURIN

consommé de bœuf

BEEF CONSOMMÉ
FOR 6 - PREPARATION TIME: 45 MINUTES
COOKING TIME: 2 HOURS 20 MINS

Oxtail..1
Leeks...2
Onions..4 whole + 1 chopped
Carrots..4 whole + 1 chopped
Celery stalks.......................................4 whole + 1 chopped
Garlic.. 2 cloves
Peppercorns...6
Peeled tomatoes 3
Cilantro...4 sprigs
Orzo .... 1 cup
Ground beef ....5½ ounces

1. Place the oxtail in a heavy saucepan and cover with cold water. Bring to a boil and skim. Add the peppercorns along with the whole leeks, onions, carrots, celery, and chopped garlic. Cook for 2 hours until the meat is falling off the bone.
2. Remove the meat and whole vegetables from the pan, and strain the beef stock through a *chinois* (fine sieve).
3. Add the chopped vegetables and ground beef, as well as tomatoes and chopped cilantro. Carefully cover all ingredients with the stock and bring to a boil. Add the orzo and cook for 10 minutes.

WINE: WITBIER

garbure

GASCON CABBAGE AND VEGETABLE SOUP
FOR 6 - PREPARATION TIME: 45 MINUTES
COOKING TIME: 2 HOURS 30 MINUTES

Green cabbage 1
White haricot beans ....10½ ounces
Carrots...6
Potatoes...6
Fava beans ....1 cup
Turnips...6
Leeks..3
Onions..3
Duck carcass..1
Confit duck *manchons* (upper wing parts) 6
Bacon ....10½-ounce slab
Ham hock 1
Duck fat...2 tablespoons
Salt, pepper

1. Slice the cabbage, removing its thick ribs. Peel all the vegetables and mince them roughly.
2. In a very large pot, melt the duck fat. Add the duck carcass and the onions and brown them.
3. Add 12 cups of water, as well as all the vegetables, the beans, bacon, and ham hock. Cook for 2 hours and then season.
4. Add the duck confit and cook for an additional 15 minutes. This soup should be thick!

WINE: MADIRAN

soupe aux fèves et aux gésiers

FAVA BEAN AND POULTRY GIZZARD SOUP
FOR 6 - PREPARATION TIME: 30 MINUTES
COOKING TIME: 45 MINUTES

Peeled fava beans	1 pound 2 ounces
Potatoes	2
Onions	3
Carrots	3
Ham hock	1
Confit poultry gizzards	10 ounces
Duck fat	2 tablespoons
Tomatoes	4

1. Peel the potatoes, onions, and carrots and chop them into small cubes.
2. Melt the duck fat in a pot, and sauté the gizzards, vegetables, ham hock, and quartered tomatoes. Add twice their volume in water, bring to a boil, and allow to reduce by half. Season.
3. Preferably to be eaten in a hunting lodge with the temperature outside at -20°F, the temperature of one's back to the stove at 90°F, and the temperature of one's cheeks at 55°F.

WINE: GRAVES ROUGE

SOUP,
POTAGE, AND CONSOMMÉ

Soup has its origins in the appearance of fire. As soon as humans learned how to boil water, they dropped meat and vegetables into it, and soup was born. Soup constituted a full meal, so it had to be nourishing. It has always followed armies into battle to warm bellies and souls. During the twelfth century, *sope* referred to the slice of bread on which the hot stock—based in meat, vegetables, fruits, honey, or wine—was poured. This single restorative meal had to sustain people for a full day's labor.

This dish of the people would, little by little, become an upper-class delight. King Louis XV—who was responsible for planting the King's kitchen garden (*le Potager du Roi*) at Versailles—transformed the *soupe populaire* into the *potage royal.* By cooking all sorts of vegetables in a pot for the pure pleasure of it rather than for "fuel," soup was given a new lease on life: it became the first course in a never-ending feast. It was also discovered to have therapeutic properties: soup does you good!

Soup became consommé: the nice chunks of vegetable were forgotten. The aim was to extract the quintessence of a carcass, to salvage the micronutrients lurking in vegetables. It was all about obtaining a clear and tasty broth, high in nutrients, low in calories. Restorative soup thus became the rejuvenating consommé.

Which to have? The choice is up to you!

LEFT
leeks with
vegetable
vinaigrette

Poireaux à la vinaigrette de légumes

LEEKS WITH VEGETABLE VINAIGRETTE
FOR 6 - PREPARATION TIME: 15 MINUTES
COOKING TIME: 35 MINUTES

Leeks 6
Bouquet garni..1
Tomatoes..2
Chives..6 blades
Scallions (or bulb green onions, if available) 1
Olive oil ....3 tablespoons
Balsamic vinegar....................................... 1 tablespoon
Dijon mustard .... 1 teaspoon
Salt, pepper

1. Cut off the top half of each leek; then cut this section into four pieces and rinse. Cook the leeks with the bouquet garni in enough water to cover for 20 minutes. Lift out the leeks with a slotted spoon.
2. Immerse the tomatoes for 30 seconds in the hot leek stock and remove their skins. Cut the tomato flesh into a small dice.
3. Let the leek stock reduce by one-quarter.
4. Finely mince the chives and green onion.
5. Make a vinaigrette by combining the mustard with the olive oil, vinegar, and 3 tablespoons of the leek stock. Season and blend in the diced tomatoes, chives, and green onion. Serve with the simmered leeks.

WINE: NO WINE—WATER AND NOTHING ELSE

tomates tout en tomates

TOMATO-STYLE TOMATOES
FOR 6 - PREPARATION TIME: 10 MINUTES

Assorted tomatoes 8
Basil.. 6 leaves
Mint .... 6 leaves
Olive oil
Balsamic vinegar
Sea salt

1. To make a tomato salad, your only problem is in choosing which tomatoes to use, since there are no less than 150 varieties! Pick four of your favorite varieties—as long as they are sweet, juicy, fully ripe, and brightly colored; select two of the finest of each variety.
2. Make a vinaigrette by mixing 1 part balsamic vinegar to 2 parts olive oil.
3. Finely chop the mint and basil.
4. Slice the tomatoes into rounds. Dress with the vinaigrette, mint and basil, and season with sea salt.

WINE: BETTER TO HAVE A BLOODY MARY

salade de lentilles aux herbes fraîches

LENTIL SALAD WITH FRESH HERBS
FOR 6 - PREPARATION TIME: 20 MINUTES
COOKING TIME: 20 MINUTES

Lentils .... 1 cup
Onion studded with 4 cloves..1
Carrots.. 2
Smoked bacon ....3½ ounces
Celery stalk 1
Cilantro.. 3 sprigs
Chives.. 10 pieces
Shallot 1
Walnut oil.. 4 tablespoons
Balsamic vinegar..1 tablespoon
Sea salt

1. Peel carrots and dice them into small cubes.
2. Put the lentils in a pot of boiling water, along with the carrots, bacon, and onion. Cook for 20 minutes; the lentils must still be firm. Then drain and rinse, removing only the onion.
3. Cut the celery into small cubes and clip the cilantro leaves. Slice the chives; peel and finely slice the shallot.
4. Season the lentils and carrots with sea salt, walnut oil, and vinegar, and combine with the herbs and celery.

WINE: CÔTES-D'AUVERGNE ROUGE

lentil salad with fresh herbs

LEFT
beet
mille-feuille

RIGHT
dandelion
salad

134

mille-feuille de betterave

BEET MILLE-FEUILLE
FOR 6 - PREPARATION TIME: 15 MINUTES

Cooked beets	3
Raw beets	1
Baby beet leaves	a good handful
Parmesan cheese	2 ounces
Cumin seeds	1 teaspoon
Olive oil	
Soy sauce	

1. Peel the beets and slice them thinly. Season with olive oil and soy sauce.
2. Using a vegetable peeler, make shavings of parmesan.
3. On a plate, arrange layers of the cooked and raw beets and beet leaves. Sprinkle with the parmesan shavings and cumin seeds.

WINE: SAUVIGNON

salade de laiterons

DANDELION SALAD
FOR 6 - PREPARATION TIME: 15 MINUTES
COOKING TIME: 10 MINUTES

Dandelion greens	10 ounces
Eggs	6
Chorizo sausage	1
Jambon cru	3 slices
Scallions (or bulb green onions if available)	3
Garlic	1 clove
Cider vinegar	1 tablespoon
Olive oil	

1. Wash the dandelion greens several times in cold running water.
2. Boil the eggs for 5 minutes and peel them.
3. Cut the chorizo sausage into matchsticks and the ham into strips. Peel and finely chop the garlic.
4. Sauté the garlic, chorizo, and ham in olive oil. Reserve the cooking oil for the dressing: combine it with the cider vinegar and a little more olive oil.
5. Chop the scallions, thinly slicing the green parts, and mix together with the dandelion greens. Toss the herbs and greens with the chorizo, ham, and dressing.
6. Cut the boiled eggs in half and arrange on top of the salad.

WINE: CAIRANNE

frisée aux lardons et aux oreilles grillées

FRISÉE WITH BACON AND CRISPY PIG'S EARS
FOR 6 - PREPARATION TIME: 20 MINUTES
COOKING TIME: 30 MINUTES

Frisée lettuce, nice and lacy	1
Hard-boiled eggs	3
Comté cheese	3½ ounces
Bacon pieces	3½ ounces
Pig's ears	2
Shallot	1
Country-style bread	1 slice
Olive oil	
Red wine vinegar	

1. Boil the pig's ears for 30 minutes (can be done the day before) and slice them very thinly.
2. Wash the frisée lettuce several times in cold running water.
3. Peel and dice the shallot. Chop the cheese into a small dice and the bread into croutons.
4. Sauté the shallots and bacon in olive oil; then sear the sliced pig's ears over high heat until they are crisp.
5. Brown the croutons in the same oil until golden. Reserve the oil.
6. Chop the hard-boiled eggs.
7. Make a vinaigrette by mixing two-thirds olive oil (plus the cooking oil) and a third of the vinegar. Toss all the ingredients together and season.

WINE: GLASS OF BEAUJOLAIS

frisée lettuce salad with bacon and crispy pig's ears

légumes inattendus

VEGETABLE SURPRISE
FOR 6 - PREPARATION TIME: 20 MINUTES
COOKING TIME: 20 MINUTES

Radishes	1 bunch
Baby pattypan squash	6
Cauliflower	3½ ounces
Broccoli	1
Fava beans	3½ ounces
Mushrooms	3½ ounces
Chanterelle mushrooms	3½ ounces
Shallots	2
Garlic	1 clove
Bouquet garni	1
White wine	½ cup
Coriander seeds	1 tablespoon
Olive oil	½ cup
Lemon	1

Salt, pepper

1. Cut off all but ½ inch of the radish tops. Cut the baby pattypan squash into quarters, and cut all the mushrooms in half and the cauliflower and broccoli into florets. Peel and chop the garlic and shallots.
2. In a large pot, sauté the garlic and shallots in the olive oil. Add the coriander seeds, then all the mushrooms and vegetables except for the fava beans. Add juice from the lemon, wine, a glass of water, and the bouquet garni. Season and simmer for 10 minutes.
3. Remove all the vegetables to a plate. Add the fava beans to the stock and allow the stock to reduce by one-third. Return the vegetables to the stock, turn off the heat, and let cool. Enjoy this dish cold.

WINE: MARSANNAY ROSÉ

petits farcis aux légumes

STUFFED BABY VEGETABLES
FOR 6 - PREPARATION TIME: 30 MINUTES
COOKING TIME: 30 MINUTES

Baby red peppers	6
Baby eggplants	6
Baby zucchini	6
Green tomatoes	6
Red tomatoes	6
Basil	1 bunch
Mint	1 bunch
Tarragon	1 bunch
Shallots	2
Garlic	2 cloves
Leftover roast veal or pork	10½ ounces
Soft white sandwich bread	3 slices
Heavy cream	½ cup
White wine	1¼ cup

Olive oil
Salt, pepper

1. Slice the tops off all the vegetables and reserve them. Remove the seeds from the red peppers and hollow out the other vegetables, reserving the flesh.
2. Peel and chop the shallots and garlic. Sauté them in the olive oil with the reserved vegetable flesh, and cook the mixture to a stew-like consistency.
3. Chop the herbs and stir into the stewed vegetables.
4. Combine the meat with the bread slices and cream. Blend with the stewed vegetables and season.
5. Fill each vegetable with the stuffing, replace the vegetable caps, and place in a baking dish. Pour the white wine over the vegetables and bake in a 350°F oven for 20 minutes. Serve hot or cooled.

WINE: ROSÉ DE PROVENCE

salade niçoise

NIÇOISE SALAD
FOR 6 - PREPARATION TIME: 20 MINUTES

Tuna in water	10½ ounces
Marinated anchovies	18
Black olives	30
Hard-boiled eggs	6
Red pepper	1
Tomatoes	6
Red onion	1

Olive oil
Sea salt

These are the basic ingredients of a *salade niçoise*. Add any raw vegetables you like, such as green beans, cucumber, salad greens. A good glug of olive oil, a little sea salt, the sound of the sea, and the deed is done!

WINE: ROSÉ DE BANDOL

SALADE NIÇOISE

LEFT
porcini
mushroom tart

RIGHT
slow-cooked
porcini
mushrooms

golden
chanterelle
and black
trumpet
mushroom
ragoût

BONS OU MÉCHAMPIGNONS?
MUSHROOMS SAVORY AND UNSAVORY

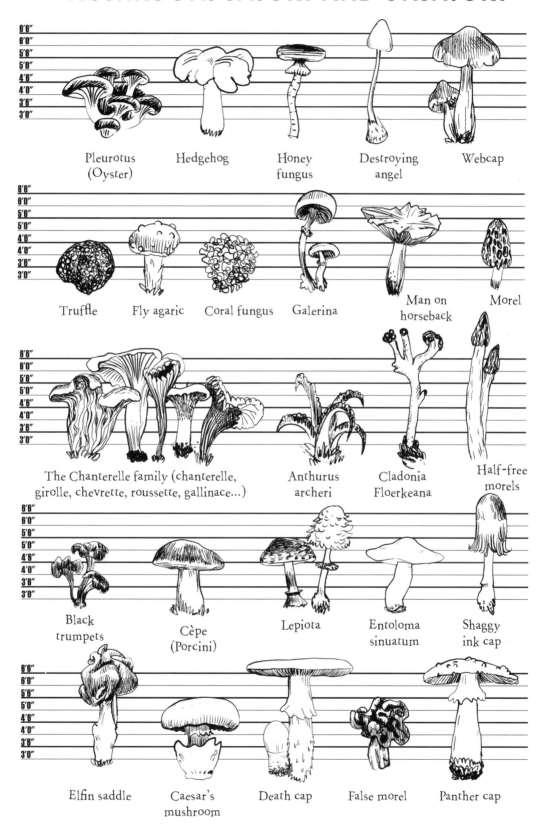

Pleurotus (Oyster)

Hedgehog

Honey fungus

Destroying angel

Webcap

Truffle

Fly agaric

Coral fungus

Galerina

Man on horseback

Morel

The Chanterelle family (chanterelle, girolle, chevrette, roussette, gallinace...)

Anthurus archeri

Cladonia Floerkeana

Half-free morels

Black trumpets

Cèpe (Porcini)

Lepiota

Entoloma sinuatum

Shaggy ink cap

Elfin saddle

Caesar's mushroom

Death cap

False morel

Panther cap

DO YOU RECOGNIZE THESE MUSHROOMS?

tarte aux cèpes

PORCINI MUSHROOM TART
FOR 6 - PREPARATION TIME: 30 MINUTES
COOKING TIME: 20 MINUTES + 15 MINUTES
REFRIGERATION TIME

Puff Pastry (see page 408 or else ready-made)	1 roll
Whole fresh porcini mushrooms	8
Smoked duck breast	3½ ounces
Walnuts	1 cup
Shallot	1
Heavy cream	½ cup
Soft white sandwich bread	2 slices
Butter	2½ tablespoons
Garlic	2 cloves
Olive oil	
Sea salt	

1. Brush the mushrooms clean and thinly slice them lengthwise.
2. Peel the shallot and sauté in olive oil. Add the smoked duck breast, cream, and cubed bread slices. Blend this mixture, adding the walnuts.
3. Roll out the pastry, prick with a fork, and cover it completely with the duck mixture. Arrange the mushrooms on top in overlapping circles. Chill for 15 minutes.
4. Peel and chop the garlic; then sauté with butter until it turns a nutty color. Brush the tart with the garlic butter, sprinkle with sea salt, and bake in a preheated 400°F oven for 20 minutes.

WINE: A BRAND-NAME APÉRITIF!

cèpes confits

SLOW-COOKED PORCINI MUSHROOMS
FOR 6 - PREPARATION TIME: 10 MINUTES
COOKING TIME: 3 HOURS

Whole porcini mushrooms	12
Shallots	4
Garlic	4 cloves
Olive oil	

1. Peel the shallots and cut each into quarters. Brush the mushrooms clean.
2. Coat the bottom of a flameproof casserole dish with olive oil. Heat gently, before adding the shallots and the unpeeled garlic.
3. Carefully arrange the whole mushrooms on top, cover, and cook in a 235°F oven for 3 hours. The mushrooms will be reduced in size by half and their flavor doubled in concentration.

WINE: UP TO YOU

ragoût de girolles et de trompettes-des-morts

GOLDEN CHANTERELLE AND BLACK TRUMPET MUSHROOM RAGOÛT
FOR 6 - PREPARATION TIME: 20 MINUTES
COOKING TIME: 20 MINUTES

Chanterelle mushrooms	10½ ounces
Black trumpet mushrooms	3½ ounces
Bacon	7-ounce slab
Onions	2
Garlic	4 cloves
Whole hazelnuts	⅓ cup
White port	⅓ cup
Heavy cream	1¼ cup
Olive oil	
Salt, pepper	

1. Wash the mushrooms several times; (black trumpets are often very dirty). Peel the onions and garlic, slice the onions, and roughly chop the garlic.
2. In a large pan, brown the onions and garlic in the olive oil. Add the mushrooms and bacon, allowing the mushrooms to give up their liquid.
3. Once the liquid has completely evaporated, deglaze the pan with the port, scraping up the bits on the bottom. Allow to reduce, and add the hazelnuts and cream. Cook for 10 minutes and season.

WINE: COTEAUX DU LAYON

feuilleté aux morilles

MOREL PUFF PASTRY SANDWICH
FOR 6 - PREPARATION TIME: 20 MINUTES
COOKING TIME: 30 MINUTES

Puff Pastry (see page 408 or else ready-made)	10½ ounces
Egg yolk	1
Frozen morels	1 pound 5 ounces
Chardonnay	¾ cup
Chicken stock	¾ cup
Shallots	3
Heavy cream	¾ cup
Oil	

1. Roll the pastry into a rectangular shape and cut into six portions. Brush each one with beaten egg yolk. Prick with a fork.
2. Bake in a preheated 350°F oven for 20 minutes.
3. Meanwhile, peel and slice the shallot. Sauté in the oil, add the frozen morels, and cook for 10 minutes so that the morels give up their water.
4. Deglaze the pan with the wine. Allow to reduce by half, and add the stock. Reduce again, then add the cream, and cook until the sauce has a syrupy consistency. Season.
5. Slice each puff pastry horizontally into two parts. Top one half with the morel cream sauce, and cover with the other pastry half.

WINE: CHARDONNAY

À LA BARIGOULE

cœurs de laitue braisés

BRAISED LETTUCE HEARTS
FOR 6 - PREPARATION TIME: 15 MINUTES
COOKING TIME: 1 HOUR

Romaine or iceberg lettuce hearts	6
Carrots	3
Onions	2
Thyme	1 large sprig
Rosemary	1 large sprig
White wine	½ cup
Chicken stock	4 cups

1. Peel and slice the carrots and onions.
2. Arrange the lettuce hearts in a gratin dish with the carrots and onions. Add the wine, rosemary, thyme, and a generous amount of stock.
3. Bake uncovered in a 350°F oven for 1 hour, adding more stock as needed.

artichauts à la barigoule

ARTICHOKES SAUTÉED IN WHITE WINE
FOR 6 - PREPARATION TIME: 20 MINUTES
COOKING TIME: 20 MINUTES

Small fresh artichokes	18
Garlic	6 unpeeled cloves
White wine	½ cup
Parsley	1 bunch
Olive oil	
Salt, pepper	

1. Remove the tough leaves and top part of the artichokes, cut them in half lengthwise, and remove the hairy "choke."
2. In a frying pan, sauté the unpeeled 6 garlic cloves in olive oil. Add the artichokes and cook gently. Add the wine and chopped parsley, allowing the liquid to reduce, and season.

ratatouille au citron de Menton

RATATOUILLE WITH LEMON
FOR 6 - PREPARATION TIME: 30 MINUTES
COOKING TIME: 2 HOURS

Tomatoes	6
Eggplants	2
Red pepper	1
Yellow pepper	1
Green pepper	1
Scallions (or bulb green onions if available)	12
Lemon (preferably from Menton!)	1
Bay leaf	1
Rosemary	1 sprig
Garlic	6 cloves
Olive oil	5 fluid ounces

1. Peel the garlic and roughly crush it. Halve the scallions lengthways and finely chop the green part. Dice the rest of the vegetables into cubes. Then combine all the vegetables, and add the olive oil, bay leaf, and rosemary.
2. Arrange the mixture in a gratin dish and place lemon wedges on top. Cover with a sheet of greased foil and bake in a 350°F oven for 2 hours, stirring at regular intervals: the more "cooked down" the vegetables, the better the ratatouille.

piperade de Monique

MONIQUE'S PIPERADE
FOR 6 - PREPARATION TIME: 20 MINUTES
COOKING TIME: 50 MINUTES

Red peppers	4
Green peppers	4
Yellow peppers	4
Ripe tomatoes	4
Shallots	3
Garlic	6 cloves
Olive oil	½ to ⅔ cup
Basque Country *fandango*	1 CD

1. Turn on the CD player and put on the disc.
2. Roast the whole peppers in the oven for 20 minutes and peel them. Blanch and peel the tomatoes, and chop the flesh.
3. Peel the garlic and shallots and finely chop them. Slice the peppers into strips—and do a couple of fandango steps.
4. Sauté all the vegetables in olive oil and let them stew for 30 minutes.
Note: The fandango is uniquely suited for the preparation of *piperade*: under no circumstances should it be used for making desserts (especially pies). In effect, dancing and cooking dessert at the same time can lead to domestic accidents: tables on fire, dropped glasses. . . . Isn't that right, Monique?

tarte aux poireaux

LEEK TART
FOR 6 - PREPARATION TIME: 20 MINUTES
COOKING TIME: 40 MINUTES

Egg 1
Puff pastry (see page 408 or else ready-made) ....9 ounces
Leeks 3
Heavy cream .... 1¼ cups
Celery stalk 1
Olive oil
Salt, pepper

1. Slice the leeks and clean them in a large amount of water. Dice the celery.
2. Soften the leeks in olive oil without browning them, and add the diced celery. Pour the cream into the mixture and let it stew; then season and allow to cool a little.
3. Roll out the pastry into a rectangular shape.
4. Add the egg to the leek mixture and blend well.
5. Generously cover the pastry with the leek mixture and bake in a preheated 350°F oven for 30 minutes.

WINE: WHATEVER'S IN THE FRIDGE

tarte aux oignons

ONION TART
FOR 6 - PREPARATION TIME: 20 MINUTES
COOKING TIME: 30 MINUTES

Puff pastry (see page 408 or else ready-made) ....9 ounces
Yellow onions 6
Pine nuts ....⅓ cup
Honey.. 1 tablespoon
Cumin seeds .... 1 tablespoon
Olive oil
Salt, pepper

1. Peel and slice the onions, and soften them in olive oil without browning. Add the honey and cook until the onions caramelize. Mix in the pine nuts and cumin, then season.
2. Roll out the pastry into a rectangular shape and prick with a fork. Cover the dough with the caramelized onions and bake in a preheated 350°F oven for 20 minutes.

WINE: WHATEVER'S IN THE FRIDGE

tarte provençale

PROVENÇAL VEGETABLE TART
FOR 6 - PREPARATION TIME: 20 MINUTES
COOKING TIME: 40 MINUTES

Puff pastry (see page 408 or else ready-made) ....9 ounces
Cherry tomatoes 6
Sundried tomatoes in oil 6
Zucchini 1
Eggplant .... 1 small
Onion 1
Basil... 1 bunch
Black olives 10
Olive oil
Sea salt, pepper

1. Peel and slice the onion, and cut the zucchini and eggplant into small cubes. Sauté all the vegetables in the olive oil, keeping them *al dente*.
2. Pick off the basil leaves and dress them in olive oil; pit the olives.
3. Roll out the pastry, and prick with a fork, then arrange the vegetables, basil, and olives on top. Season.
4. Bake in a preheated 350°F oven for 30 minutes.

WINE: WHATEVER'S IN THE FRIDGE

LEFT
leek tart

ABOVE
onion tart

LEFT
provençal vegetable tart

LE GRATIN DES GRATINS
THE GRATIN OF ALL GRATINS

macaronis

MACARONI
FOR 6 - PREPARATION TIME: 20 MINUTES
COOKING TIME: 30 MINUTES
Macaroni being Mère Brazier's favorite vegetable, we couldn't leave it out!

Macaroni .... 1 pound 2 ounces
Heavy cream .... 2½ cups
Butter...1 tablespoon
Flour .... 2 tablespoons
Grated nutmeg.............................1 teaspoon
Comté cheese ....5½ ounces
Salt, pepper

1. Cook the macaroni in salted boiling water for 8 minutes: it must be *al dente*.
2. Make a roux by melting the butter in a pan and stirring in flour. Pour in the cream and cook for 5 minutes. Add nutmeg and season.
3. Arrange the macaroni in a gratin dish, cover with the cream sauce, and top with shavings of the cheese. Bake for 15 minutes in a 350°F oven.

Dauphinois

POTATOES DAUPHINOIS
FOR 6 - PREPARATION TIME: 30 MINUTES
COOKING TIME: 1 HOUR

Potatoes............................ 4 pounds 8 ounces
Heavy cream .... 2½ cups
Grated nutmeg.............................1 teaspoon
Salt, pepper

1. Peel the potatoes and slice into rounds. Toss them in the cream and nutmeg, and season well.
2. In a gratin dish, arrange layers of potatoes covered by cream. Bake for 1 hour in a 350°F oven.

côtes de cardon

CARDOON STALKS
FOR 6 - PREPARATION TIME: 45 MINUTES
COOKING TIME: 50 MINUTES

Bunch of cardoon stalks 1
Marrow bones.. 6
Flour.. 2 tablespoons
Butter.................................1½ tablespoons
Chicken stock .... 4 cups
Salt, pepper

1. The cardoon is related to the artichoke. Peel the cardoon stalks, slice them on the diagonal, and then cook them with the marrow bones for 25 minutes in a pot of salted water.
2. Drain the stalks and remove the marrow from the bones. Reserve the marrow.
3. Make a roux by melting butter in a pan and stirring in the flour. Pour in the stock and simmer for 5 minutes.
4. Arrange the cardoon stalks in a gratin dish, cover with the sauce, and top with the marrow. Bake for 15 minutes in a 350°F oven.

pommes boulangère

BAKER'S WIFE'S POTATOES
FOR 6 - PREPARATION TIME: 20 MINUTES
COOKING TIME: 1 HOUR

Potatoes............................ 4 pounds 8 ounces
Onions.. 4
Chicken stock .... 4 cups
Thyme ....1 large sprig
Rosemary ....1 large sprig
Bay leaf 1
Salt, pepper

1. Peel the potatoes and onions, slice them into rounds, and arrange them in layers in a gratin dish.
2. Season the stock and completely cover the gratin with the stock. Then add the thyme, rosemary, and bay leaf.
3. Bake for 1 hour in a 350°F oven.

potimarron et cannelle

PUMPKIN AND CINNAMON
FOR 6 - PREPARATION TIME: 20 MINUTES
COOKING TIME: 45 MINUTES

Cheese or sugar pumpkins 3
Eggs 4
Soft brown sugar .... 2 tablespoons
Heavy cream .... ¾ cup
Ground cinnamon ....1 teaspoon
Salt, pepper

1. Cut the pumpkins into eight pieces, remove their seeds, and cook them in a saucepan of water. Drain, purée, and add the cream, sugar, and cinnamon, then the whole eggs, and season.
2. Pour the pumpkin mixture into a gratin dish and bake for 20 minutes in a 350°F oven.

légumes niçois

NIÇOISE-STYLE VEGETABLES
FOR 6 - PREPARATION TIME: 30 MINUTES
COOKING TIME: 1 HOUR

Tomatoes..8
Onions.. 4
Zucchini 4
Eggplants.. 3
Thyme ....2 large sprigs
Bay leaves 3
Garlic...6 cloves
Olive oil
Sea salt

1. Slice the vegetables into rounds; peel and chop the garlic.
2. In a gratin dish, arrange the sliced vegetables on their sides, alternating the different kinds and tightly packing them together. Arrange the thyme and bay leaves on top, and sprinkle with garlic and sea salt, along with a generous drizzle of olive oil. Bake for 1 hour in a 300°F oven.

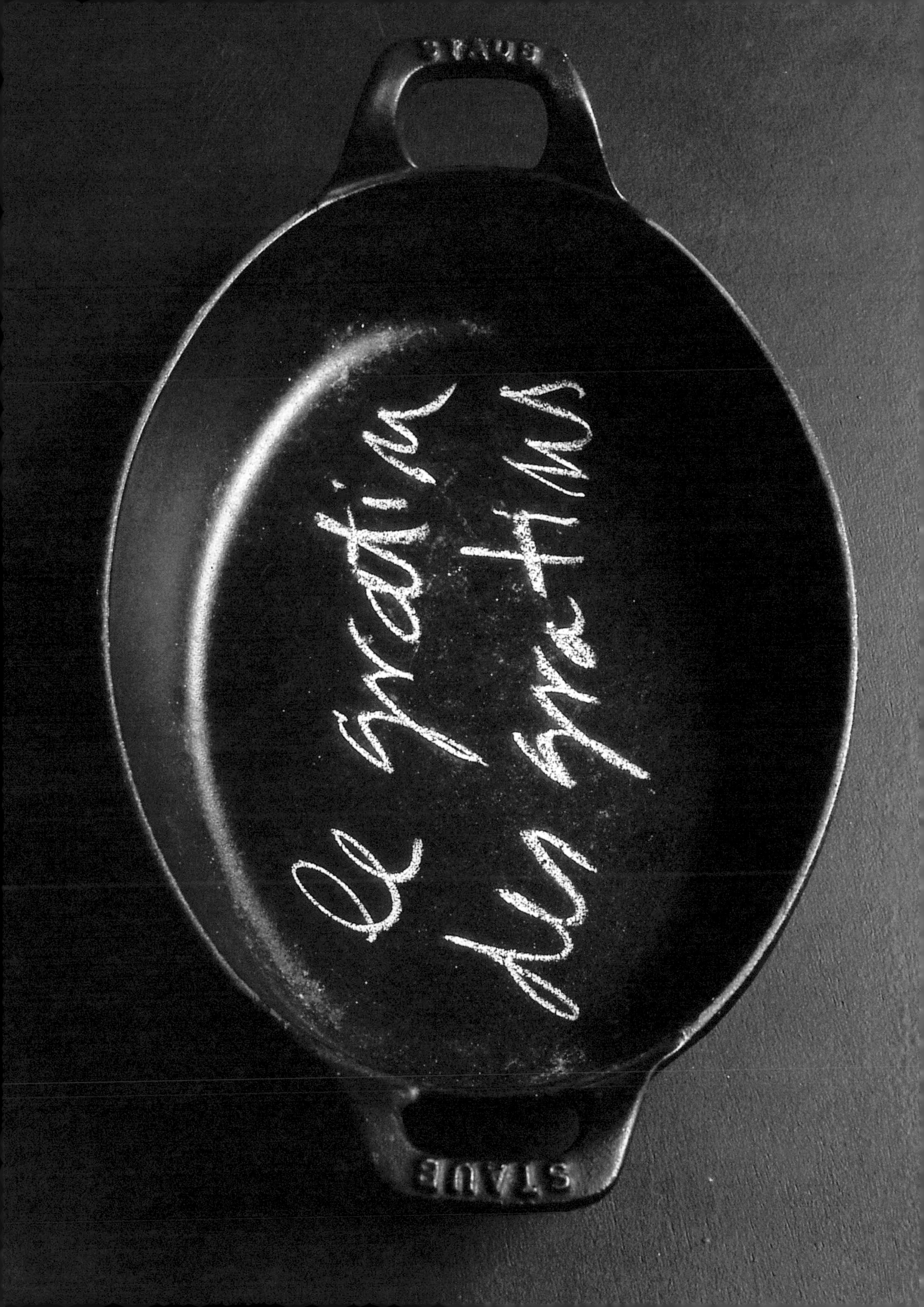
le gratin
les gratins
STAUB
STAUB

PETIT PENSE-BÊTE
D'AIDE À LA CUISSON
QUICK CRIB SHEET ON COOKING METHODS

DES A.O.C. VACHES
REGISTERED COWS

Le Gavroche
Nicolas ou l'esprit de Paname
Nicolas or the spirit of Panama

LA SÜRKRÜT
(CHOUCROUTE EN ALSACIEN)
(ALSATIAN SAUERKRAUT)

DES A.O.C. COCHONNES
REGISTERED SWINE

JOUONS : LES MONUMENTS
DE PARIS
LET'S PLAY: MONUMENTS OF PARIS

LES VINS DE LA
VALLÉE DU RHÔNE
THE WINES OF THE RHONE VALLEY

MEUHH
- Bêêhhh -
GROINK

MOO - BAA - OINK

PETIT PENSE-BÊTE
D'AIDE À LA CUISSON
QUICK CRIB SHEET ON COOKING METHODS

THERE ARE FOUR MAIN COOKING METHODS.

ROASTING

The piece of meat is cooked in a preheated oven in a dry atmosphere
with only a small amount of added fat. The sensory properties of the food
(taste, texture, etc.) are perfectly preserved.

GRILLING

The piece of meat is in direct contact with the heat source. The idea is to
sear the meat quickly to caramelize its surface and lock in its juices. Pan-frying and
deep-frying belong to this category of cooking.

BOILING

The meat is cooked in a volume of water so that
the nutrients in the meat are dispersed to flavor the broth.
This mode of cooking is often lengthy in order to obtain a tender piece of meat.
The broth often has vegetables and aromatic herbs added to it, as in
a *pot-au-feu* or *blanquette*.

BRAISING

Pieces of meat to be cooked by braising must have a high water content.
The cooking process in effect uses the water already in the food to cook it inside
a closed receptacle with only a small amount of fat added. The condensation
of the cooking liquid produces a sauce rich in nutrients.

BEEF	ROASTING	GRILLING	BOILING	BRAISING
CHUCK, NECK				•
CROSS-RIB	•	•		
RIB	•	•		
ENTRECÔTE	•	•		
FILET (TENDERLOIN)	•	•		
RUMP	•	•		
ROUND				•
SILVERSIDE				•
KNUCKLE				•
SHIN (HIND)			•	•
SKIRT			•	•
FLANK			•	•
BRISKET			•	•
SHORT RIB				•
BLADE			•	•
SHIN (FRONT)			•	•
LAMB	ROASTING	GRILLING	BOILING	BRAISING
NECK			•	•
CROSS-RIB		•		
SECOND RACK		•		
FIRST RACK		•		
LOIN		•		
RUMP	•			
LEG	•			•
BREAST			•	•
SHOULDER	•		•	•
PORK	ROASTING	GRILLING	BOILING	BRAISING
RACK	•	•		•
LOIN	•	•		•
SHOULDER				
EYE FILET	•	•		•
LEG			•	•
HOCK, SHANK			•	
BACON, SIDE			•	
SNOUT			•	
EAR			•	
TROTTER			•	
BELLY RACK	•		•	•
RUMP	•			•
BELLY			•	
TAIL			•	
HEAD			•	
SPARERIBS		•	•	•

DES A.O.C. VACHES
REGISTERED COWS

Vosgienne

Ferrandaise

Salers

Charolaise

Gasconne

1	Chuck, neck	6c	Knuckle
2	Cross-rib	6d	Round
3a	Rib	7	Shin (hind)
3b	Entrecôte	8	Skirt
4	Filet (tenderloin)	9	Flank
5	Rump	10	Brisket
6a	Eye of silverside for escalopes	11	Short rib
		12	Blade
6b	Eye of topside for escalopes	13	Shin (front)

Bazadaise

LEFT
roast beef,
pure and
simple

RIGHT
poached
rump steak
(sirloin)

bœuf rôti tout simplement

ROAST BEEF, PURE AND SIMPLE
FOR 6 - PREPARATION TIME: 30 MINUTES
COOKING TIME: 40 MINUTES

Beef roast	2 pounds 11 ounces
Potatoes	6
Shallots	3
Garlic	4 unpeeled cloves
Butter	2½ tablespoons
White wine	½ cup
Olive oil	
Sea salt	

1. In a roasting pan over high heat, caramelize the surface of the roast on all sides in some olive oil.
2. Peel the shallots and add them to the pan with the unpeeled garlic cloves.
3. Peel the potatoes, cut them in eight portions lengthwise, and arrange them around the roast. Pour in the wine.
4. Cover and cook in a 350°F oven for 25 minutes. Add the butter and cook an additional 5 minutes.
5. Season and let rest for 5 minutes before serving.

WINE: SAINT-JOSEPH

bœuf à la ficelle

POACHED RUMP STEAK (SIRLOIN)
FOR 6 - PREPARATION TIME: 45 MINUTES
COOKING TIME: 45 MINUTES

Rump steak (sirloin)	6 thick pieces
Carrots	6
Turnips	6
Potatoes	6
Onions	3
Leeks	3
Rutabagas	2
Celery stalks	6
Celeriac (celery root)	½
Bouquet garni	1
Sea salt	

1. Peel and chop the vegetables, and cook in a large volume of water with the bouquet garni. Ten minutes before the end of cooking, tie up the steak pieces and attach them to a wooden spoon.
2. Set the spoon over the pot with the steaks dipping into the vegetable stock—they mustn't touch the pot. Cook for 5 minutes for rare meat or to your liking.
3. Season the steaks with sea salt. Slice them and serve with the vegetables, some stock, and a béarnaise sauce.

WINE: PINOT NOIR FROM ALSACE

filet de bœuf Rossini

BEEF FILET WITH FOIE GRAS
FOR 6 - PREPARATION TIME: 20 MINUTES
COOKING TIME: 20 MINUTES

Beef filets (tenderloins)	6 (about 7 ounces each)
Fresh foie gras	1 pound 5 ounces
Potatoes	5
Butter	⅓ cup
White wine	⅓ to ½ cup
Oil for deep-frying	
Peanut oil	
Salt, pepper	

1. Peel the potatoes, cut them into thin straws, then rinse and dry on a cloth.
2. In a cast-iron pan, melt half the butter with a spoonful of peanut oil, and sear the beef filets on both sides to brown them. Remove the filets and keep in a warm place.
3. Deglaze the pan with white wine, scraping up the bits on the bottom. Whisk in the remaining butter, and season.
4. Deep-fry the straw potatoes in oil at 350°F until golden.
5. Cut the foie gras into six slices and pan-fry them on both sides in a nonstick pan without any fat. Blot them on paper towels and place them on the beef filets. Drizzle with the pan juices before serving.

WINE: ALOXE-CORTON

eye filet steak with foie gras

LEFT
filet of
beef in a
pastry case
with
mushrooms

RIGHT
beef carpaccio

166

filet de bœuf en croûte de champignons

FILET OF BEEF IN A PASTRY CASE WITH MUSHROOMS
FOR 6 - PREPARATION TIME: 60 MINUTES
COOKING TIME: 40 MINUTES + 30 MINUTES RESTING TIME

Whole tenderloin of beef, trimmed	2¾ pounds
Mushrooms	1 pound 5 ounces
Garlic	2 cloves
Tarragon	1 bunch
Parsley	1 bunch
Shallots	4
Puff pastry (see page 408 or else ready-made)	1 pound 2 ounces
Egg yolk	1
Olive oil	
Salt, pepper	

1. Pan-fry the tenderloin on all sides for 10 minutes; then let it rest for 30 minutes on a rack so that the blood can drip down.
2. Chop the mushrooms, tarragon, and parsley. Peel and chop the garlic and shallots, and sauté in olive oil. Add the mushrooms and herbs, and cook until the mixture has a fairly dry consistency. Season generously.
3. Roll out the pastry to a rectangle, prick with a fork and enclose the tenderloin. Cover the meat with the mushroom mixture, roll it up in the pastry, and seal the edges with the beaten egg yolk. Create a vent on top so that steam can escape.
4. Using the pastry trimmings, make strips to decorate the pastry case. Brush with the egg yolk and bake in a preheated 350°F oven for 20 minutes.

WINE: SAINT-JULIEN

filet de bœuf en carpaccio

BEEF CARPACCIO
FOR 6 - PREPARATION TIME: 2 MINUTES
COOKING TIME: 45 MINUTES

Beef filet	1 pound 5 ounces
Shiraz (preferably from the Cornas region or the Rhône valley)	1 cup
Veal stock	¾ cup
Butter	3 tablespoons
Hazelnuts	⅓ cup
Chives	12 stems
Radishes	6
Sea salt	

1. Reduce the wine by one-quarter in a saucepan. Stir in the stock, and allow it to reduce until the sauce is syrupy. Whisk in the butter.
2. Pan-fry the beef filet on a very high heat to color it—not cook it!—all over. Rest the beef for 5 minutes.
3. Cut the beef into very thin slices. Arrange on plates and dress with the wine sauce, chopped hazelnuts, julienned radishes, chives, and sea salt.

WINE: CORNAC

côte de bœuf, beurre d'echalote et moelle

RIB STEAK WITH SHALLOT BUTTER AND MARROW
FOR 6 - PREPARATION TIME: 15 MINUTES
COOKING TIME: 25 MINUTES

Rib steak with some marrow	2 pounds 11 ounces
Butter	7 ounces
Shallots	2
Chives	1 bunch
Coarsely ground black pepper	1 teaspoon
Sea salt	

1. Buy a house in the country, build a stone barbecue, open a good bottle of wine, and have a glass . . .
2. Start up the barbecue with wood gathered from the forest, find some matches (hard because you quit smoking), finish your glass of wine before the bee buzzing around decides to have a bath in it, place the grilling rack over the fire, and wait for embers to form. . . . While you're waiting, prepare the vegetables: dice the shallots, snip the chives, and work them into the butter with a fork, add salt and the pepper.
3. Cook the marrow in simmering water for 20 minutes.
4. All you need to do now is grill the rib steak, open a second bottle (we saw you quietly finish off the first one using the hot barbecue as an excuse), and serve the rib steak topped with its marrow and the shallot butter.

WINE: IT ALL DEPENDS ON THE WEATHER! IF IT'S 100°F OUTSIDE, A GOOD MORGON; IF IT'S 65°F INSIDE, A NUITS-SAINT-GEORGES!

entrecôte à la bordelaise

RIB-EYE STEAK WITH BORDELAISE SAUCE
FOR 6 - PREPARATION TIME: 15 MINUTES
COOKING TIME: 20 MINUTES

Rib-eye steaks	6 (about 7 ounces each)
Shallots	6
Bordeaux wine	1 cup
Cognac	2½ tablespoons
Butter	2½ tablespoons
Salt, pepper	

1. Pan-fry the steaks over high heat for 5 minutes on each side. Remove, set on a plate, and keep warm.
2. Peel and chop the shallots and sauté them in the same pan. Flambé the pan with the cognac, and deglaze with the Bordeaux, scraping up the bits on the bottom. Allow the sauce to reduce by half; then whisk in the chopped butter and season.
3. Drizzle the bordelaise sauce over the steaks and serve.

WINE: PAUILLAC

TARTARE DE BŒUF BISTROT

LEFT
beef tartare
bistro-style

RIGHT
flank steak
with grilled
shallots

tartare de bœuf bistrot

BEEF TARTARE BISTRO-STYLE
FOR 6 - PREPARATION TIME: 15 MINUTES

Whole piece of beef filet ....1¾ pound
Mild onions..2
Capers .... 1 tablespoon
Chives, snipped .... 1 tablespoon
Tomato ketchup...2 tablespoons
Olive oil ....½ cup
Mustard .... 1 tablespoon
Egg yolks...3
Tabasco
Salt, pepper

1. Chop the beef into small, evenly sized cubes.
2. Dice the onions.
3. Combine the mustard with tomato ketchup, olive oil, and egg yolks. Add capers, chives, and onion.
4. Combine the dressing and meat gently, and season with salt, pepper, and Tabasco.
5. Shape into a mound and serve with a salad of fresh herbs.

WINE: THE HOST'S PLEASURE!

bavette aux echalotes grillées

FLANK STEAK WITH GRILLED SHALLOTS
FOR 6 - PREPARATION TIME: 10 MINUTES
COOKING TIME: 10 MINUTES

Flank steaks .... 6 (about 6 ounces each)
Shallots...12
Butter...2½ tablespoons
White wine..2½ tablespoons
Salt, coarsely ground black pepper

1. Pan-fry the steaks over a high heat on both sides: they must be seared to seal in all their juices. Set them on a plate and keep warm.
2. Peel and slice the shallots. Sauté them in the same pan and deglaze with wine, scraping up all the bits on the bottom. Whisk in the butter and season.
3. Top the steaks with the softened shallots, and serve with thick-cut french fries.

WINE: THE HOSTESS'S PLEASURE!

bavette au saint—marcellin

FLANK STEAK WITH SAINT-MARCELLIN CHEESE
FOR 6 - PREPARATION TIME: 10 MINUTES
COOKING TIME: 10 MINUTES

Flank steaks .... 6 (about 6 ounces each)
Saint-Marcellin cheeses 3
Butter..1 tablespoon
Salt, pepper

1. Pan-fry the steaks in butter over a high heat on both sides: they must be seared to seal in all their juices. Set them on a plate, season, and keep in a warm place.
2. Cut each cheese in two horizontally. Place half a Saint Marcellin on each of the steaks
3. Place the steaks under a hot broiler for 5 minutes to melt the cheese. Serve with a *gratin dauphinois* (page 154).

WINE: THE HOST'S CELLAR!

onglet

HANGER STEAK
FOR 6 - PREPARATION TIME: 15 MINUTES
COOKING TIME: 15 MINUTES

Hanger steaks 6
Shallots..3
Mushrooms ....10 ounces
Parsley, chopped .... 1 tablespoon
White wine..½ cup
Butter..1 tablespoon
Oil
Salt, pepper

1. Melt the butter with a tablespoon of oil. Sear the steaks over a high heat to brown the surface well; set them on a plate and keep warm.
2. Slice the shallots and mushrooms, and sauté in the same pan. Deglaze the pan with the wine, scraping up the bits on the bottom. Let the liquid reduce, then add the parsley, and season.
3. Add the juice that has leaked from the steaks to the sauce, season, and pour over the meat.

WINE: THE HOSTESS'S CELLAR!

flank steak with Saint-Marcellin cheese

pot-au-feu

BOILED BEEF AND VEGETABLES
FOR 6 - COOKING TIME: 3 HOURS

Beef short ribs	1 pound 2 ounces
Beef shin	1 pound 2 ounces
Oxtail	1
Marrow bones	3
Carrots	6
Onions studded with 4 cloves	3
Potatoes	6
Round green cabbage	½
Turnips	6
Leeks	3
Bouquet garni	1
Celery stalks	4
Coarse salt	
Cornichons	

1. Tie the pieces of meat with string so that they don't fall apart during cooking. Place in a pot, cover with a large quantity of water, and bring to a boil, taking care to skim regularly.
2. Add the bouquet garni, onions, and chunks of celery and simmer for 2 hours.
3. Add the peeled and chopped carrots, turnips, leeks, cabbage, and marrow bones. Season with coarse salt and cook for an additional hour. Cook the potatoes separately.
4. Gently remove the meat and vegetables from the broth. Serve them with coarse salt and cornichons.

WINE: CHÂTEAUNEUF-DU-PAPE

faire un fond

HOW TO MAKE STOCK

In cooking, stock is the essential foundation for making sauces. It is indispensable. To make a stock you need a friendly butcher, some patience, and a recipe that is worth your all.

FOR VEAL STOCK YOU NEED:

Veal bones	4 pounds 8 ounces
Carrots	4
Onions	4
Cloves	4
Bay leaves	2
Thyme	1 large sprig
Parsley	4 sprigs

1. Have your butcher crack the veal bones.
2. Peel the carrots and onions. Stud one of the onions with the cloves and cut the rest into large chunks.
3. Sweat the veal bones in a roasting pan with the carrots and onions; then roast them in a 400°F oven for 30 minutes.
4. Meanwhile, in a large stock pot, bring 16 cups of water to the boil with the herbs and clove-studded onion.
5. Add the bones and vegetables to the pot; moisten the roasting tin with a little water to scrape up the bits on the bottom, and add this to the pot. Cook at a very low simmer for 4 hours, skimming the fat at regular intervals.
6. Strain the liquid through a *chinois* (fine sieve) and cook further to reach your desired consistency for the stock.

The method is identical for making chicken stock (use chicken or duck carcasses); the only difficulty is finding the carcasses.

POT AU FEU

Le Gavroche

NICOLAS, OR THE SPIRIT OF PANAMA

He's like a kid fresh from the streets who decided to enter the bistro world the way others enter the church. "Nothing shoddy about it, *m'sieur*, it's the real deal, one of those things that's been around since . . . oh, who knows!" He's got the cockiness of a market seller, the smile of a well-groomed hostess, and an utter determination to please. The menu, for its part, is like the place, rooted in all that is good and reassuring, leaving no room for the "tasteless."

The *oeuf mayo* (eggs with mayonnaise) is fully realized; the *côte de boeuf* (rib steak) is as marbled as one could wish, plump as a down quilt, crunchy on the outside and juicy in the middle; the *frites* (French fries) are as golden as a young girl in the sun. Everyone at the table is, of course, friendly; the Chenas is passed from table to table; conversation flows. We forget ourselves, we feel good. "It's true there's a spirit about the place, *m'sieur*, it's alive. Some have even seen it move!"

MOULIN ROUGE
(THE SONG FROM MOULIN ROUGE)
de
GEORGES AURIC & JACQUES LARUE

Paroles anglaises de
WILLIAM ENGVICK

LES MONUMENTS DE PARIS
THE MONUMENTS OF PARIS

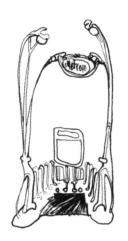

The Guimard metro station

The Grande Arche

The Moulin Rouge

Notre Dame Cathedral

The Louvre and its pyramid

The Arc de Triomphe as
seen from the Champs-Élysées

The iron lady
(also known as
the Eiffel Tower)

LEFT
beef cheeks
bourguignon

RIGHT
braised beef
with carrots

bourguignon de joues de bœuf

BEEF CHEEKS BOURGUIGNON
FOR 6 - PREPARATION TIME: 30 MINUTES
COOKING TIME: 1 HOUR 40 MINUTES +
24 HOURS MARINATING TIME

Beef cheeks	4
Scallions (bulb green onions if available)	8
Carrots	2
Juniper berries	10
Bay leaves	2
Red wine	2 cups
Veal stock	2 cups
Cognac	2½ tablespoons
Bouquet garni	1
Flour	4 teaspoons
Bacon	3½ ounces, diced

Oil
Salt, pepper

1. The day before cooking, trim the fat from the beef cheeks and cut each one into three pieces. Let them marinate in the red wine, crushed juniper berries, cognac, and bay leaves in the refrigerator.
2. The next day, peel the carrots and scallions. Sauté them in oil with the drained meat (reserving the marinade), and allow the meat and vegetables to brown. Then add the flour and cook for 5 minutes, stirring regularly.
3. Pour in the marinade, bring to a boil, and skim. Add the bouquet garni and veal stock, simmering the meat and vegetables for 1 hour 30 minutes until the meat is very tender; add water if necessary. Season and add the fried bacon.

WINE: NUITS-SAINT-GEORGES

bœuf braisé aux carrots

BRAISED BEEF WITH CARROTS
FOR 6 - PREPARATION TIME: 45 MINUTES
COOKING TIME: 1 HOUR 50 MINUTES

Stewing beef	2 pounds 4 ounces
Pork belly	7 ounces
Carrots	6
Red wine	1 cup
White wine	1 cup
Onions	6
Garlic	6 cloves
Celery stalks	4
Bouquet garni	1
Concentrated tomato purée	1 tablespoon

Olive oil

1. Cut the meat into 1½-inch cubes and brown the meat in a flameproof casserole dish along with the cubed pork belly and sliced onions. Deglaze the pan with the red and white wine, scraping up the bits on the bottom, and flambé.
2. Add the crushed garlic, bouquet garni, cubed celery, and tomato purée to the beef. Cover with 4 cups of water and cook for 1 hour.
3. Peel the carrots and slice them thickly on the diagonal. Add them to the casserole and cook an additional 45 minutes. Season and serve.

WINE: FAUGÈRES

bœuf mironton

BOILED BEEF IN ONION AND VINEGAR SAUCE
FOR 6 - PREPARATION TIME: 45 MINUTES
COOKING TIME: 30 MINUTES

Leftover *pot-au-feu* meat (page 174)	1 pound 12 ounces
Leftover *pot-au-feu* carrots (page 174)	4
Onions	6
Beef consommé	2 cups
Concentrated tomato purée	3 tablespoons
Flour	4 teaspoons
Parsley	1 bunch
Balsamic vinegar	½ cup

Olive oil
Salt, pepper

1. Peel and slice the onions. In a saucepan, gently brown them in olive oil, stir in the flour, and let them cook down for about 20 minutes.
2. Deglaze the pan with the balsamic vinegar, scraping up the bits on the bottom. Stir in the consommé and tomato purée, and season.
3. Thinly slice the beef and carrots, arrange them in a gratin dish, and cover with the onion mixture. Bake in a 350°F oven for 20 minutes. Sprinkled with chopped parsley and serve.

WINE: MEIGNIER

BŒUF MIRONTON

LEFT
roast veal,
pure and
simple

RIGHT
veal filet
with creamed
leeks

rôti de veau tout simplement

ROAST VEAL, PURE AND SIMPLE
FOR 6 - PREPARATION TIME: 10 MINUTES
COOKING TIME: 1 HOUR 10 MINUTES +
15 MINUTES RESTING TIME

Veal roast	2 pounds 11 ounces
Shallots	3
New potatoes	1 pound 2 ounces
Baby turnips	6
Garlic	4 cloves
White wine	½ cup
Bouquet garni	1
Thyme	1 large sprig
Butter	2½ tablespoons
Olive oil	

1. Sear the meat in olive oil over high heat in a flameproof casserole dish or Dutch oven. Add the shallots and unpeeled garlic, and pour in the wine; toss in add the thyme and bouquet garni.
2. Cover and bake in a 400°F oven for 30 minutes, adding a little water now and then, if needed, so that ½-inch of liquid always remains in the dish.
3. Trim the turnip tops, and halve the potatoes, arranging them around the roast. Bake for an additional 30 minutes, then allow the roast to rest for 15 minutes.
4. Arrange the roast and the vegetables on a platter. Add butter to the casserole dish and bring the cooking juices to the boil. Season the gravy and serve with the roast.

WINE: WINE, PURE AND SIMPLE!

mignon au blanc de poireaux

VEAL TENDERLOIN WITH CREAMED LEEKS
FOR 6 - PREPARATION TIME: 30 MINUTES
COOKING TIME: 20 MINUTES

Veal tenderloin	1 pound 12 ounces
Leeks	3
Heavy cream	1¼ cups
Fennel seeds	1 tablespoon
Veal stock	¾ cup
White wine	⅓ to ½ cup
Olive oil	
Salt, pepper	

1. Trim the tenderloin to remove any veins.
2. Slice the leeks and wash them well. Soften the leeks in olive oil, and add the fennel seeds, veal stock, and cream. Let the mixture stew for 15 minutes, and season.
3. Meanwhile, brown the veal on all sides in a roasting pan in a 350°F oven for 15 minutes—the inside of the veal should remain pink.
4. Deglaze the roasting pan with the white wine, scraping up all the bits on the bottom. Add the creamed leeks to the dish.
5. Serve the tenderloin cut into medallions.

WINE: VIOGNIER DE L'ARDÈCHE

carré de veau à la graine de moutarde

RACK OF VEAL WITH WHOLE-GRAIN MUSTARD
FOR 6–8 - PREPARATION TIME: 20 MINUTES
COOKING TIME: 2 HOURS 15 MINUTES

Rack of veal with 4 ribs	1
Potatoes	6
Celery stalks	2
Bouquet garni	1
Scallions (bulb green onions if available)	12
Garlic	6 cloves
White wine	1½ tablespoons
Moutarde de Meaux (wholegrain mustard)	3 tablespoons
Butter	1½ tablespoons
Olive oil	
Salt, pepper	

1. In a flameproof casserole dish or Dutch oven, brown the rack of veal on all sides in butter and olive oil over high heat. Season.
2. Add the scallions to the dish, along with the unpeeled garlic, the bouquet garni, and celery. Deglaze the baking dish with the wine, scraping up all the bits on the bottom.
3. Cover and bake in a 315°F oven for 1 hour 15 minutes, turning the rack at regular intervals and adding water, if needed to keep the veal moist.
4. Add the peeled potatoes and the mustard to the cooking juices and bake for an additional 40 minutes.
5. Place the casserole dish on the stove and let it simmer, uncovered, for 5 minutes more.

WINE: SANTENAY

LEFT
veal rolls with
Bayonne ham

RIGHT
veal paupiettes
with tarragon

190

PAUPIETTES

escalope de veau au jambon de Bayonne

VEAL ROLLS WITH BAYONNE HAM
FOR 6 - PREPARATION TIME: 30 MINUTES
COOKING TIME: 20 MINUTES

Veal escalopes	6
Jambon de Bayonne (air-dried Bayonne ham)	12 slices
Zucchini	2
Eggplant	1
Red peppers	2
Scallions (bulb green onions if available)	6
Garlic	1 clove
Dried thyme leaves	1 teaspoon
Rosemary	1 large sprig
White wine	½ cup
Olive oil	

1. Peel and chop the garlic. Spread out the ham slices in slightly overlapping pairs. Place a veal escalope on each pair and trim the ham. Sprinkle garlic and thyme over the escalopes, then roll and tie them up.
2. Place the escalopes in a gratin dish, adding all the chopped vegetables, and drizzle with olive oil. Add the rosemary and ham trimmings and season.
3. Bake in a 350°F oven for 20 minutes.
4. Deglaze the gratin dish with the wine, scraping up the bits on the bottom. Serve.

WINE: IROULIGNY

paupiettes à l'estragon

VEAL PAUPIETTES WITH TARRAGON
FOR 6 - PREPARATION TIME: 45 MINUTES
COOKING TIME: 35 MINUTES

Veal escalopes	7
Tarragon	1 bunch
Soft white sandwich bread	2 slices
Heavy cream	⅓ cup
Garlic	3 cloves
Parsley	1 bunch
Shallots	6
Tomatoes	8
Cherry tomatoes	12
White wine	¾ cup
Tomato ketchup	1 tablespoon
Olive oil	
Salt, pepper	

1. Using the flat side of a cleaver, flatten six of the escalopes so that they are as thin as possible. Trim them into rectangular shapes.
2. Peel and chop the garlic and pick off the tarragon leaves.
3. Combine the remaining veal escalope, veal trimmings, bread slices, cream, parsley, and half the tarragon leaves, and season. Place a good spoonful of the stuffing in the center of each escalope, fold it up like a wallet and tie with string to make a *paupiette*.
4. Place the *paupiettes* in a heavy pan and sauté them in the olive oil. Add the diced shallots, quartered tomatoes, the cherry tomatoes, and the rest of the tarragon.
5. Moisten the *paupiettes* with the wine, cover, and cook for 30 minutes on a low heat. Add the tomato ketchup and season.

WINE: CHÂTEAUNEUF-DU-PAPE

LES VINS DE LA
VALLÉE DU RHÔNE

THE WINES OF THE RHÔNE VALLEY

OF ALL THE ROADS OF FRANCE AND EUROPE,
MY FAVORITE IS THE ONE THAT I DRIVE
BY CAR OR BY HITCHING A RIDE
TOWARD THE SHORES OF THE SOUTH OF FRANCE

On the slopes of côte-rôtie

You need it whether going to Rome or to Sète

There's more to come after Condrieu

Whether you're two, three, four, five, six, or seven

the trunk filled with château-grillet

And the saint-joseph in your cups

It's a road that's a recipe

A holiday road

turning off to crozes-hermitage

and hermitage like a mirage

Cutting across the Rhône and through Provence

Making Paris no more than a suburb of Valence

a district of cornas and saint-Péray

and the outskirts of Saint-Paul-de-Vence

The summer sky

between the coteaux-du-tricastin

and the early morning côtes-du-vivarais

Fills our hearts with its clarity

and our bags with gigondas

Chases away the bitterness and bite

Which are the plague of the big city

hurray for côtes-du-ventoux

and vacqueyras

So excited

we drink châteauneuf-du-pape

and on the next leg some lirac

We sing, we celebrate

the olive trees are blue my little Lisette

the tavel is pink my little Lison

costières-de-nîmes or

côtes-du-luberon

Love and good cheer makes everyone beam

On Route Nationale 7, we're very happy!

193

LEFT
stuffed veal
breast

RIGHT
garlic-studded
veal tenderloin

194

poitrine farcie

STUFFED VEAL BREAST
FOR 6 - PREPARATION TIME: 30 MINUTES
COOKING TIME: 3 HOURS

Boned veal breast	4 pounds 8 ounces
Sausage meat	14 ounces
Garlic	6 cloves
Paprika	1 tablespoon
Aniseed	1 tablespoon
Sage	20 sprigs
Piment d'Espelette (hot paprika)	1 teaspoon
Sea salt	
Olive oil	

1. Lay the veal breast out flat and trim off the excess fat if necessary. Rub the outside of the meat with paprika and *piment d'Espelette*. Season with sea salt.
2. Peel and chop the garlic, finely shred the sage, and combine with the sausage meat and aniseed. Spread the sausage mixture on the veal, roll up, and tie.
3. Oil the rolled breast and roast in a 235°F oven for 3 hours. This dish is good eaten hot or cold.

WINE: SAINT-NICOLAS DE BOURGUEIL

filet clouté d'ail

GARLIC-STUDDED VEAL FILET
FOR 6 - PREPARATION TIME: 20 MINUTES
COOKING TIME: 20 MINUTES + 1 HOUR REFRIGERATION TIME

Veal filet medallions	12
Garlic	12 cloves
Veal stock	½ cup
Potatoes	6
Onions	2
Duck fat	3 tablespoons
Parsley	1 bunch
Butter	2½ tablespoons
Salt, pepper	

1. Peel the garlic, cut each clove into six, and remove the sprout in the middle. Make slits in each veal medallion using a pointed knife. Insert six pieces of garlic into each medallion. Chill for 1 hour.
2. Peel the potatoes and onions and cut them into thin rounds. Melt the duck fat in a large pan and brown the potatoes and onions, stirring regularly. Chop the parsley, stir it in, and season.
3. Melt the butter in a pan. Brown the medallions on both sides and deglaze the pan with the stock. Cook the medallions for 5 minutes and season. Serve with the sautéed potatoes.

WINE: SANCERRE ROUGE

tendron grillé

GRILLED VEAL FLANK STEAK
FOR 6 - PREPARATION TIME: 30 MINUTES
COOKING TIME: 20 MINUTES + 1 HOUR MARINATING TIME

Veal flank steaks	6
Scallions (bulb green onions if available)	3
Zucchini	2
Red peppers	2
Fennel	1 bulb
Garlic	3 cloves
Soy sauce	2 tablespoons
Tomato ketchup	2 tablespoons
Olive oil	2 tablespoons

1. Now that you've built your barbecue (see the *Côte de boeuf*, page 168), it's time to make it pay for itself. Prepare a marinade by blending the soy sauce, tomato ketchup, olive oil, and chopped garlic. Marinate the flank steaks in this mixture for 1 hour.
2. Cut the scallions in two; slice the zucchini, peppers, and fennel very thinly. Coat them all in olive oil.
3. Over gentle embers (watch out for flames), cook the steaks for about 10 minutes on each side; grill the vegetables and serve with a dash of soy sauce for seasoning.

WINE: BOURGOGNE IRANCY, CHILLED BUT NOT OVER CHILLED

quasi de sept heures

SEVEN-HOUR ROAST VEAL
FOR 6 - PREPARATION TIME: 10 MINUTES
COOKING TIME: 7 HOURS + 24 HOURS MARINATING TIME

Veal rump roast	2 pounds 11 ounces
Onions	3
Carrots	3
Bay leaves	2
Garlic	6 cloves
Thyme	3 sprigs
Dry white wine	1 bottle
Olive oil	
Salt, pepper	

1. The day before cooking, marinate the veal rump. To make the marinade, mix together the wine, finely chopped onions and carrots, bay leaves, thyme, and the roughly crushed garlic. Add the veal and let marinate overnight.
2. The next day, sear the roast in a roasting pan on all sides. Deglaze the roasting pan with the marinade, scraping up all the bits on the bottom.
3. Place in a 195°F oven and roast for 7 hours, basting regularly with the marinade juices.

WINE: HAUT MÉDOC

LEFT
veal stewed
with cream

RIGHT
slow-cooked
veal shank

blanquette de veau

VEAL STEWED WITH CREAM
FOR 6 - PREPARATION TIME: 30 MINUTES
COOKING TIME: 1 HOUR 30 MINUTES

Veal shoulder and breast, cut into pieces	2 pounds 11 ounces
Carrots	3
Onions	3
White baby onions	10
Bouquet garni	1
Pork belly, cubed	5½ ounces
Leeks	2
Garlic	3 cloves
Celery stalks	3
Butter	½ cup
Flour	1½ tablespoons
Heavy cream	1¼ cups
Egg yolks	4
Lemon	1
Salt, pepper	

1. Peel and chop the garlic and onions (not the baby onions); peel the carrots and slice into rounds. Wash and thinly slice the white part of the leek and the celery stalks.
2. In a heavy saucepan, gently sauté the veal pieces without browning them. Add the pork belly, vegetables, and bouquet garni. Sauté together, and cover with a large volume of water. Add the baby onions and cook over a low heat for 1 hour.
3. When the meat is cooked, remove and set aside, along with the vegetables. Strain the stock through a *chinois* (fine sieve) and reduce if necessary. Moisten the meat and vegetables with a bit of hot stock from the pan.
4. Make a roux by melting the butter in a pan and stirring in the flour. Add the stock and cook to a smooth sauce. Remove from the heat.
5. Mix together the cream and egg yolks, stir into the stock (the sauce must not boil), and season. Add the juice of a lemon and pour this sauce over the reserved meat and vegetables. Serve immediately.

WINE: POUILLY FUMÉ

jarret de veau en cuisson lente

SLOW-COOKED VEAL SHANK
FOR 1 SHANK - PREPARATION TIME: 30 MINUTES
COOKING TIME: 3 HOURS 15 MINUTES

Veal shank	1
Bouquet garni	1
Leek	1
Carrots	4
Onions	4
Veal stock	2 cups
Honey	2 tablespoons
Butter	½ cup
Salt, pepper	

1. Cook the veal shank in boiling water, along with the bouquet garni and sliced leek for 2 hours. Cook until the meat is starting to fall off the bones.
2. In a roasting pan, sauté the diced carrots and thinly sliced onions in butter. Add the honey, and deglaze the roasting pan with the stock, scraping up the bits on the bottom.
3. Place the shank in the roasting pan and bake in a 350°F oven for 1 hour, basting the meat regularly. Serve hot.

WINE: HAUT MÉDOC

côte de veau grand-mère

GRANDMOTHER'S VEAL CHOPS
(IN A MUSHROOM, BACON, AND ONION CREAM SAUCE)
FOR 6 - PREPARATION TIME: 10 MINUTES
COOKING TIME: 25 MINUTES

Individual veal rib chops	6
Flour	2½ tablespoons
Mushrooms	1 pound 2 ounces
Smoked bacon pieces	7 ounces
Baby onions	12
Madeira	⅓ to ½ cup
Heavy cream	1¼ cups
Butter	
Salt, pepper	

1. Cut the mushrooms into quarters. Sauté with the bacon and baby onions.
2. Flour the veal chops; then sauté them in butter for 5 minutes on each side, until they are well-browned.
3. Add the mushroom mixture, and deglaze the pan with the Madeira.
4. Stir in the cream. Cook gently for an additional 10 minutes, and season. Serve immediately.

WINE: AN "OLD" WINE, AS MY GRANDMOTHER WOULD SAY

grandmother's veal chops (in a bacon, mushroom, and onion cream sauce)

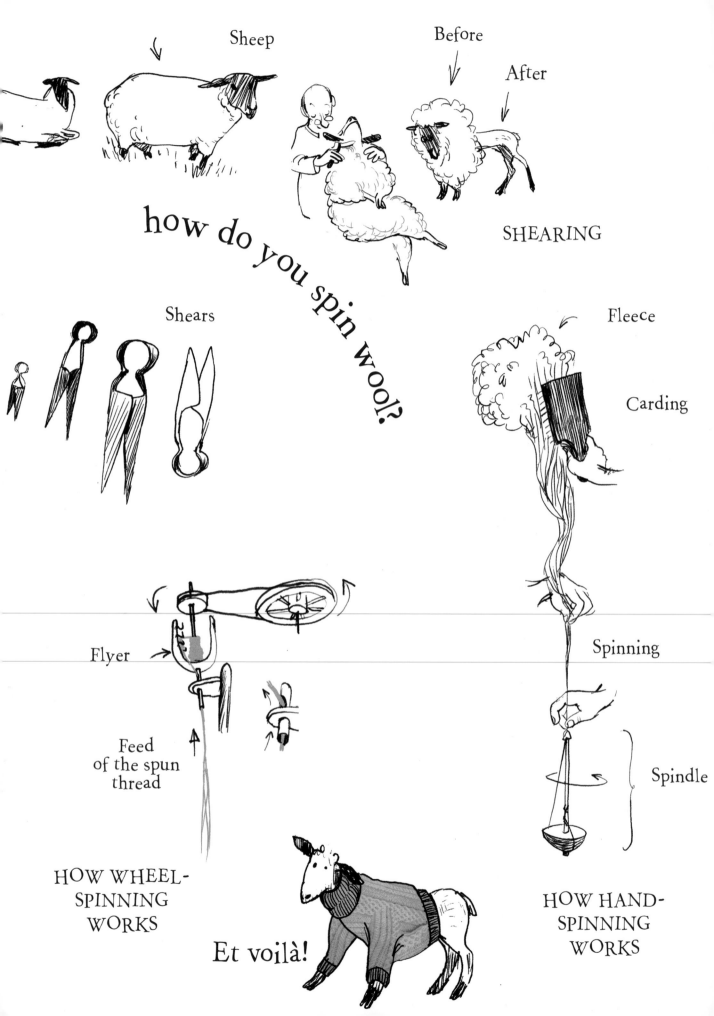

Sheep

Before

After

how do you spin wool?

SHEARING

Shears

Fleece

Carding

Flyer

Spinning

Feed
of the spun
thread

Spindle

HOW WHEEL-
SPINNING
WORKS

Et voilà!

HOW HAND-
SPINNING
WORKS

DES A.O.C. BÊÊHHHHH
REGISTERED BAA-BAAS (SHEEP)

Rouge de l'ouest

Tarasconnaise

Suffolk

Noire du velay

Southdown

Merino

Solognote

Texel

Raïole

1 Neck
2 Cross-rib
3a First rack
3b Second rack
4 Loin
5 Rump
6 Leg
7 Breast and short ribs
8 Shoulder

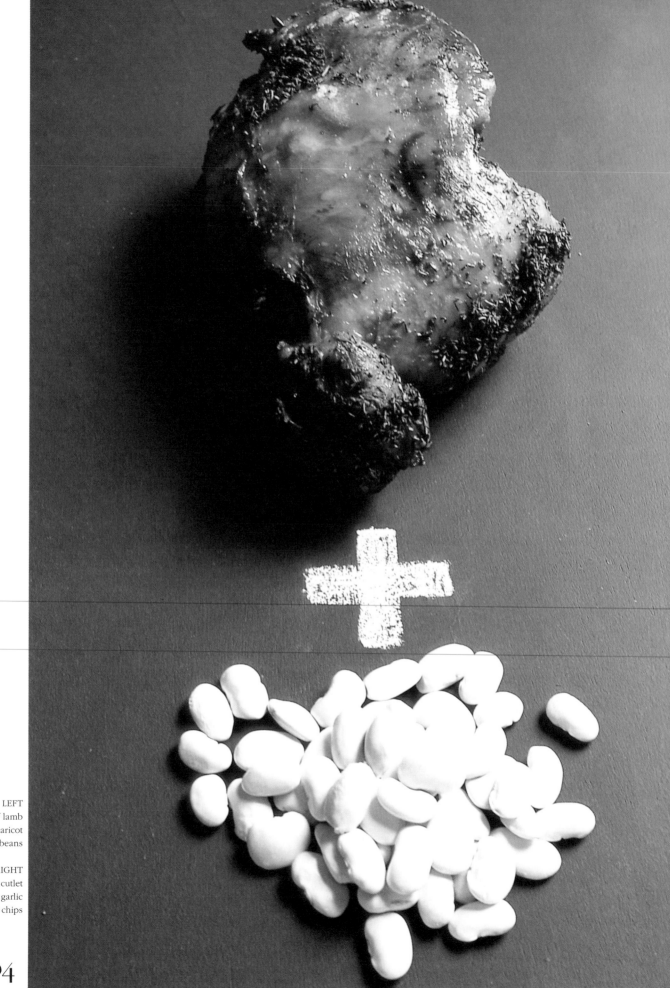

LEFT
leg of lamb
with haricot
beans

RIGHT
lamb cutlet
with garlic
chips

gigot aux haricots tarbais

LEG OF LAMB WITH DRIED WHITE BEANS
FOR 6 - PREPARATION TIME: 20 MINUTES
COOKING TIME: 2 HOURS + 12 HOURS SOAKING TIME

Leg of lamb	1
Bacon slices	7 ounces
Garlic	6 cloves
Olive oil	2½ tablespoons
White dessert wine (Muscat)	½ cup
Dried haricot beans (or other small white beans)	1½ cups
Bouquet garni	1
Carrots	3
Onion studded with 4 cloves	1
Dried thyme leaves	
Salt, pepper	

1. The day before cooking, soak the beans in cold water.
2. Meanwhile, peel and chop the garlic with thyme and mix with the olive oil. Make cuts all over the lamb leg and rub with the garlic oil mixture. Wrap the leg in plastic wrap and keep in the refrigerator.
3. The next day put the beans in a saucepan of water with the bouquet garni, onion, sliced carrots, and bacon. Cook for 2 hours, or until the beans are tender, and drain.
4. Meanwhile, place the leg of lamb in a roasting pan and roast in a 400°F oven for 45 minutes, moistening the meat with water occasionally—the meat should still be pink.
5. Deglaze the roasting pan with the wine, scraping up the bits on the bottom. Add the bean mixture to the cooking juices and season. Slice the meat and serve with the beans.

WINE: PAUILLAC

côtelette aux chips d'ail

LAMB CUTLETS WITH GARLIC CHIPS
FOR 6 - PREPARATION TIME: 30 MINUTES
COOKING TIME: 50 MINUTES

Lamb cutlets	12
Onions	6
Fennel	2 bulbs
Zucchini	3
Sun-dried tomatoes in oil	1 cup
Garlic	6 cloves
Thyme	1 large sprig
Bay leaf	1
White wine	½ cup
Olive oil	
Salt, pepper	

1. Peel the onions and garlic and slice them into rounds along with the fennel and zucchini.
2. In a gratin dish, arrange the zucchini, onion, sun-dried tomatoes, and fennel. Drizzle with the olive oil and wine, add the thyme and bay leaf, and season. Bake in a 350°F oven for 30 minutes.

3. In a frying pan, brown the veal cutlets on both sides and season. Lightly brown the garlic chips in the cooking fat.
4. Arrange the cutlets on top of the baked vegetables. Drizzle with the cooking fat, top with the garlic chips, and bake for an additional 10 minutes.

WINE: PAUILLAC

navarin d'agneau

LAMB NAVARIN
FOR 6 - PREPARATION TIME: 45 MINUTES
COOKING TIME: 1 HOUR 45 MINS

Boned lamb shoulder	2 pounds 11 ounces
Bouquet garni	1
Leek	1
Onions	2
Baby carrots	6
Scallions (bulb green onions if available)	6
Snow peas	18
Shelled fava beans	1 cup
Tomatoes	3
Flour	4 teaspoons
Heavy cream	1¼ cups
White wine	½ cup
Butter	2½ tablespoons
Salt, pepper	

1. Cut the lamb into 1½ inch cubes. Peel and slice the onions and the white part of the leek.
2. In a heavy casserole, brown the lamb pieces in the butter with the onion and leek. Add the flour and cook for 5 minutes. Deglaze the pan with the wine, scraping up all the bits on the bottom, letting the liquid reduce until it has completely evaporated.
3. Cover with an inch of water, add the bouquet garni, and cook for 1 hour, skimming regularly. Stir in the cream and let it simmer for an additional 30 minutes.
4. Meanwhile, cook the rest of the vegetables separately in a saucepan filled with salted boiling water—the carrots for 20 minutes; scallions (or bulb green onions) for 15 minutes; snow peas for 5 minutes; and fava beans for just a minute or two.
5. Plunge the tomatoes into boiling water for 10 seconds and peel them. Then chop the flesh into cubes.
6. Mix all the vegetables into the casserole and season. Serve hot.

WINE: SAINT-JULIEN

LEFT
mutton and
bean stew

RIGHT
neck of
mutton stew

haricot de mouton

MUTTON AND BEAN STEW
FOR 6 - PREPARATION TIME: 20 MINUTES
COOKING TIME: 2 HOURS 40 MINUTES +
12 HOURS SOAKING TIME

Breast of mutton	4 pounds 8 ounces
Dried white beans	1 cup
Bouquet garni	1
Onion studded with 4 cloves	1
Carrots	4
Ripe tomatoes	6
Shallots	6
Concentrated tomato purée	2 tablespoons
White wine	½ cup

Olive oil
Salt, pepper

1. A day before cooking, soak the beans in cold water.
2. The next day cook the beans in a large volume of water with the bouquet garni, onion, and sliced carrots for 1 hour.
3. Cut the mutton into cubes and add to the beans. Cook for an additional hour.
4. In a casserole or Dutch oven, soften the shallots and add the quartered tomatoes in olive oil. Pour in the wine and concentrated tomato purée.
5. Remove the mutton breast from the bean mixture. Add to the casserole containing the shallots and tomato mixture. Cover and cook for 30 minutes, then add the beans, and season.

WINE: LIRAC

ragoût de mouton

NECK OF MUTTON STEW
FOR 6 - PREPARATION TIME: 20 MINUTES
COOKING TIME: 1 HOUR 40 MINUTES

Neck of mutton	4 pounds 8 ounces
Potatoes	6
Carrots	2
Bay leaves	2
Rosemary	2 large sprigs
Garlic	4 cloves
Flour	4 teaspoons

Olive oil
Salt, pepper

1. Cut the mutton neck into small pieces. Sauté them in olive oil in a Dutch oven or casserole until lightly browned; then add the flour and cook for another 5 minutes.
2. Add 2 cups of water, the sliced carrots, unpeeled garlic, bay leaves, and rosemary. Cover and cook at low heat for 1 hour.
3. Peel and cut the potatoes into quarters, add them to the mutton and vegetables, and cook for an additional 30 minutes. Season and serve.

WINE: COSTIÈRES-DE-NÎMES

épaule farcie

STUFFED LAMB SHOULDER
FOR 6 - PREPARATION TIME: 30 MINUTES
COOKING TIME: 1 HOUR

Boned lamb shoulder	1
Veal shoulder	7 ounces
Pork belly	3½ ounces
Dried thyme leaves	1 teaspoon
Shallot	1
Chopped black olives	⅓ cup
Rosemary	3 sprigs
Bay leaves	1 large sprig
Lovage (wild celery)	2 large sprigs
Cognac	2½ tablespoons

Olive oil
Salt, pepper

1. Finely chop the veal and pork belly. Peel and dice the shallot and mix into the diced meat. Add the thyme, chopped olives, and cognac, and season.
2. Spread the stuffing on top of the boned lamb shoulder. Place the herbs in the center, letting them stick out one side. Then roll up the breast, which is filled with the stuffing, tie it up, brush it with olive oil, and season.
3. Roast in a 350°F oven for 1 hour, slice, and serve.

WINE: CORBIÈRES

Salima Aissaoua

COUSCOUS LIKE OURS!

Yes, indeed! The second favorite dish of our fellow French citizens is couscous. It follows close on the heels of *blanquette* (a traditional stew) on the list of delicacies dear to us all. What a friendly poke in the ribs of our gastronomy, and what a magnificent symbol of openness to other cultures. Borders may well stand firm, but culinary sharing is international. We share another country's culture and it becomes part of our heritage; we eat its food and it becomes part of our everyday lives. Salima upholds her culture in its traditions and knowledge, but she, too, has this notion of sharing, both in her generosity in giving and her generosity in learning. This double sharing, at once strong and so simple (and so natural), is the cornerstone of a functioning society.

le couscous de Salima

SALIMA'S COUSCOUS
FOR 6 - PREPARATION TIME: 20 MINUTES
COOKING TIME: 1 HOUR 10 MINUTES

Instant couscous	2 pounds 4 ounces
Zucchini	3
Carrots	3
Turnips	3
Onions	2
Dried chickpeas, soaked overnight	½ cup
Paprika	1 tablespoon
Saffron	1 pinch
Quatre-épices (spice blend)	1 teaspoon
Concentrated tomato purée	3 tablespoons
Lamb shoulder	1
Butter	2½ tablespoons

Olive oil
Salt, pepper

1. Cut the lamb into large pieces. Chop the onion, and peel and cut the vegetables into large pieces. Season the lamb with the paprika, saffron, and *quatre-épices,* a blend of four spices.

2. Sauté the meat in olive oil. Cover with a large volume of water (three times the volume of the meat). Add the chickpeas, all the vegetables, and the concentrated tomato purée. Put the meat and vegetable mixture into a *couscoussier* (couscous pot) or large saucepan to steam for 50 minutes, until the lamb is tender.

3. Pour enough boiling water over the couscous to cover it. Stir, cover, and let it sit for 10 minutes until cooked. Fluff the grains with a fork, mix in melted butter and some olive oil, and season.

4. Taste the sauce, and serve the couscous with the lamb and vegetables.

WINE: SALIMA DOESN'T DRINK WINE WITH HER COUSCOUS

DES A.O.C. COCHONNES
REGISTERED HOGS

Gascon

Black Limousin

French Landrace

Piétrain

Large white-him

Large white-her

Basque

Bayeux

1	Rack	9	Ears
2	Loin	10	Trotters
3	Shoulder (butt, blade)	11	Belly rack
4	Eye filet	12	Rump
5	Leg	13	Belly
6	Hock	14	Tail
7	Side (bacon)	15	Head
8	Snout	16	Spare ribs

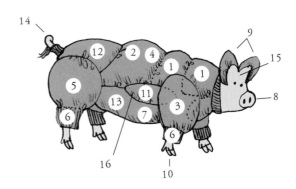

217

LEFT
roast pork,
pure and
simple

RIGHT
rack of pork
in casserole

218

rôti De cochon tout simplement

ROAST PORK, PURE AND SIMPLE
FOR 6 - PREPARATION TIME: 20 MINUTES
COOKING TIME: 1 HOUR 40 MINUTES

Pork loin roast ....2 pounds 11 ounces
White wine...1¼ cups
Celery stalks..4
Baby carrots 6
Baby turnips 6
Scallions (bulb green onions if available)......................6
Garlic...1 bulb
Shallots..6
Bay leaf 1
Rosemary ....1 large sprig
Butter...1½ tablespoons
Olive oil ....2 tablespoons
Salt, pepper

1. In a gratin dish, brown the entire roast in butter and olive oil over high heat.
2. Cut the celery into sticks and add to the pork with the wine, shallots, garlic bulb, and herbs.
3. Roast in a 350°F oven for 45 minutes.
4. Add the carrots, turnips, bulb spring onions, and some more water if necessary. Season and roast for a further 45 minutes, basting the pork regularly.

WINE: **SAINT-JOSEPH**

carré De cochon en cocotte

RACK OF PORK IN CASSEROLE
FOR 6 - PREPARATION TIME: 30 MINUTES
COOKING TIME: 2 HOURS 10 MINUTES

4-rib rack of pork 1
Onions..4
Scallions (bulb green onions if available)......................6
Fresh peas..2 pounds 4 ounces
Finger potatoes ....1 pound 2 ounces
Granny Smith apples..3
Dry hard cider ....2 cups
Butter...⅓ cup
Salt, pepper

1. In a flameproof casserole dish or Dutch oven, brown the rack of pork in butter over high heat. Add the sliced onions. Pour in half the cider, cover, and cook over low heat for 1 hour 30 minutes. Season.
2. Add the potatoes in their skins and the scallions. Cook for 20 minutes.
3. Chop the Granny Smith apples into cubes. Add to the casserole with the peas and the remaining cider, and cook for an additional 10 minutes.

WINE: **DRY HARD CIDER**

filet De cochon à la Dijonnaise

PORK LOIN WITH DIJON MUSTARD
FOR 6 - PREPARATION TIME: 15 MINUTES
COOKING TIME: 1 HOUR 40 MINUTES

Pork loin roast ....2 pounds 4 ounces
Shallots..2
Garlic...2 cloves
Veal stock...1¼ cups
White port..½ to ⅔ cup
Heavy cream...1¼ cups
Dijon mustard...3 tablespoons
Butter...2½ tablespoons
Salt, pepper

1. Peel and chop the shallots and garlic.
2. In a heavy pan or Dutch oven, brown the pork loin on all sides in the butter over high heat. Add the shallots and garlic. Deglaze the pan with the port, scraping up the bits on the bottom. Cover and cook over low heat for 30 minutes.
3. Add the veal stock and cook for an additional 30 minutes.
4. Stir in the cream and cook for another 30 minutes. Season.
5. Just before serving, stir in the Dijon mustard.

WINE: **HAUTES-CÔTES-DE-NUITS**

LEFT
salt pork
with lentils

RIGHT
Auvergne
pork pot

potée auvergnate

AUVERGNE PORK POT
FOR 6 - PREPARATION TIME: 45 MINUTES
COOKING TIME: 3 HOURS

Pork belly rack	1 pound 5 ounces
Pork butt	1
Country-style sausages	6
Bacon	14-ounce slab
Garlic sausage	1
Bouquet garni	1
Onions	4
Round green cabbage	1
Carrots	6
Leeks	3
Turnips	6
Potatoes	6

1. Cut the cabbage into six pieces. Peel the vegetables and carefully wash the leeks.
2. In a large stock pot, simmer the pork butt for 1 hour with the onions and bouquet garni.
3. Add the belly rack, piece of bacon, cabbage, and leeks, and cook another hour.
4. Now add the sausages, carrots, and turnips, and cook for 30 minutes; at that time, add the potatoes and cook for a further 30 minutes.
5. Carve the meats and serve very hot. Add salt at the table, since the meats are already very salty.

WINE: CÔTES-D'AUVERGNE

petit salé aux lentilles

SALT PORK WITH LENTILS
FOR 6 - PREPARATION TIME: 20 MINUTES
COOKING TIME: 1 HOUR 40 MINUTES

Salt-cured pork spare ribs	1 pound 5 ounces
Pork butt	1
Bacon	7-ounce slab
Garlic sausage	1
Salt-cured pork loin	1 pound 5 ounces
Bouquet garni	1
Leek	1
Lentils	1 cup
Onion studded with 4 cloves	1
Carrots	2
Bay leaves	2
Duck fat	3 tablespoons

1. Cook the meats, except for the sausage, for 1 hour in a large volume of water with the bouquet garni and leek. Then add the sausage and cook for another 30 minutes.
2. Meanwhile, peel the carrots and cut into large dice. Simmer the lentils with the carrots, onion, and bay leaves for 30 minutes. Drain.
3. Melt the duck fat and stir through the lentil mixture. Season and serve with the carved meats.

WINE: CROZES-HERMITAGE

kig ha fars

BRETON "MEAT AND PUDDING"
FOR 6 - PREPARATION TIME: 45 MINUTES
COOKING TIME: 3 HOURS

POT-AU-FEU

Beef shin	1 pound 5 ounces
Salt pork	1 pound 5 ounces
Bacon	6 thick slices
Pork hocks	2
White cabbage	1
Carrots	6
Leeks	3
Onion studded with 4 cloves	1
Bouquet garni	1
Salt, pepper	

BUCKWHEAT *FAR* (PUDDING)

Buckwheat flour	1½ cups
Eggs	2
Salted butter, melted	⅓ cup
Milk	1 cup
Raisins	1 handful
Salt, pepper	

WHEAT *FAR* (PUDDING)

All-purpose flour	2 cups
Eggs	2
Milk	1 cup
Salted butter, melted	3½ tablespoons
Superfine sugar	2 tablespoons

LIPIG (BUTTER SAUCE)

Butter	1 cup
Shallots	4

1. Make a *pot-au-feu* by cooking all the meats together with the roughly chopped leeks, cabbage, onion, and bouquet garni and water to cover. Cook for 1 hour.
2. Meanwhile, dampen two cotton cloths and prepare the *fars*. To make the buckwheat *fars*, form a mound of buckwheat flour, make a hollow in the middle, and add the eggs, melted butter, milk, and raisins. Combine all the ingredients, place the mixture on one of the two cloths, and tie it up with string.
3. Follow the same procedure for the wheat *far*, placing it on the second damp cloth.
4. Add the two puddings to the *pot-au-feu* stock and cook for 1 hour. Then add the carrots and cook for a further 1 hour.
5. Prepare the *lipig* by cooking the sliced shallots in the butter.
6. Remove the puddings from the stock and rest for 5 minutes. Serve the meats on a warmed plate, surrounded by the vegetables. Open the pudding cloths, crumble the *fars*, and serve the broth and the *lipig* separately.

WINE: DRY HARD CIDER

kig ha fars at Hervé and Michou's place

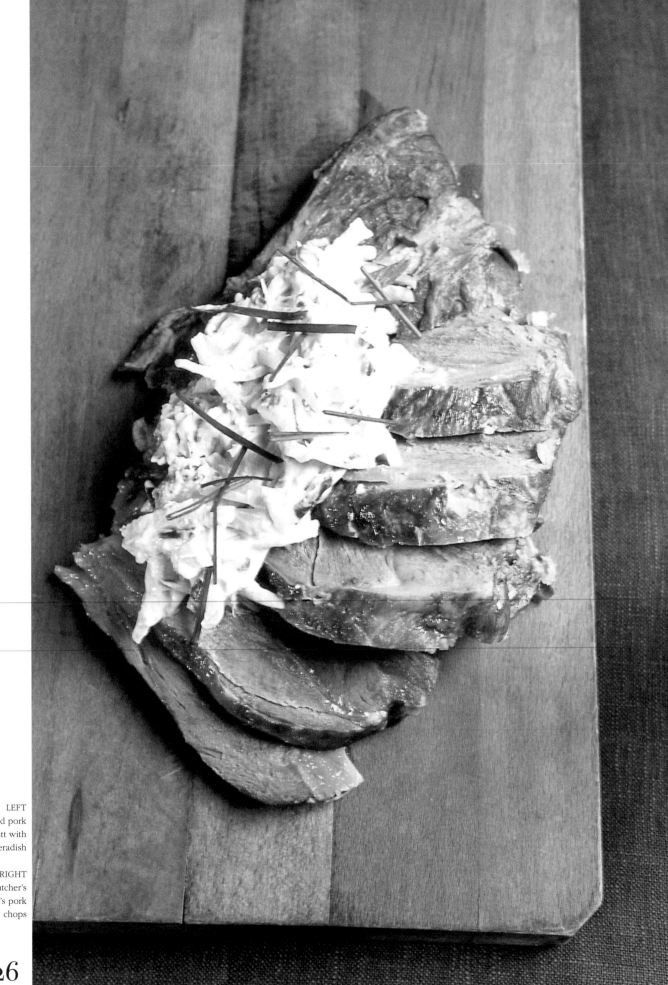

LEFT
smoked pork
butt with
horseradish

RIGHT
butcher's
wife's pork
chops

palette fumée au raifort

SMOKED PORK BUTT WITH HORSERADISH
FOR 6 - PREPARATION TIME: 20 MINUTES
COOKING TIME: 2 HOURS

Smoked pork butt (from the shoulder)	1
Bouquet garni	1
Crème fraîche	⅓ cup
Horseradish	1 tablespoon
Radishes	1 bunch
Chives	1 bunch
Shallot	1

Salt, pepper

1. Boil the smoked pork with the bouquet garni in a large pot of water for 2 hours.
2. To make the horseradish sauce, julienne the radishes, peel and finely chop the shallot, and snip off the chives. Mix them all together with the horseradish and crème fraîche; then season.
3. Carve the slices of smoked pork (hot or cold) and dress with the horseradish sauce.

WINE: PINOT GRIS

côte de cochon charcutière

BUTCHER'S WIFE'S PORK CHOPS
FOR 6 - PREPARATION TIME: 30 MINUTES
COOKING TIME: 20 MINUTES

Pork chops	6
Bacon strips	3½ ounces
Onion	1
Baby spinach leaves	1 pound 5 ounces
Cornichons	3½ ounces
Tomatoes	2
Red port wine	2½ tablespoons
Butter	
Salt, pepper	

1. Drop the tomatoes into boiling water for 10 seconds. Peel the tomatoes, and chop the flesh into cubes. Julienne the cornichons.
2. Pan-fry the pork chops in butter for 10 minutes on each side. Keep in a warm place.
3. In the same pan, brown the bacon strips with the chopped onion and add the spinach and cornichons. Deglaze the pan with the port, add the diced tomato, and season.
4. Serve the pork chops topped with the vegetables.

WINE: SYLVANER

sauerkraut

SAUERKRAUT
FOR 6- PREPARATION TIME: 15 MINUTES
COOKING TIME: 2 HOURS 15 MINUTES

Sauerkraut	2 pounds 11 ounces
Duck fat or lard	2 tablespoons
Onion	1
Bay leaf	1
Cloves	2
Cumin	1 teaspoon
Juniper berries	8
Riesling	½ cup
Water or vegetable broth	2 cups
Smoked ham	1 pound 2 ounces
Speck (smoked)	9 ounces
Pork shoulder	14 ounces
Potatoes	6
Wiener sausages	3
Hiri sausages	3

Salt, pepper

1. Wash the sauerkraut two or three times in warm water.
2. Finely chop the onion, and brown it in a saucepan in the duck fat. Add the onion to the sauerkraut with some salt and pepper, bay leaf, cloves, cumin, juniper berries, and water or broth. Cover and cook over low heat for 40 minutes.
3. Then add the smoked ham, speck, and pork shoulder, and cook for 1 hour.
4. Add the wine and diced potatoes and cook for 15 minutes; then add the sausages and cook for a final 15 minutes.
5. Warm up a serving dish for the sauerkraut. Arrange the potatoes and meat on top of the sauerkraut.

WINE: RIESLING

NOTE: This Alsatian recipe was passed on to me by Suzanne Roth, a superb master of Alsatian cooking and the author of many cookbooks.

LES VINS D'ALSACE
THE WINES OF ALSACE

The Alsatian wine region stretches between the Vosges mountains and the Alsace plain. This highly individual *terroir* enjoys one of the lowest rainfalls in France, with a warm and dry climate—a real pleasure for the grape. The vines are planted up to an altitude of 1300 feet (400 meters) on the buttresses of the Vosges mountains, maximizing their exposure to the sun. The grape grows slowly and also ripens slowly, its flavor concentrated to produce a wine of international renown. This viticultural history, lodged deep in the region's memory, dates back to the first millennium. The geographical sitiuation of the vineyards has been the source of numerous problems during times of international conflict. The sacking of the vines during the Second World War enabled the region to return even stronger, setting out a quality charter for both the varieties and winemaking process. This resurrection was capped by recognition of Alsace as a registered designation of origin (AOC) in 1962; the Alsace *Grand Cru* in 1975 for exceptional wines derived from noble varieties; and the *crémant d'Alsace* in 1976 for sparkling wines.

THERE ARE EIGHT DIFFERENT ALSATIAN VARIETIES:

- Sylvaner
- Riesling
- Gewürztraminer
- Pinot Blanc
- Pinot Gris
- Muscat
- Pinot Noir
- Klevener de Heiligenstein
- And, finally, Edelzwicker, which is a blend of white varieties

All of these different varieties carry their own specific nuance of flavor and aroma. From a dry and sharp white like the Sylvaner to the exuberant Gewürztraminer, let yourself be seduced by the complexity. Let us not forget either the *vendanges tardives* (late-harvested grapes) gathered at the over-ripe stage, and the *grain noble* selection, involving a successive sorting of grapes affected by noble rot: the quality of product is literally magic.

A FEW PAIRINGS OF DISHES WITH ALSATIAN WINES

Seafood:	Pinot Blanc, Riesling, Sylvaner
White meat:	Pinot Gris, Crémant
Game:	Pinot Noir
Sauerkraut:	Riesling
Munster cheese:	*Vendange tardive* Gewürztraminer
For sheer pleasure:	A *grain noble* selection

Es Kummt e Schähreschiffer in's Land

De Jungfere schlief ich sie um' sunscht,
Mit minnre scheene Schlifferkunscht,
Feleteri un feletera !
Mit minnre scheene Schlifferkunscht,
Fidi, fidi, ràlele, riolälä !
Schliff ich's Messer un die Schähr !

Ich hab' inn Sinn uff Colmer ze gehn,
Mit mim scheene Schlifferkarich,
Feleteri...

In Colmer sinn an richi Litt,
Wie mir ebbs ze verdiene gänn.
Feleteri...

Dheim haw ich gar e ganz füeles Wieb
Drum haw ich an kenn Hemd am Lieb !
Feleteri...

Sie kocht sehr selte mir d'Suppe warm,
Un's g'miess isch gschmeltzt das Gotterbarm.
Feleteri...

Wo ich nur geh' un wo ich nur steh,
So bisse mich die Lies un Fleh !
Feleteri...

Ach ! Schähreschliffer schliff nurre zü
Denn scheeni Maidle gibt 's genü
Feleteri...

VINIFICATION

OU FAIRE SON VIN SOI-MÊME !

VINIFICATION, OR MAKE YOUR OWN WINE!

LES VINS DU JURA

THE WINES OF THE JURA

CONFIT DE CANARD

EN CONSERVE

PRESERVED DUCK CONFIT

Chantons ! Let's sing!

Il est un coin de France

Chanson Basque de l'Opérette
«Le chanteur de Mexico» de Francis Lopez

Basque song "There's a corner of France", from the operetta *Le chanteur de Mexico*
by Francis Lopez

poules, poulets, canards
hens, chickens, ducks

VOLAILLES
POULTRY

+

dinde et pigeon
turkey and pigeon

LE SECRET DE FAMILLE DE LILLET

THE LILLET FAMILY SECRET

POULES, POULETS...

HENS, CHICKENS...

Turkey-cock and turkey-hen

Chicken
(poulet – for eating)

Hen (poule –
for laying & boiling)

Rooster

Duck

Guinea hen

A rooster...

...a capon

LEFT
chicken
chasseur

RIGHT
bresse chicken
with *vin jaune*

236

poulet sauté chasseur

CHICKEN CHASSEUR
FOR 4 - PREPARATION TIME: 30 MINUTES
COOKING TIME: 40 MINUTES

A well-muscled free-range chicken that is
acquainted with nature, having skipped about
every day of its life for earthworms 1
Ripe tomatoes 6
Mushrooms .... 10 ounces
Shallots 3
Bouquet garni 1
White wine .... ½ cup
Tarragon .... 1 bunch
Flat-leaf parsley .... 3 sprigs
Flour .... 4 teaspoons
Finger potatoes 6
Olive oil
Salt, pepper

1. Cut the chicken into eight pieces.
2. Plunge the tomatoes into boiling water for 10 seconds.
Peel the tomatoes and set aside the flesh. Peel and chop
the shallots.
3. In a heavy pan, sauté the chicken, shallots, and
mushrooms over high heat until brown. Add the flour, then
the wine. Then add the tomato flesh, bouquet garni, and
peeled potatoes, and season. Cover and cook over medium-
low heat for 30 minutes.
4. Serve with chopped herbs on top.

WINE: SAINT-AMOUR

poulet De Bresse au vin jaune

BRESSE CHICKEN WITH VIN JAUNE
FOR 4 - PREPARATION TIME: 30 MINUTES
COOKING TIME: 1 HOUR

Bresse chicken, or the best quality you can buy 1
Morel mushrooms .... 7 ounces
Vin jaune (sherry-like white wine) from the Jura .... 1¼ cups
Heavy cream .... 1¼ cups
Shallots 5
Garlic .... 3 cloves
Bouquet garni 1
Chicken stock .... ¾ cup
Flour .... 4 teaspoons
Butter .... 2½ tablespoons
Oil
Salt, pepper

1. Cut the chicken into eight pieces, and peel and slice
the shallots.
2. Sauté the chicken in a mixture of butter and oil. Add the
shallots and morels, and drain off the fat.
3. Return the chicken and shallots to the pan, and coat with
the flour. Add the wine and chicken stock.
4. Add the peeled garlic and bouquet garni; then cook at a
low simmer for 45 minutes. Stir in the cream and cook an
additional 15 minutes.

WINE: SOME VIN JAUNE, OBVIOUSLY

poulet rôti tout simplement

ROAST CHICKEN, PURE AND SIMPLE
FOR 4 - PREPARATION TIME: 15 MINUTES
COOKING TIME: 1 HOUR

The twin brother of the previous chicken 1
Boursin-style cheese with garlic and *fines herbes* 1
Tarragon .... 1 bunch
Garlic .... 3 cloves
Sea salt
Olive oil

1. Remove the chicken's innards, and reserve the heart and
liver.
2. Chop the heart and liver and combine well with the
cheese, tarragon, and chopped garlic.
3. Fill the chicken with the cheese mixture.
4. Oil the chicken and sprinkle with sea salt.
5. Roast uncovered in a 400°F oven for 1 hour, basting the
chicken regularly.
6. To serve, cut the chicken into portions and dress it with a
mixture of melted cheese and the cooking juices.

**WINE: SOME SODA FOR THE CHILDREN. I KNOW,
IT'S NOT GOOD, BUT WHAT CAN YOU DO!**

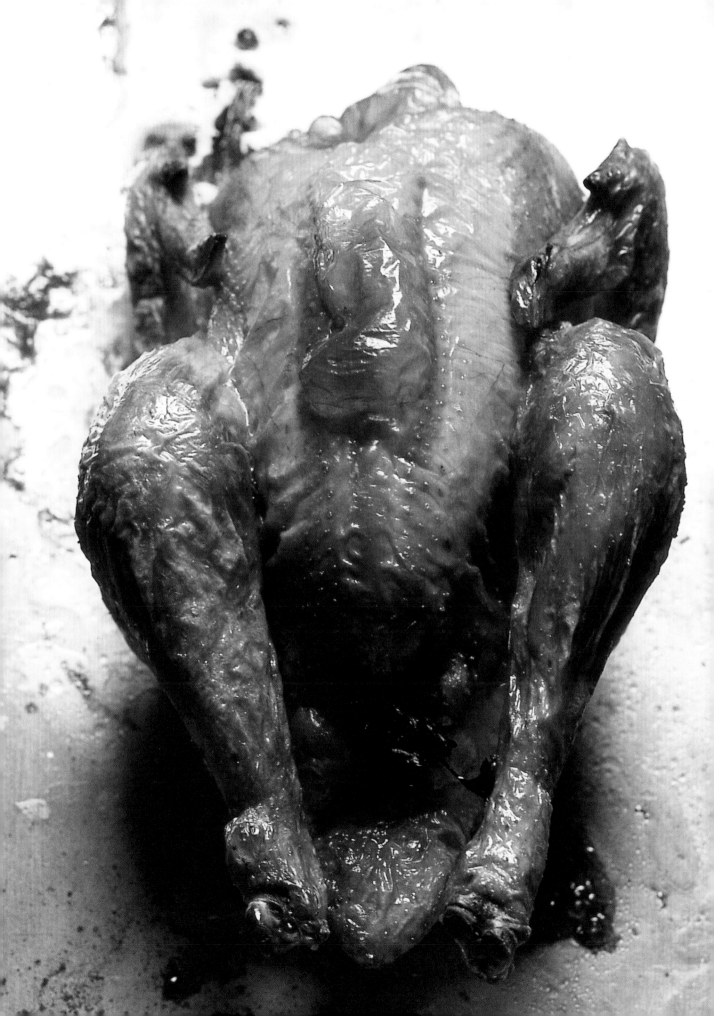

LES VINS DU JURA
THE WINES OF THE JURA

The Jura wine-growing region is undoubtedly the smallest in France. Small in area, but high in quality. Like many wine-growing regions, Jura has had its troubled times, in particular the phylloxera crisis at the end of the nineteenth century, which led to this region being crossed off the French wine menu. Through work and self-sacrifice, 4,600 acres were replanted. This work was rewarded in 1936 when the registered appellation Arbois AOC was secured.

TODAY THERE ARE SIX REGISTERED WINES IN THE JURA:

ARBOIS
Made from 70 percent red wines and 30 percent white wines, the Arbois AOC covers 13 *communes* (municipalities) with 5 authorized grape varieties—Poulsad, Pinot Noir, Trousseau, Chardonnay, and Savagnin.

CHÂTEAU-CHALON
Made from 100 percent *vins jaunes*, from the Savagnin grape variety, the Château-Chalon AOC is the most well known wine and the most mysterious. The *vin jaune* must age for six years and three months in oak barrels. It's during this period that a *voile* ("veil") of yeast develops on the wine's surface, thus protecting it from oxidation and bestowing its particular character.

L'ÉTOILE
A region surrounded by five hills forming the points of a star, it produces white wines of great finesse.

CÔTES-DU-JURA
This appellation is the broadest in the Jura region, which includes a very wide range of wine production.

MACVIN DU JURA
This appellation belongs to the family of *mistelles*, liqueurs obtained by adding one-third of the local *marc* (pomace brandy) to unfermented grape juice. It will then spend 12 months in an oak barrel and should be between 16° and 22° proof to lay claim to the name.

CRÉMANT DU JURA
White or rosé in color, the *crémant du Jura* enjoys a very broad appellation; this sparkling wine can be produced either from white varieties (50 percent Chardonnay), or from red varieties (50 percent Pinot Noir or Poulsard).

As in many regions, the culinary identity of the Jura marries perfectly with its viticultural identity. So get ready for a *soirée* of *comté* cheese and Château-Chalon!

VINIFICATION
OR: MAKE YOUR OWN WINE!

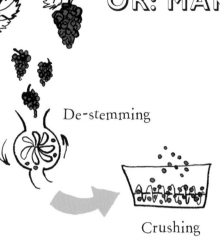

De-stemming

Crushing

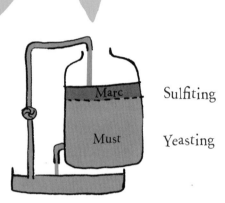

Marc

Must

Sulfiting

Yeasting

Pressing

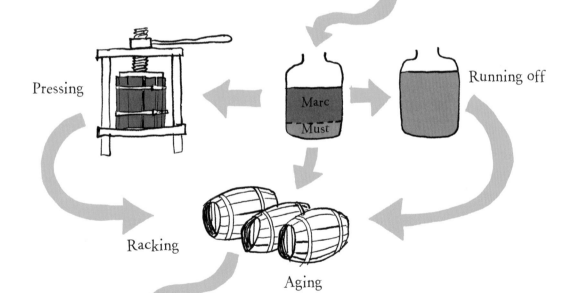

Marc

Must

Running off

Racking

Aging

Bottling

Labeling

Sealing

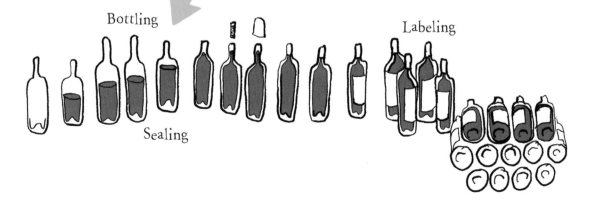

Storing

LEFT
chicken with
crayfish

RIGHT
coq au vin

242

poulet aux écrevisses

CHICKEN WITH CRAYFISH
FOR 4 - PREPARATION TIME: 45 MINUTES
COOKING TIME: 1 HOUR

A very close cousin of the previous chickens	1
Small crayfish	12
Onions	3
Ripe tomatoes	6
Saffron	1 pinch
Garlic	6 cloves
Cognac	2½ tablespoons
White wine	1 cup
Lobster bisque or seafood chowder	¾ cup
Heavy cream	¾ cup
Olive oil	
Salt, pepper	

1. Remove the intestinal tract of the crayfish. Peel and slice the garlic and onions. Cut the chicken into eight pieces.
2. In a heavy pot, sauté the chicken pieces until browned, then add the garlic and onions, and season. Cook for a few minutes. Deglaze the pan with the wine, scraping up the bits on the bottom. Add the saffron and chopped tomatoes, then cover, and simmer on a low flame for 30 minutes.
3. In a frying pan, sauté the crayfish in olive oil; then flambé with the cognac. Add them to the chicken pot with the pan juices. Then add the cream and lobster bisque and cook for an additional 15 minutes.

WINE: CROZES-HERMITAGE

coq au vin

CHICKEN IN RED WINE
FOR 6 - PREPARATION TIME: 30 MINUTES
COOKING TIME: 1 HOUR 15 MINUTES

Stewing chicken	1
Bacon	7-ounce slab
Mushrooms	7 ounces
Baby onions	12
Red wine from Chambertin	1 bottle
Red wine from Burgundy	1 bottle
Bouquet garni	1
Butter	2½ tablespoons
Flour	4 teaspoons
Sugar	1 tablespoon
Cognac	⅓ to ½ cup
Salt, pepper	

1. Cut the stewing chicken into eight pieces. Coat the chicken lightly with flour. Sauté the pieces in butter with the cubed bacon and peeled baby onions. Flambé the pan with cognac and cover with the Burgundy; then season and add the sugar and bouquet garni.
2. Sauté the mushrooms separately, letting them brown well, and add them to the chicken. Cover and cook at a low simmer for 1 hour.

3. Check the chicken to see if it is done—the meat must begin to fall off the bones. Remove the bouquet garni and serve in the pot.
4. P.S. The bottle of Chambertin has disappeared! Why is everyone staring at me?

WINE: CHAMBERTIN

poule au pot

CHICKEN POT-AU-FEU
FOR 6 - PREPARATION TIME: 30 MINUTES
COOKING TIME: 1 HOUR 40 MINS

Stewing hen	1
Carrots	6
Celery stalks	3
Celeriac (celery root)	½
Turnips	6
Leeks	3
Bouquet garni	1
Onion studded with 4 cloves	1
Cornichons	
Coarse sea salt	

1. Place the chicken, innards removed, in a large pot and cover with water. Bring to a boil for 5 minutes, drain, and rinse.
2. Put the chicken back in the pot and cover with clean water. Peel all the vegetables, wash them well, and add them to the pot. Season.
3. Cook on a low simmer for about 1 hour 30 minutes. If there is too much liquid, simmer the stock until reduced.
4. Serve with coarse sea salt and cornichons!

WINE: PULIGNY-MONTRACHET

dinde farcie de bonnes choses

TURKEY STUFFED WITH GOOD THINGS
FOR 10 - PREPARATION TIME: 60 MINUTES
COOKING TIME: 3 HOURS

Turkey, deboned (backbone removed)	
by your butcher	1 (11-pound)
Bacon	3½-ounce slab
Pork belly	3½ ounces
Pork loin	14 ounces
Veal meat	7 ounces
Tinned chestnuts	5 ounces
Garlic	6 cloves
Shallots	3
Heavy cream	¾ cup
Pistachio nuts	⅓ cup
Armagnac	2½ tablespoons
White port	⅓ to ½ cup
Olive oil	
Salt, pepper	

1. Peel and dice the garlic and shallots, and sauté in olive oil.
2. Chop the bacon, pork meat, and veal with the heart and liver of the turkey. Roughly crush the chestnuts, and combine with the cream, pistachio nuts, Armagnac, port, and the softened garlic and shallots. Add the chopped meats, mix together well, and season.
3. Spoon the stuffing into the turkey cavity. Close it up and tie with string. Oil the turkey and season.
4. Roast in a 235°F oven for 3 hours, basting regularly.

WINE: HERMITAGE ROUGE; IT'S CHRISTMAS, ISN'T IT?

pigeons Lucien Tendret

LUCIEN TENDRET'S SQUAB
FOR 6 - PREPARATION TIME: 20 MINUTES
COOKING TIME: 30 MINUTES

Squab	6
Green asparagus spears	18
Slices of country-style bread	6
Butter	2½ tablespoons
Juniper berries	6
Shallot	1
Olive oil	
Salt, pepper	

1. Remove the squab innards, reserving the hearts and livers.
2. Sauté the livers with the hearts, chopped shallot, and juniper berries until just cooked. Process the mixture with the butter and season.
3. Boil the asparagus spears in salted water, keeping them crisp.
4. Season the squab and cook in a heavy saucepan for about 15 minutes (depending on their size). Allow them to rest for 5 minutes.
5. Fry the bread slices in olive oil until golden, and spread with the liver mixture. Place the squab on top, pour on the cooking juices, and arrange the asparagus around.

WINE: SAINT-ÉMILION

squab au muscat

SQUAB IN MUSCAT
FOR 6 - PREPARATION TIME: 20 MINUTES
COOKING TIME: 15 MINUTES

Squab	6
Bacon	6 thin slices
Muscat de Rivesaltes	¾ cup
Green and red grapes	10 ounces
Butter	2½ tablespoons
Salt, pepper	

1. Remove the squab innards, reserving the hearts and livers. Wrap each pigeon in a slice of bacon and tie with string. Slice the grapes in two and remove the seeds.
2. In a large pan, sauté the squab in butter with the reserved giblets. Deglaze the pan with the Muscat, scraping up the bits on the bottom. Allow the liquid to reduce by half before adding the grapes. Cover and cook for 10 minutes over low heat. Season with salt and pepper.

WINE: MUSCAT SEC

LEFT
duck with
turnips
and other
vegetables

RIGHT
salmi of duck

canard aux navets et autres légumes

DUCK WITH TURNIPS AND OTHER VEGETABLES
FOR 6 - PREPARATION TIME: 30 MINUTES
COOKING TIME: 40 MINUTES + 15 MINUTES RESTING TIME

Wild duck..1
Turnips..6
Green tomatoes..6
Small red peppers..6
Baby zucchini...6
Baby eggplants...6
Thyme..3 large sprigs
Rosemary...1 sprig
Tarragon...1 bunch
Garlic...6 cloves
Mild onions..3
Olive oil
Salt, pepper

1. Remove the innards of the duck, reserving the liver and heart. Roughly chop the liver and heart, along with the garlic and peeled onions.
2. Spoon the mixture into the duck cavity. Add the aromatic herbs, drizzle generously with olive oil, and season.
3. Place the duck in a roasting pan and roast at 350°F for 20 minutes, basting regularly with the cooking juices.
4. Arrange the vegetables around the duck and season. Roast for a further 20 minutes.
5. Let the duck rest for 15 minutes before serving.

WINE: MINERVOIS ROUGE

salmis de canard

SALMI OF DUCK
FOR 6 - PREPARATION TIME: 30 MINUTES
COOKING TIME: 45 MINUTES

Duck..1
Bacon...7-ounce slab
Carrots..3
Red wine..1¼ cups
Chicken stock..1¼ cups
Armagnac...2½ tablespoons
Bay leaf...1
Flour..4 teaspoons
Butter...1½ tablespoons
Scallions (bulb green onions if available)...........................6

1. Remove the innards of the duck, reserving the liver. Cut the duck into eight pieces and coat lightly with flour. Sauté in butter with the peeled, diced carrots and cubed bacon. Flambé with the Armagnac.
2. Add the wine, stock, and bay leaf and cook for 20 minutes. Add the scallions, and cook for a further 20 minutes. Season.
3. Chop the liver very finely and incorporate into the sauce. *Salmi* keeps very well as a preserve.

WINE: BUZET ROUGE

pintade au chou

GUINEA HEN WITH CABBAGE
FOR 4 - PREPARATION TIME: 20 MINUTES
COOKING TIME: 50 MINUTES

Guinea hen, giblets removed..1
Green cabbage 1
Bacon pieces...9 ounces
White wine...½ cup
Sage leaves...6
Carrots..3
Duck fat ....3 tablespoons
Chicken stock...¾ cup
Salt, pepper

1. In a heavy pot, melt the duck fat. Season the guinea hen and brown until nice and golden.
2. Add the bacon pieces and sage along with the peeled, diced carrots.
3. Cut the cabbage into six pieces and wash well. Add the cabbage to the pot, pour in the wine and stock, then cover and cook for 45 minutes over low heat, stirring regularly.

WINE: SAUMUR BLANC

LILLET, SECRET DE FAMILLE

LILLET, A FAMILY SECRET

Bordeaux and its wines are exported throughout the world, among them Lillet, one of the oldest French apéritifs still in production. Lillet, a timeless classic whose durability is simply due to its quality, is found near Podensac, in Graves. Don't go asking for the Lillet recipe since it is a closely guarded secret, a genuine relic with international cult status—James Bond being the No. 1 fan. On winemaking day, everything is padlocked. Just a few aromatic vapors let you know that something is indeed happening, a metamorphosis that mingles orange peel and Bordeaux wines, distilled who knows how. Lillet and its unique posters on display in every bistro remind consumers that they are effectively sipping an institution.

LEFT
duck *à l'orange*

RIGHT
duck breast
with
black currants

CANARD À L'ORANGE

canard à l'orange

DUCK À L'ORANGE
FOR 6 - PREPARATION TIME: 20 MINUTES
COOKING TIME: 15 MINUTES + 24 HOURS REFRIGERATION TIME

Fat duck breasts	3
Oranges	4
Honey	1 tablespoon
Soy sauce	¾ cup
Ground cinnamon	1 tablespoon
Butter	2½ tablespoons

1. Start the prep for this dish one day before serving. Slash the fatty side of the duck breasts in a crisscross pattern (the flesh should show through).
2. Take the zest from two of the oranges and the juice from three. Mix the juice with the zest, cinnamon, honey, and soy sauce. Reserve 1 orange.
3. Place the duck breasts in a dish, skin side up, and pour the orange marinade over them. Chill for 24 hours.
4. Pan-fry the duck, skin side down, for 10 minutes on a gentle heat; the fat needs to render and brown. Drain off the fat and return the breasts to the pan. Peel and segment the remaining orange.
5. Add the orange segments and half the marinade to the pan, and let reduce for 5 minutes. Remove the meat and whisk in butter to make a sauce to serve with the duck.

WINE: RULLY BLANC

magret de canard au cassis

DUCK BREAST WITH BLACK CURRANTS
FOR 6 - PREPARATION TIME: 20 MINUTES
COOKING TIME: 30 MINUTES

Fat duck breasts	3
Shallot	1
Red wine	1¼ cups
Crème de cassis	⅓ to ½ cup
Black currants	1 tablespoon
Butter	⅔ cup
Celeriac (celery root)	1
Lemon	1

Salt, pepper

1. Peel the celeriac, cut into cubes, and cook in boiling water with the juice of a lemon. Purée the cooked celeriac, add two-thirds of the butter, and season.
2. Peel and finely chop the shallot. Bring the wine to a boil, add the shallot, and allow the liquid to reduce by half. Add the *crème de cassis* and black currants, and reduce again. The sauce should be syrupy. Whisk in the remaining butter to make a sauce.
3. Slash the fatty side of the duck breasts in a crisscross pattern. Pan-fry them, skin side down, for 10 minutes over gentle heat (the fat needs to melt and brown). Turn the breasts over and cook an additional 5 minutes.
4. Slice the breasts into six pieces, dress with the black currant sauce, and serve with the celeriac purée.

WINE: VOLNAY

LES VINS DE BOURGOGNE
THE WINES OF BURGUNDY

Burgundy is the region of France that offers the greatest number of appellations, the territory carved up in a way that is quasi-Lilliputian. It stretches from south of Paris to north of Lyon and is divided into five major *terroirs*: Chablis, Côte de Nuits, Côte de Beaune, Côte Chalonnaise, and Mâconnais. Some will say that Beaujolais forms part of this viticultural region, but I prefer to reserve for it an identity of its own: *vive le Beaujolais libre!* Some productions, narrowly defined, are limited to a few acres of vines, two or three arranged on well-defined soil, masterfully cultivated to obtain a specific result. Chardonnay and Pinot Noir fight for the attention of winemakers and supply the cellars of wine lovers.

In **Chablis**, it's easy: they make Chablis. This Chardonnay, in from the cold, lives in fear of the spring frosts that can be fatal to it.

The **Côte de Nuits** produces reds of rare elegance and finesse. Pinot Noir in all of its splendor. From north to south, the various appellations are:

- Côte-de-Nuits-Villages
- Marsannay-la-Côte
- Fixin
- Gevrey-Chambertin
- Morey-Saint-Denis
- Chambolle-Musigny
- Vougeot
- Vosne-Romanée
- Nuits-Saint-Georges

The winemakers of **Côtes de Beaune** produce white wines known the world over. This is the reign of Chardonnay, undisputed emperor of the French viticultural legacy. The reds have great intensity and cheerfully compete with the hegemony of Chardonnay. From north to south, the different appellations are:

- Côte-de-Beaune-Villages
- Ladoix
- Pernand-Vergelesses
- Aloxe-Corton
- Savigny-lès-Beaune
- Chorey-lès-Beaune
- Beaune
- Côte-de-Beaune
- Pommard
- Volnay
- Monthélie
- Saint-Romain
- Auxey-Duresses
- Meursault
- Blagny
- Puligny-Montrachet
- Chassagne-Montrachet
- Saint-Aubin
- Santenay
- Maranges

The **Côte Chalonnaise** is considered the second fiddle of the Burgundy region, with less prestigious appellations but some very wonderful surprises for those who take the time to taste them. From north to south, the appellations are:

- Bourgogne Côte-chalonnaise
- Bouzeron
- Givry
- Mercurey
- Montagny
- Rully

The **Mâconnais** is the southernmost *terroir* in Burgundy, where Pinot Noir gives way to Gamay. It's a more rural region that doesn't have any *premiers* or *grands crus* (the first-growth wines or highest-quality vineyards). From north to south, the appellations are:

- Mâcon
- Mâcon supérieur
- Mâcon-Villages
- Saint-Véran
- Pouilly-Vinzelles
- Viré-Clessé

LEFT
duck confit

RIGHT
cassoulet
with duck
confit

258

confit de canard

DUCK CONFIT
FOR 6 - PREPARATION TIME: 10 MINUTES
COOKING TIME: 2 HOURS + 24 HOURS REFRIGERATION TIME

Drumsticks from a fat duck 2
Duck breasts 2
Duck fat .... 2 pounds 4 ounces
Thyme .... 2 large sprigs
Bay leaves 2
Sea salt
Coarsely ground black pepper

1. The day before cooking, salt the flesh side of the duck
pieces generously and season with pepper. Chill for 24 hours.
2. Rinse the duck and wipe dry. Melt the duck fat in a pot
large enough to hold the duck and add the bay leaves and
thyme. Immerse the duck in the fat and cook over a very
low flame for 2 hours, with the fat just barely simmering.
The flesh should flake off the bone.
3. Store the duck confit covered with duck fat.

WINE: FITOU

gésier et cœur confit

GIZZARD AND HEART CONFIT
Proceed as for duck confit. Confit hearts and gizzards
are excellent sliced in salads.

cassoulet au confit

CASSOULET WITH DUCK CONFIT
FOR 6 - PREPARATION TIME: 45 MINUTES
COOKING TIME: 3 HOURS 30 MINUTES +
12 HOURS SOAKING TIME

Duck breast confit 2
Upper wing confit 6
Toulouse sausages (or good pork sausages) 6
Dried white beans .... 3 cups
Bacon .... 7-ounce slab
Onion studded with 1 clove 1
Onions 3
Garlic .... 6 cloves
Pork rind .... 7 ounces
Carrots 2
Duck fat .... 3 tablespoons
Concentrated tomato purée .... 2 tablespoons
Breadcrumbs .... ½ cup
Salt, pepper

1. Soak the beans in cold water a day before cooking.
2. Peel and slice the onions and carrots. Place in a
flameproof casserole along with the drained beans, peeled
garlic, pork rind, bacon, and clove-studded onion. Cover
with water, bring to a boil, and simmer slowly for 2 hours.
3. Add the concentrated tomato purée and sausages. Cook
for an additional 1 hour, barely simmering. Season the
cassoulet once the beans are cooked.
4. Place the pieces of duck confit in a baking dish with the
duck fat. Add the pork rind and sausages, pour in the beans,
and sprinkle with the breadcrumbs. Bake in a 350°F oven for
20 minutes.

WINE: SAINT-CHINIAN

CONFIT DE CANARD
EN CONSERVE
PRESERVED DUCK CONFIT

1

A day before cooking, generously salt the flesh side of the duck and season with pepper.

Chill for 24 hours. The following day, rinse and wipe the pieces dry.

2

Cook the duck for 2 hours in barely simmering duck fat, melted beforehand. Add bay leaves and thyme.

3

Place in the jar.

4

Pour the duck fat on top.

5 Close the jar, not forgetting the rubber seal.

6 Fill the sterilizer with hot water.

7

Cook for 1 hour in the sterilizer or in a large pot filled with boiling water.

8 Let it cool.

And keep for 6 months in a cool place.

Or in the bottom of the refrigerator.

Il est un coin de France

"There is a corner of France": Basque song from Francis Lopez's
operetta, *Le chanteur de Mexico* (The Mexican Singer)

1-Il est un coin de France____ Où le bonheur fleur_it,____ Où l'on con__naît d'a
2-Le jour de sa nais__san_ce____ on est Pe__lo_ta__ri____ dès la pre__mière en_

vance,____ Les joies du pa_ra__dis,____ Et quand on a la chance____
fan_ce____ le doua_nier vous pour__suit____ Quand vient l'a_do_les__cen_ce____

D'ê_tre de ce pa__ys,____ On est comme en va__can_ces,____ Du_rant tou_
Les fil_les vous sou__rient____ Et l'on chante et l'on dan_se,____ Mê_me quand

_te sa vie____ Ai_re tun Txikitun____ Ai_re tun La_ï_re____ Ai_re tun Txikitun____ Ai_re tun La_ï_re_
_on vieil__lit____

____ Ai_re tun_Txiki tun___ Ai_re tun La_ï_re____ Ai_re tun Txi ki tun La_ï____re O___lé ___ré O__

_lé 3-Et la nuit_____ dans nos mon_ta__gnes__ nous chant__ons_____ autour du feu_____ et le

vent,_____ qui vient d'Espa_____gne, Porte au loin_____ cet air____ joy__eux_____ Ai_re

263

Couplet no 1
Il est un coin de France
Où le bonheur fleurit,
Où l'on connaît d'avance,
Les joies du paradis,
Et quand on a la chance
D'être de ce pays,
On est comme en vacances,
Durant toute sa vie

Couplet no 2
Le jour de sa naissance,
On est pelotari
Dès la première enfance,
Le douanier vous poursuit,
Quand vient l'adolescence,
Les filles vous sourient,
Et l'on chante et l'on danse,
Même quand on vieillit

Refrain
Aire tun Txikitun
Aire tun Laïre
Aire tun Txikitun
Aire tun Laïre
Aire tun Txikitun
Aire tun Laïre
Aire tun Txikitun Laïre - Olé

Couplet no 3
Et la nuit dans nos montagnes,
Nous chantons autour du feu,
Et le vent qui vient d'Espagne,
Porte au loin cet air joyeux

Aire tun Txikitun
Aire tun Laïre
Aire tun Txikitun
Aire tun Laïre
Aire tun Txikitun
Aire tun Laïre
Aire tun Txikitun Laïre - Olé

Aire tun Txikitun
Aire tun Laïre
Aire tun Txikitun
Aire tun Laïre
Aire tun Txikitun
Aire tun Laïre
Aire tun Txikitun Laïre - Olé

La Palombière :
Pierrette & Claude Faugère
Le plan de la palombière

The pigeon-hide diagram

Les appeaux

The calls

La panoplie du chasseur
The hunter's array of tools

GIBIER À GOGO

GAME GALORE

À POIL ET À PLUME

FURRED AND FEATHERED

LE XV DE FRANCE
SUR SON 32

FRANCES XV OUT OF 32

Le tournoi des six nations

The six nations championship

FURRED GAME...

Roe deer

Doe

Stag

Woodcock

Grouse

Partridge

Wood pigeon

Pheasant

Duck

...AND FEATHERED!

Doe

Doe

Doe

Boar

Thrush

Hare

Duck

Rabbit

Pierrette and Claude Faugère

OR THE EXTRA CHROMOSOME

An old scientific study, no one knows from when or by whom any more, demonstrated, after anatomical testing, that Pierrette and Claude Faugère are carriers of an extra chromosome, the CAWP: "Crazy about wood pigeons". This genetic modification is common in southwestern France and expresses itself in a set of symptoms we shall describe below.

AN INFINITE LOVE FOR THEIR REGION
CAWPs have boundless affection for their region and its the natural world. They have a tendency to disappear into the pine forest every weekend, or in a moment of spare time, to tend to it, chop it, prune it, clear it. They are one with their environment.

WITH THE CAWP, THE JUNIOR WOODCHUCKS
GUIDEBOOK CAN STAY IN THE CUPBOARD
The CAWP is as cunning as a monkey, resourceful like no other, and as handy as Robinson Crusoe. They know the art of building a cabin in the middle of a pine forest you would happily spend several holidays

in; climbing trees, hiding in the fern corridors, pulling out all the old tricks, and enjoying the silence.
The wood pigeon still has some great days ahead of it.

What about the hunting, I hear you say! CAWPs spend their time on the lookout for flocks of wood pigeons; throughout the year they try to draw the birds down to the ground using pet decoys. But it very often happens that the bird simply passes them by, throwing a mocking glance their way and calling out to their domesticated brethren from the tops of the pine trees.

THEY KNOW HOW TO ENTERTAIN
And when by chance the CAWP captures a few wood pigeons, often tired from an overlong journey, and invites you to his table, well, believe me, the wood pigeons *à la ficelle* (which they call *palombe— au string*, or string-tied pigeon)—cooked golden brown using a flaming *capucin* (a cast-iron basting instrument) and served on a crunchy roast—take on a dimension that is beyond belief.

The principle
behind the "palombière"
(pigeon trap)

LEFT
rabbit
fricassee

RIGHT
rabbit with
smoky bacon

276

gibelotte de lapin

RABBIT FRICASSEE
FOR 6 - PREPARATION TIME: 30 MINUTES
COOKING TIME: 1 HOUR 15 MINUTES

Rabbit	1
Pork belly	7 ounces
Parsnips	6
Baby spinach	14 ounces
Onions	4
Garlic	6 cloves
Bouquet garni	1
Chardonnay-style white wine	1 bottle
Red port	⅓ to ½ cup
Marc de Bourgogne (or grappa or brandy)	2½ tablespoons
Moutarde de Meaux (wholegrain mustard)	1 tablespoon
Flour	4 teaspoons
Olive oil	
Salt, pepper	

1. Cut the rabbit into 6 pieces. Peel and slice the onions. Peel the parsnips and cut into four pieces.
2. Chop the pork belly into cubes. Sauté the rabbit in the olive oil with the pork belly, onion, and unpeeled garlic until brown; then add the flour to coat.
3. Flambé with the *marc*, and deglaze the pan with the port, scraping up the bits on the bottom. Stir in the wine.
4. Add the bouquet garni and season. After 30 minutes, add the parsnips and cook for another 30 minutes.
5. Bind the sauce with the mustard and add the spinach, then cover and cook for a final 5 minutes.

WINE: CHARDONNAY

lapin au lard fumé

RABBIT WITH SMOKY BACON
FOR 6 - PREPARATION TIME: 20 MINUTES
COOKING TIME: 2 HOURS

Rabbit	1
Bacon	6 slices
Onions	6
Tomatoes	6
White wine	1 cup
Bay leaves	3
Thyme	3 sprigs
Salt, pepper	

1. Cut the rabbit into 6 pieces. Peel the onions and slice them, along with the tomatoes.
2. Arrange a layer of tomato and onion in a casserole dish. Add the rabbit pieces and top with the bacon slices before adding another tomato-onion layer, the bay leaves, and thyme. Pour in the wine and season.
3. Bake in a 350°F oven for 1 hour; then uncover and cook for another hour. The vegetables must be stewed well.

WINE: BOURGOGNE IRANCY

palombe à la ficelle (dite palombe au string)

FIRE-ROASTED WOOD PIGEON ("PALOMBE AU STRING")
FOR 6 - PREPARATION TIME: 15 MINUTES
COOKING TIME: 1 BOTTLE OF WHITE AND 3 OF RED

Wood pigeons	6
Butter	7 ounces
Capucin (cast-iron basting instrument)	1
Thick toasted bread slices	6
Pierrette and Claude Faugère	
Salt, pepper	

1. Remove the insides of the wood pigeons, reserving the liver and heart. Soak some kitchen string in cold salted water. Tie the string around the pigeons' necks and hang them up on a nail in front of a fireplace. Be careful: the heat of the fireplace can cause sudden dehydration in susceptible and non-susceptible individuals. Remember to carry a bottle opener to avoid any unpleasantness.
2. Set a container underneath the pigeons to catch the juices. Turn the strings around to cook the pigeons and remember to rehydrate yourself. Cook the livers and hearts in the juices, and flambé the pigeons in butter using the *capucin*. Enjoy on the toasted bread with some wine—if there's any left.

WINE: GRAVES ROUGE

LES 12 APPEAUX
THE 12 CALLS

Roe deer

Red-legged
partridge

Quail

White goose

Woodcock

Boar

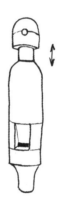

Cuckoo

Fox

Whistler (male)

Blackbird

Duck

Hunter

LEFT
sautéed rabbit
with Riesling

RIGHT
rabbit
flambéed with
cognac

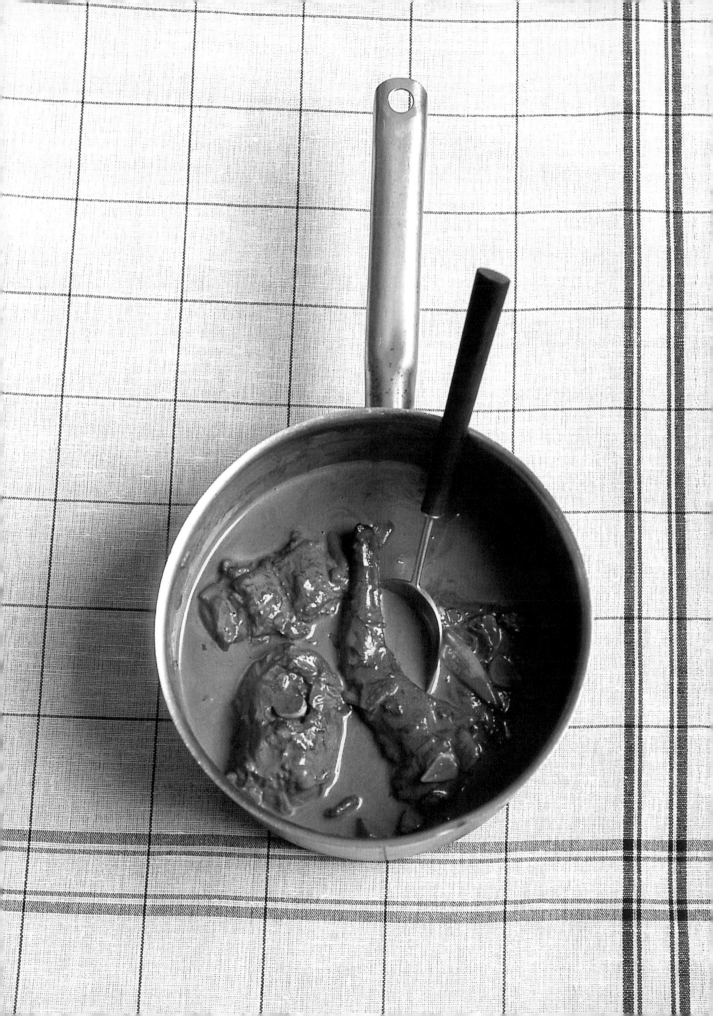

lapin sauté au riesling

SAUTÉED RABBIT WITH RIESLING
FOR 6 - PREPARATION TIME: 30 MINUTES
COOKING TIME: 1 HOUR

Rabbit	1
Shallots	6
Riesling	1 bottle
Heavy cream	1¼ cups
Flour	4 teaspoons
Cooked spaghetti	enough for 6 little "nests"
Butter	⅓ cup

Cold-pressed oil
Salt, pepper

1. Cut the rabbit into 6 pieces. Peel and slice the shallots.
2. Sauté the shallots and the rabbit in oil without browning, and add the flour, stirring well. Pour in the wine and simmer for 45 minutes. Stir in the cream and season.
3. Shape the cooked spaghetti into little "nests." Make little spaghetti "cakes" by browning them in butter in a nonstick pan.

WINE: RIESLING

lapin flambé au cognac

RABBIT FLAMBÉED WITH COGNAC
FOR 6 - PREPARATION TIME: 20 MINUTES
COOKING TIME: 1 HOUR 15 MINUTES

Rabbit	1
Onions	4
Garlic	6 cloves
Veal stock	1 cup
Heavy cream	1¼ cups
Cognac	⅓ to ½ cup

Olive oil
Salt, pepper

1. Peel and slice the onions and garlic. Cut the rabbit into 6 pieces.
2. Sauté the rabbit, onions, and garlic in olive oil until golden. Flambé with the cognac and deglaze the pan with the stock.
3. Cover and cook on a low heat for 45 minutes. Stir in the cream and cook for an additional 15 minutes. Season.

WINE: LIRAC

LA PANOPLIE DU CHASSEUR
THE HUNTER'S ARRAY OF TOOLS

The shotguns

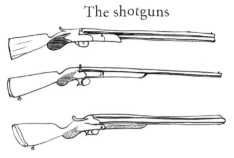

Over/under barrels

Repeating

Side-by-side barrels

Hunting horn

Calling horn

Barrel brush with a twisted stem

The case

The knife

Eccentric cartridge extractor

Ring mechanism

Shotgun shell

 Daniel

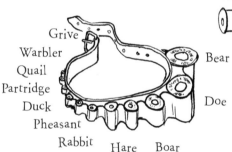

Grive
Warbler
Quail
Partridge
Duck
Pheasant
Rabbit   Hare   Boar

Bear

Doe

Cartridge belt and its cartridges

Mirror lure for larks

Plastic decoy

Enlarging tactical scope

The water canteen

Camouflage-print tent

The dog

Trap for big game

saddle of hare
with pepper

râble de lièvre au poivre

SADDLE OF HARE WITH PEPPER
FOR 6 - PREPARATION TIME: 20 MINUTES
COOKING TIME: 15 MINUTES

Saddle of hare	2 pounds
Cognac	1½ tablespoons
White wine	⅓ to ½ cup
Coarsely ground black pepper	½ teaspoon
Butter	⅓ cup
Cooked beets	3
Baby spinach	10 ounces
Salt	

1. Peel the membrane from the hare saddle. Pan-fry the hare in 1½ tablespoons of butter and brown on all sides for 5 minutes. Remove and keep warm.
2. Add the pepper to the pan, flambé with the cognac, and then deglaze with the wine, scraping up the bits on the bottom. Whisk in the remaining butter.
3. Wilt the spinach in the sauce and add the beets, sliced into rounds, to warm. Slice the saddle into medallions and dress with the peppery sauce.

WINE: VOSNE-ROMANÉE

lièvre à la royale

HARE "ROYALE" (BONED, STUFFED, AND BRAISED)
FOR 8 - PREPARATION TIME: 60 MINUTES
COOKING TIME: 3 HOURS 10 MINUTES

Hare	6 pounds 12 ounces
Pork loin	7 ounces
Veal meat	7 ounces
Fresh foie gras	3½ ounces
Pork fatback	3½ ounces
Amber rum	2½ tablespoons
Onions	6
Carrots	6
Shallots	2
Garlic	6 cloves
Sheets of pork fat (bards)	4
Good red wine	1 bottle (for cooking)
Oil	
Salt, pepper	

1. Ask your butcher to completely debone the hare, taking care not to pierce the skin and reserving the bones and blood.
2. Finely chop the pork loin, fatback, veal, foie gras, as well as the hare's liver, heart, and kidneys. Peel and chop the shallots, mix everything together, add the rum, and season.
3. Lay the hare flat on its back and season. Arrange the stuffing down the middle. Fold the hare over; then wrap the sheets of pork fat (bards) around it lengthwise and crosswise. Tie it all up with string.
4. Oil a large flameproof casserole dish. Place the hare inside and surround it with the onions, carrots, and garlic. Add the bones, pour in the wine, and season. Cook, uncovered, on a low heat for 3 hours.

5. Remove the hare to a plate. Reduce the sauce to obtain a syrupy consistency, then bind the sauce with the hare's blood.
6. Carve the hare carefully into slices. Serve surrounded by the drizzled sauce.

WINE: CHAMBOLLE-MUSIGNY

cailles au foie gras

QUAIL WITH FOIE GRAS
FOR 6 - PREPARATION TIME: 45 MINUTES
COOKING TIME: 10 MINUTES

Quail	6
Fresh foie gras	7 ounces
Raisins	⅓ cup
Chives	10 sprigs
Armagnac	1½ tablespoons
Butter	⅓ cup
Salt, pepper	

1. Debone the quails, taking care not to pierce the skin. Lay them out flat on their backs and season.
2. Combine the raisins and Armagnac. Finely snip the chives and add to the mixture.
3. Cut the foie gras into six pieces; mold them in your hands into the shape of the quail cavities. Roll them in the raisin mixture and season.
4. Stuff the foie gras inside each quail; after the foie gras is enclosed in each quail, the birds should be tied with string.
5. Melt the butter in a hot ovenproof pan. Arrange the quails in the pan and roast in a 400°F oven for 8 minutes, basting the birds regularly.

WINE: CONRIEUX

LEFT
fillet of boar
with juniper
berries

RIGHT
stewed boar
in a fruity
wine sauce

filet de sanglier au genièvre

TENDERLOIN OF BOAR WITH JUNIPER BERRIES
FOR 6 - PREPARATION TIME: 15 MINUTES
COOKING TIME: 25 MINUTES + 10 MINUTES RESTING TIME

Boar tenderloin..2 pounds 4 ounces
Juniper berries 10
Garlic..3 cloves
Baby carrots with their tops..6
Bulb spring onions 6
Butter...2½ tablespoons
White wine...1¼ cups
Olive oil
Salt, pepper

1. In a heavy pan, caramelize the surface of the boar
tenderloin over high heat. Add the crushed juniper berries
and crushed garlic and season. Pour in the wine, add all the
vegetables, then cover and cook for 20 minutes on a gentle
heat. Allow to rest for 10 minutes.
2. Remove the meat from the pan and keep warm. Bring the
cooking juices to the boil and whisk in the butter. Serve with
the sliced tenderloin.

WINE: MADIRAN

civet de sanglier acidulé

STEWED BOAR IN A FRUITY WINE SAUCE
FOR 6 - PREPARATION TIME: 20 MINUTES
COOKING TIME: 2 HOURS 15 MINUTES

Boar shoulder ....4 pounds 8 ounces
Bacon ....10½-ounce slab
Veal stock ....1⅓ cups
Red wine ....1 bottle
Kirsch ....2½ tablespoons
Crème de mûres (blackberry liqueur) ....⅓ to ½ cup
Shallots..6
Garlic...6 cloves
Carrots..3
Bouquet garni 1
Dark chocolate ....2 squares
Chanterelle mushrooms ....1 pound 2 ounces
New potatoes...1 pound 2 ounces
Olive oil
Salt, pepper

1. Peel the shallots, garlic, and carrots, and then chop them
roughly. Cut the boar into 2-inch cubes.
2. Sauté the boar with the diced bacon, shallots, garlic, and
carrots. Flambé with the kirsch. Pour in the wine, add the
stock and bouquet garni, and season. Cook for 1 hour
30 minutes on a gentle heat, covered.
3. Add the new potatoes and blackberry liqueur and cook
further for 30 minutes.
4. Pan-fry the mushrooms separately. Add them to the boar
with the chocolate and mix well.

WINE: CAHORS

gigue de chevreuil grand veneur

"GREAT HUNTER'S" ROAST VENISON
FOR 8 - PREPARATION TIME: 45 MINUTES
COOKING TIME: 1 HOUR 45 MINUTES +
24 HOURS MARINATING TIME

Haunch of venison ....4 pounds 8 ounces
Onions..4
Carrots..4
Shallots...4
Garlic..4 cloves
Cloves...4
Thyme ....1 sprig
Rosemary ....1 sprig
Bay leaves 2
Coarsely ground black pepper ....1 teaspoon
Red wine ....4 cups
Marc de Bourgogne (or grappa or brandy) ....2½ tablespoons
Cornstarch ....4 teaspoons
Heavy cream ....1⅓ cups
Butter...⅓ cup
Olive oil
Salt

1. The day before cooking, peel all the vegetables and slice
them thickly. Marinate the venison in the wine, marc,
vegetables, pepper, bay leaves, thyme, rosemary, and cloves.
2. The next day, rub the venison with the butter and season.
Roast in a 350°F oven for 1 hour 30 minutes (about
20 minutes per pound), basting regularly. Strain the marinade
through a chinois (fine sieve), removing the thyme,
rosemary, and bay leaf.
3. Sauté the strained vegetables in olive oil, pour in the
strained marinade, and allow to reduce by half. Strain the
sauce again through the chinois. Combine the cornstarch
with a little water and stir it into the sauce. Add the cream,
stirring, and cook for a final 10 minutes.
4. Carve the venison and serve with the sauce.

WINE: CHASSAGNE-MONTRACHET ROUGE

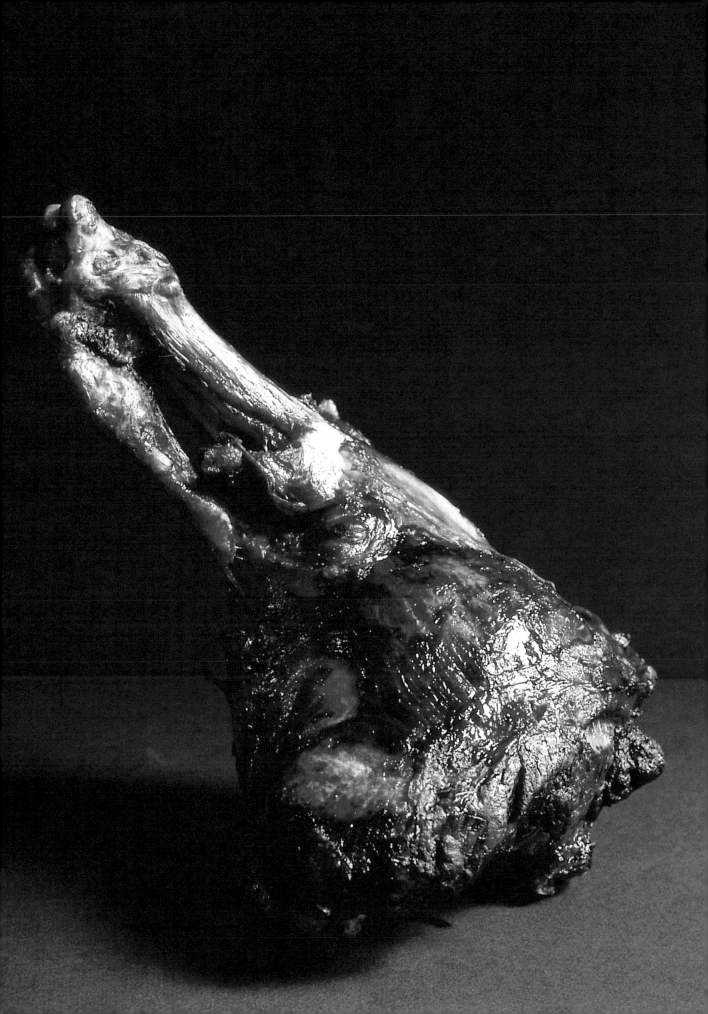

LE TOURNOI
DES SIX NATIONS
THE SIX NATIONS CHAMPIONSHIP

*But what would the southwest be without rugby—
or what would rugby be without the southwest?*

When sports and philosophy hit it off, when sports and gastronomy unite as one, then it's obvious we're close to talking about rugby. Rugby is a bit like the happy lung of an entire region, and now an entire country.

The north-south divide has disappeared to give way to a rugby nation. It's true that we can't help taking on a southwestern accent as soon as we say the word *ruuugby,* and that inevitably we soon dream of *cassoulet de confit de canard* (cassoulet with duck confit) as soon as we hear it. Never has a sport had such a stupendous identity.

GRAND SLAMS
victory in every match

WOODEN SPOON
defeat every match

TRIPLE CROWN
*honorific title awarded when one of the four British teams
wins all of its matches against the three other British teams*

	CHAMPION-SHIPS PLAYED	GRAND SLAMS	OUTRIGHT WINS	SHARED WINS	WOODEN SPOONS	TRIPLE CROWN
ENGLAND	105	12	25	10	7	23
WALES	107	9	23	11	5	18
FRANCE	77	8	16	8	8	—
SCOTLAND	107	3	14	8	13	10
IRELAND	107	1	10	8	13	9
ITALY	8	0	0	0	3	—

LE XV DE FRANCE SUR SON 32
THE FRENCH XV OUT OF 32

Clément Poitrenaud
Fullback
(6 ft. 2 in.) (216 lb)

Aurélien Rougerie
Wing
(6 ft. 4½ in.) (227 lb)

Cédric Heymans
Wing
(5 ft. 11 in.) (211.6 lb)

Christophe Dominici
Wing
(5 ft. 8 in.) (185 lb)

Vincent Clerc
Wing
(5 ft. 10 in.) (196 lb)

Yannick Jauzion
Center
(6 ft. 4 in.) (231 lb)

Damien Traille
Center
(6 ft. 3½ in.) (220 lb)

David Marty
Center
(5 ft. 11 in.) (196 lb)

David Skrela
Fly-half
(6 ft. 3 in.) (200 lb)

Frédérick Michalak
Fly-half
(5 ft. 11 in.) (172 lb)

Lionel Bauxis
Fly-half
(5 ft. 11 in.) (194 lb)

Pierre Mignoni
Scrum-half
(5 ft. 7 in.) (159 lb)

Jean-Baptiste Elissalde
Scrum-half
(5 ft. 8 in.) (161 lb)

Serge Betsen
Flanker
(6 ft.) (211.6 lb)

Julien Bonnaire
Flanker
(6 ft. 4 in.) (220 lb)

Rémy Martin
Flanker
(6 ft. 5 in.) (238 lb)

Yannick Nyanga
Flanker
(6 ft. 5½ in.) (202.8 lb)

Imanol Harinordoquy
Flanker
(6 ft. 3½ in.) (231 lb)

Thierry Dusautoir
Flanker
(6 ft. 2 in.) (220 lb)

Sébastien Chabal
Lock/Flanker
(6 ft. 3½ in.) (253.5 lb)

Lionel Mallet
Lock
(6 ft. 5½ in.) (251 lb)

Fabien Pelous
Lock
(6 ft. 6 in.) (238 lb)

Jérôme Thion
Lock
(6 ft. 6½ in.) (253.5 lb)

Sébastien Bruno
Hooker
(5 ft. 9 in.) (235.80 lb)

Rapohaël Ibanez
Hooker
(5 ft. 10 in.) (225 lb)

Dimitri Szarzewski
Hooker
(5 ft. 11 in.) (225 lb)

Pieter De Villiers
Prop
(6 ft. ½ in.) (235.80 lb)

Sylvain Marconnet
Prop
(6 ft.) (244.7 lb)

Olivier Miloud
Prop
(6 ft. 1 in.) (238 lb)

Jean-Baptiste Poux
Prop
(5 feet 11 in.) (231 lb)

Bernard Laporte
Selector

Nicolas Mas
Prop
(5 feet 11 in.) (242.5 lb)

« Quand la mouette a pied, paré à virer ! »
"When the seagulls touch bottom,
think about turning around"

découvrir les crustacés
et les poissons
discover crustaceans and fish

COMMENT OUVRIR
LES HUÎTRES ?
HOW TO OPEN OYSTERS

Les châteaux de la Loire
The châteaux of the Loire

les vins du Val de Loire
ET LEURS CHÂTEAUX

The wines of the Loire Valley
AND THEIR CASTLES

POISSONS, COQUILLAGES, ET CRUSTACÉS...

FISH, SHELLFISH, AND CRUSTACEANS

FRUITS DE MER
SEAFOOD

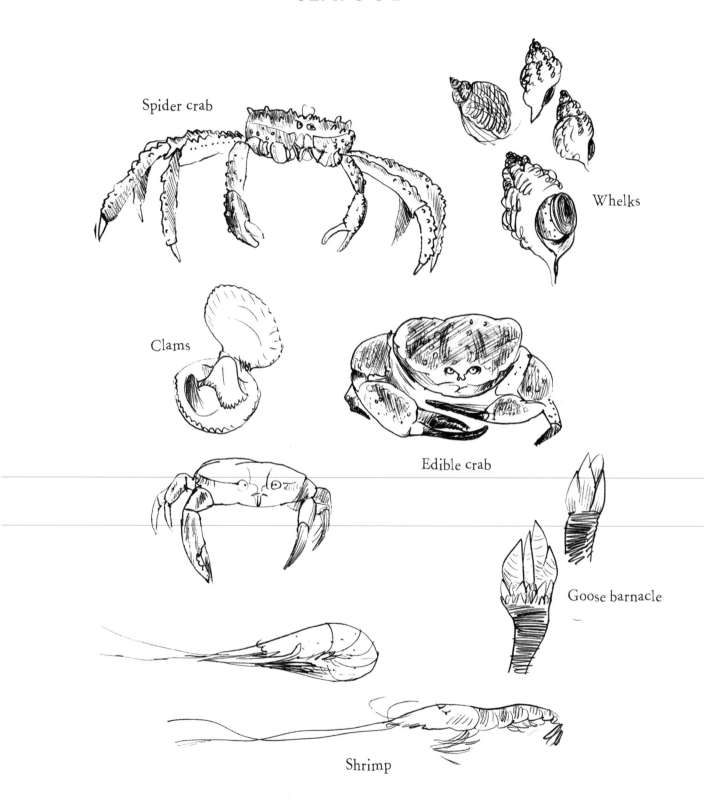

Spider crab

Whelks

Clams

Edible crab

Goose barnacle

Shrimp

Edible crab

Clams

Spider crab

Velvet crab

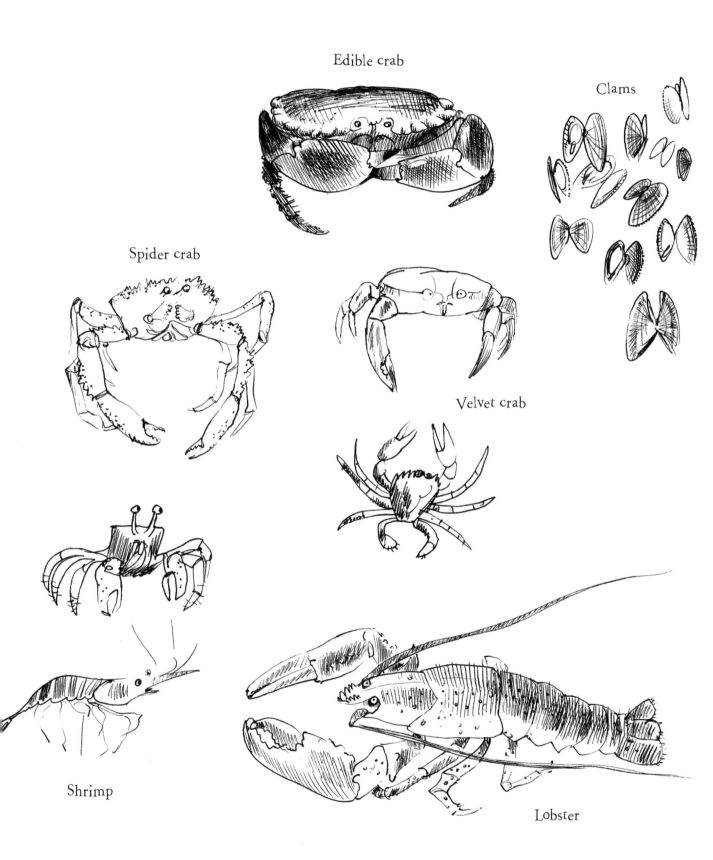

Shrimp

Lobster

moules marinières

MUSSELS STEAMED IN WHITE WINE
FOR 6 - PREPARATION TIME: 10 MINUTES
COOKING TIME: 15 MINUTES

Mussels	9 pounds
Garlic	6 cloves
Shallots	3
Parsley	1 bunch
White wine	1¼ cups
Unsalted butter	⅓ cup

1. Peel the garlic and shallots and chop them with the parsley.
2. Bring the wine to a boil in a very large pot. Add the butter, garlic, shallots, and parsley, and allow to barely simmer for 5 minutes.
3. Add the cleaned mussels, cover, and cook for 10 minutes, stirring regularly. The mussels are cooked when they open. Discard any mussels that have not opened by this time since they are unsafe to eat.

WINE: GROS-PLANT FROM THE NANTAIS REGION

moules à la crème de safran

MUSSELS IN SAFFRON CREAM
FOR 6 - PREPARATION TIME: 30 MINUTES
COOKING TIME: 30 MINUTES

Mussels	9 pounds
Garlic	6 cloves
Shallots	3
White wine	1¼ cups
Parsley	1 bunch
Unsalted butter	⅓ cup
Heavy cream	1¼ cups
Saffron	1 pinch

1. Prepare and cook the mussels as in the previous recipe.
2. Reserve the cooking juices. Remove the mussels from their shells, but keep 30 in the shell for decoration.
3. Add the cream and saffron to the cooking juices with half the shelled mussels and cook for 10 minutes. Purée this mixture and strain through a *chinois* (fine sieve).
4. Heat the remaining mussels in the puréed saffron cream and decorate with the reserved mussels in their shells.

WINE: BOURGOGNE ALIGOTÉ

MOULES MARINIÈRES

DE LA PLAGE

HUITRES
FRUITS de ME
Cuits ou Crus

Trescarte

QUAND LA MOUETTE A PIED, PARÉ À VIRER!

French proverb: "When the seagulls touch bottom, think about turning around"

On Arcachon Bay, on the southwest coast, the oyster farmers' huts are squeezed between vacationers hungry for the sun and the sea hungry for vacationers.

A little blue shelter, the color of the landscape, is occupied by a force of nature named Trescarte (this is a man you want on your team!), standing surrounded by empty shells, ready to attend to the day's harvest. The oysters taste of the moment; they have the flavor of the view, the smell of the bay. We order them by the dozens, opened for a few extra cents (less than the cost of a Band-Aid) by the expert hands of Trescarte, a man proud of his work. Don't forget the well-chilled dose of white wine to definitively settle the pleasure of the morning. *"Huîtres au petit déjeuner, bonne journée assurée."* "Oysters for breakfast guarantee a good day."

LEFT
scallops tartare
with poppy
seeds

RIGHT
hot oysters
with fennel-
seed sabayon

Saint-Jacques crues à la graine de pavot

SCALLOP TARTARE WITH POPPY SEEDS
FOR 6 - PREPARATION TIME: 10 MINUTES

Scallops	12
Poppy seeds	1 teaspoon
Lime	1
Olive oil	2 tablespoons
Soy sauce	1 teaspoon
Sea salt	

1. Thinly slice the scallops and arrange in a rosette pattern on the plate.
2. Zest the lime and chop the zest finely. Make a vinaigrette by mixing together the olive oil, soy sauce, and lime zest.
3. Glaze the scallops with the vinaigrette using a brush, sprinkle with poppy seeds, and season.

WINE: MUSCADET

huîtres chaudes, sabayon à la graine de fenouil

HOT OYSTERS WITH FENNEL-SEED SABAYON
FOR 6 - PREPARATION TIME: 15 MINUTES
COOKING TIME: 10 MINUTES

Spéciales (fleshy oysters, in the shell)	18
Dry white wine	¾ cup
Shallot	½
Heavy cream	¾ cup
Egg yolks	2
Fennel seeds	1 teaspoon

1. Peel and chop the shallot. Bring the wine to a boil, add the shallot, and allow to cook for 5 minutes.
2. Arrange the oysters in a wide pan. Add the wine mixture and cover, heating gently until the oysters open.
3. Strain the oyster juice and wine through a muslin-lined *chinois* (fine sieve), then stir in the cream, and let the liquid reduce by half.
4. Remove from the heat, add the egg yolks, and emulsify using a mixer.
5. Sprinkle the fennel seeds over the oysters, top with a spoonful of the sabayon (egg-yolk cream), and bake for 2 minutes in a 350°F oven. Serve immediately.

WINE: GRAVES BLANC

Saint-Jacques poêlées

SEARED SCALLOPS
FOR 6 - PREPARATION TIME: 15 MINUTES
COOKING TIME: 25 MINUTES

Scallops	18
Garlic	6 cloves
Cauliflower	1
Arugula leaves	3 cups
Lemon	½
Olive oil	¾ cup
Salt, pepper	

1. Chop the cauliflower and cook in boiling salted water for 20 minutes. Drain, then process briefly into a rough purée, and season.
2. Purée the arugula leaves with the olive oil and juice of the lemon to make a coulis, or sauce.
3. Peel and slice the garlic and fry until golden.
4. Sear the scallops on each side in olive oil.
5. Place a mound of cauliflower purée on each plate. Arrange three scallops on top, then a few garlic chips, and dress with the arugula coulis.

WINE: SANCERRE BLANC

brochettes de Saint-Jacques à la crème de corail

SCALLOP BROCHETTES WITH CORAL CREAM
FOR 6 - PREPARATION TIME: 30 MINUTES
COOKING TIME: 15 MINUTES

Scallops (with the coral)	18
Carrots	2
Zucchini	2
Black radish	2
Bulb spring onions	2
Shallot	1
Heavy cream	¾ cup
Soy sauce	1 tablespoon
Olive oil	

1. Remove the coral from the scallops. Thread the scallops onto skewers (three scallops per skewer) and oil them.
2. Finely chop the shallot, and sauté in olive oil with the scallop coral. Purée this mixture and strain through a *chinois* (fine sieve). Add the cream and let it reduce.
3. Julienne all the vegetables. Stir-fry them quickly in a hot wok and stir in the soy sauce.
4. Sear the scallops, arrange on a bed of stir-fried vegetables, and serve with the coral cream.

WINE: MUSCADET

LA MARÉE
THE TIDE

Pull on some rubber boots, and grab a rake and net—here comes the time of the tides, the time for *la pêche à pied* ("fishing with your feet"). These tides are perfectly calculated today thanks to the use of harmonics.

These harmonics enable us to assign a value to the tidal range that varies from one port to the next. The tidal ranges fall between 20 and 120.

EQUINOCTIAL SPRING TIDE: 120
AVERAGE SPRING TIDE: 95
AVERAGE TIDE: 70
AVERAGE NEAP TIDE: 45

TO ENSURE THAT FISH BASKETS ARE FILLED IN COMPLETE SAFETY, IT'S ESSENTIAL TO BE COMPLETELY FAMILIAR WITH THE MEANING OF THE TERMS USED WHEN TALKING ABOUT TIDES.

COEFFICIENT: A factor enabling us to compare the intensity of tides from one place to another.

SEMI-DIURNAL TIDE: This refers to a tide with two low tides and two high tides with the same height during the same day.

TIDAL RANGE: The difference in height between high tide and low tide.

TIDAL AMPLITUDE: Corresponds to half the tidal range.

NEAP TIDE: The period when the difference between high and low tide is low during the first and third quarters of the moon.

AMPHIDROMIC POINT: The tidal point where the tidal range is zero.

SPRING TIDE: The period when the difference between high and low tide is greatest, corresponding to the period when the Earth, Moon, and Sun are aligned.

LES HUÎTRES
COMMENT LES OUVRIR ?
OYSTERS: HOW DO YOU OPEN THEM?

For the clumsier
ones among us, protect
your hands.

1 Place your thumb half an inch
from the end of the blade.

2 Insert the blade between the two shell halves at the
level of the muscle located in the upper two-thirds.

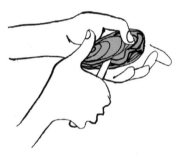

3 Cut through the muscle horizontally.

4 Lift and remove the upper half-shell without
tearing the oyster meat, which must remain whole.

If you haven't found any
pearls, make yourself a necklace from
different grades of oyster shells.

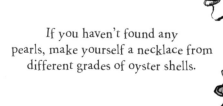

n°5: 1–1½ oz

n°4: 1½–2½ oz

n°3: 2½–3 oz

n°2: 3–4 oz

n°1: 4–5½ oz

Anne-Marie and Yves

WHICH WAY TO THE *COQUILLES SAINT-JACQUES?*

Sailing from the direction of Landevennec as far as Moulin-à-Mer is a small boat equipped with two sails in order to do without the now-too-expensive diesel, its belly full with a precious catch of scallops. Yves, the captain, and Anne-Marie, looking the perfect sailor's wife, are wearing outfits drenched in wax and salt that bear witness to the day's wild sea sprays. Each year, for a few days, they're granted a license to bring in a catch that must pay the bills for the coming months.

The scallop, then, is something that is eagerly awaited, sought out, seduced, respected. Fishing is work that leaves its mark on you, hardens you, makes you strong. Looking at Yves' hands, you tell yourself he must have pulled a few cords and sorted a few scallops to turn these two piano-playing instruments into power tools! But seeing the permanent smile on Anne-Marie's face, you also tell yourself that they must enjoy sharing these marine moments as husband and wife. They are beautiful—these Breton scallops—the meat firm and iodine-rich, the coral orange and well formed. They are good eaten raw on the deck of the moored boat, sheltered from the open sea, as we wait to disembark.

LEFT
breton lobster
à l'américaine
(in tomato
cream sauce)

RIGHT
cockles in
butter sauce

310

homard breton à l'américaine

BRETON LOBSTER IN TOMATO CREAM SAUCE
FOR 6 - PREPARATION TIME: 45 MINUTES
COOKING TIME: 30 MINUTES

Lobsters	3 (each 1 pound 9 ounces)
Shallots	4
Garlic	3 cloves
White wine	2¾ cups
Cognac	2½ tablespoons
Tomatoes	8
Heavy cream	1⅓ cups
Olive oil	

1. Cut the lobsters in two. Remove and reserve the coral and all of the liquid. Separate the claws from the heads.
2. Sauté the lobsters in olive oil in a sauté pan for 5 minutes until the shells become very red. Flambé them with the cognac, allow to cool, then shell completely.
3. Plunge the tomatoes into boiling water for 10 seconds. Peel the tomatoes and chop the flesh.
4. Dice the shallots and garlic, sauté them in olive oil, then add the tomato pulp, and allow the mixture to stew.
5. Pour in the wine, add the lobster, and cook for 10 minutes. Stir in the cream and cook for an additional 5 minutes.
6. Remove the lobster and set aside in a warm place. Add the coral to the sauce and cook for another 5 minutes; then purée the whole mixture. Dress the lobster with the tomato cream sauce.

WINE: CHÂTEAUNEUF-DU-PAPE BLANC

coques au beurre blanc

COCKLES IN BUTTER SAUCE
FOR A GOOD SNACK WITH APERITIFS
PREPARATION TIME: 10 MINUTES
COOKING TIME: 15 MINUTES

Cockles	2 pounds 4 ounces
Shallot	1
White wine	⅓ to ½ cup
Butter	⅓ cup

1. Rinse the cockles well—they need several water baths.
2. Dice the shallot and cook in the white wine until the liquid has completely evaporated.
3. Dice the butter and whisk it in piece by piece over a very low flame. The butter will emulsify.
4. Place the cockles in a pot. Cover and cook until they open; then drizzle with the butter sauce.

WINE: A GOOD APERITIF

langoustines rôties, panures briochées

ROASTED SCAMPI WITH BRIOCHE CRUMBS
FOR 6 - PREPARATION TIME: 15 MINUTES
COOKING TIME: 10 MINUTES

Scampi or large shrimp	18
Brioche	2 slices
Salted butter	3 tablespoons
Unsalted butter	2½ tablespoons
Piment d'Espelette (hot paprika or chili powder)	1 pinch

1. Dry out the brioche in a moderately hot oven. Crush the brioche into crumbs and mix in the *piment d'Espelette*.
2. Cut the scampi in two lengthwise and remove the central intestinal tract.
3. Melt the butter until it turns a nutty color.
4. Using a brush, glaze the scampi flesh with the melted butter. Then dip each one in the brioche crumbs.
5. Place the scampi, shell side down, in a hot, buttered, oven-proof pan on top of the stove and cook for 3 minutes. Transfer to the oven and cook for another 2 minutes.

WINE: CROZES-HERMITAGE BLANC

roasted scampi with brioche crumbs

Hervé

THE CALL OF THE BAGPIPE

This Breton native has this magnificent habit of always having his instrument close by.

Et dans dix ans je m'en irai
J'entends le loup et le renard chanter
Et dans dix ans je m'en irai
J'entends le loup et le renard chanter

… so he's always able to sing, to play…

J'entends le loup, le renard et la belette
J'entends le loup et le renard chanter
J'entends le loup, le renard et la belette
J'entends le loup et le renard chanter
Et dans dix ans je m'en irai
Et dans dix ans je m'en irai

… he likes to be with friends…

La jument de Michao et son petit poulain
Sont passés dans le pré, ont mangé tout le foin
La jument de Michao et son petit poulain
Sont passés dans le pré, ont mangé tout le foin

… the kig ha fars needs a few hours…

L'hiver viendra, les gars, l'hiver viendra
La jument de Michao, elle s'en repentira
L'hiver viendra, les gars, l'hiver viendra
La jument de Michao, elle s'en repentira

Et dans neuf ans je m'en irai
J'entends le loup le renard et la belette
Et dans neuf ans je m'en irai
J'entends le loup et le renard chanter

J'entends le loup, le renard et la belette
J'entends le loup et le renard chanter
J'entends le loup, le renard et la belette
J'entends le loup et le renard chanter.

… with his deep-water oysters, he's too much, that Hervé !

LEFT
shellfish

RIGHT
squid with
*piment
d'Espelette*

coquillages au vinaigre

SHELLFISH WITH VINEGAR
ANOTHER GOOD SNACK WITH APERITIFS
PREPARATION TIME: 20 MINUTES
COOKING TIME: 15 MINUTES

Soft-shell clams	12
Hard-shell clams	12
Mussels	12
Sea urchins	6
Dog cockles	12
Cockles	12
Razor clams	12
Butter	⅔ cup
Balsamic vinegar	⅓ to ½ cup
Tarragon	1 bunch
Shallots	2
White wine	¾ cup

1. You can use just about any selection of shellfish for this dish. . . . Just find the freshest varieties that you enjoy!
2. Pick off the tarragon leaves and chop them with the shallots. Place in a pan with the vinegar and cook until the liquid has evaporated.
3. Dice the butter and add it piece by piece to the pan with the tarragon over very low heat, whisking all the time.
4. Open the sea urchins and detach the meat from the shell. Place all the shellfish in a large pan with the wine and cook over gentle heat until they all open.
5. Spoon 1 teaspoon of the vinegared butter into the sea-urchin shells and drizzle the other shellfish with the rest.

WINE: POUILLY-FUISSÉ

calamars au piment d'Espelette

SQUID WITH PIMENT D'ESPELETTE
FOR 6 - PREPARATION TIME: 30 MINUTES
COOKING TIME: 10 MINUTES

Baby squid	60
All-purpose flour	¾ cup
Piment d'Espelette (hot paprika)	1 teaspoon
Olive oil	

1. Prepare the squid by removing the internal cartilage and beak. Pat dry with paper towels.
2. Combine the flour and *piment d'Espelette* and use it to coat the squid.
3. Heat the olive oil in a frying pan and briefly pan-fry the squid over high heat until cooked but still tender.

WINE: JURANÇON SEC

supions à l'encre

CUTTLEFISH IN INK
FOR 6 - PREPARATION TIME: 30 MINUTES
COOKING TIME: 30 MINUTES

Cuttlefish	2 pounds 4 ounces
Garlic	6 cloves
White wine	1 cup
Heavy cream	1¼ cups
Cuttlefish ink	3 sachets
Olive oil	

1. Prepare the cuttlefish by removing the internal cartilage and beak.
2. Finely chop the garlic and sauté in olive oil.
3. Add the cuttlefish and let it cook for 15 minutes. Deglaze the pan with the wine, scraping up the bits on the bottom. Stir in the cream and ink, and cook additionally for 15 minutes, until the cuttlefish is very tender.

WINE: TARIQUET

grilled
cuttlefish

blanc de seiche grillé

GRILLED CUTTLEFISH
FOR 6 - PREPARATION TIME: 10 MINUTES
COOKING TIME: 8 MINUTES + 12 HOURS MARINATING

Cuttlefish "fillets" (cleaned whole cuttlefish)	2 pounds 4 ounces
Soy sauce	2 tablespoons
Paprika	1 tablespoon
Lime	1
Scallions (bulb green onions if available)	3

Olive oil

1. A day before cooking, slash 18 triangles into each of the cuttlefish fillets, cross-hatching the flesh. Place in a dish, slashed side up, and dress with the soy sauce, lime juice, paprika, and olive oil.
2. The next day, sear the cuttlefish in olive oil in a hot pan for 4 minutes on each side.
3. Serve drizzled with a dash of olive oil and sprinkled with the sliced scallions.

WINE: MENETOU-SALON BLANC

rouille du pêcheur

STEWED OCTOPUS WITH ROUILLE SAUCE
FOR 6 - PREPARATION TIME: 45 MINUTES
COOKING TIME: 2 HOURS 10 MINUTES

Octopus	4 pounds 8 ounces
Bay leaves	1 branch
Bouquet garni	1
White wine	1 cup
Onions	3
Fennel	1 bulb
Celery stalk	1
Potatoes	1 pound 12 ounces
Olive oil	⅓ to ½ cup
Garlic	3 cloves
Mustard	1 teaspoon
Saffron	1 pinch
Eggs	2
Olive oil	¾ cup

Salt, pepper

1. Skin and clean the octopus, and cut the tentacles into sections.
2. Slice the onions, fennel, and celery. Sauté the vegetables in olive oil, adding the octopus, bay leaves, and bouquet garni. Pour in the wine, cover, and cook, barely simmering for 2 hours.
3. Peel the potatoes and chop them into cubes. Cook them in salted boiling water.
4. Using a mortar and pestle, make a paste from the garlic, mustard, saffron, egg yolk, and a pinch of salt. Gradually drizzle in the olive oil.
5. Drain the octopus, reserving ¾ cup of the cooking liquid. Strain this liquid through a muslin-lined *chinois* (fine sieve). Combine the liquid, potatoes, and octopus, add the rouille sauce, and season.

WINE: ROSÉ DE PROVENCE

écrevisses pattes rouges à la nage

POACHED CRAYFISH
FOR 6 - PREPARATION TIME: 30 MINUTES
COOKING TIME: 45 MINUTES

Crayfish	30
Shallots	3
Red pepper	1
Celery stalks	3
Lemongrass	3 stems
Baby pattypan squash	6
Leeks	2
White wine	1 cup

Salt, pepper
Olive oil

1. Devein the crayfish.
2. Wash the leeks well; then slice the vegetables and the lemongrass. Place in a large saucepan with the wine and 2 cups water, and cook until reduced by half.
3. Plunge the crayfish into the vegetable broth and cook for 15 minutes.
4. Serve in a shallow bowl with a drizzle of olive oil.

WINE: SAINT-VÉRAN

LES POISSONS

FISH

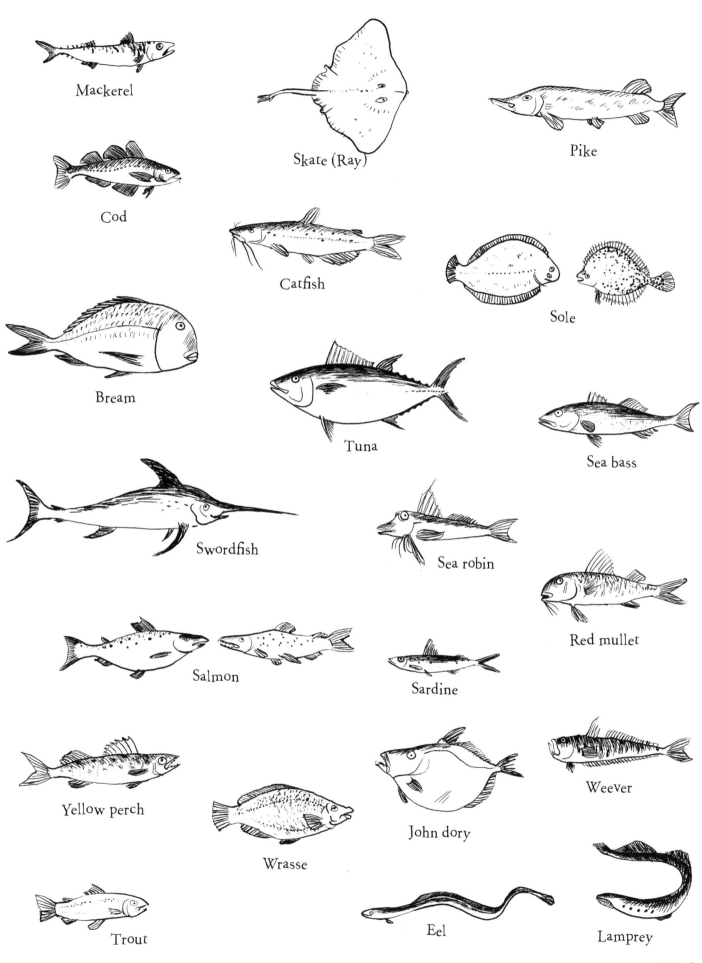

Mackerel

Skate (Ray)

Pike

Cod

Catfish

Sole

Bream

Tuna

Sea bass

Swordfish

Sea robin

Red mullet

Salmon

Sardine

Yellow perch

Wrasse

John dory

Weever

Trout

Eel

Lamprey

LEFT
pike
quenelles

RIGHT
pike terrine

326

quenelles de brochet

PIKE QUENELLES
FOR 6 - PREPARATION TIME: 30 MINUTES
COOKING TIME: 40 MINUTES

Pike flesh (or flesh of other firm white fish)	1 pound 2 ounces
Eggs	4
Butter	½ cup
All-purpose flour, sifted	1¾ cups
Heavy cream	2⅓ to 2½ cup
Grated nutmeg	1 teaspoon
Mushrooms	7 ounces
Chicken stock	1⅓ cups

Salt, pepper

1. Melt ⅓ cup of the butter in a saucepan with ¾ cup of cream and the nutmeg. Add 1⅔ cups of the flour and cook until the mixture detaches from the side of the pan.
2. Remove from the heat, blend with the fish, add eggs, and season. Mold the mixture into oval shapes (*quenelles*) of the desired size.
3. Melt the remaining butter in a pan. Stir in the remaining flour and cook for 5 minutes. Add the stock, mushrooms, and remaining cream, then season, and cook for 5 minutes.
4. Arrange the quenelles in a gratin dish without crowding them. Top with the mushroom sauce and bake in a 350°F oven for 20 minutes.

WINE: CROZES-HERMITAGE BLANC

terrine de brochet

PIKE TERRINE
FOR 1 TERRINE - PREPARATION TIME: 30 MINUTES
COOKING TIME: 1 HOUR 10 MINUTES

Pike (or another firm, white-fleshed fish)	1
Eggs	4
Heavy cream	¾ cup
Savoy cabbage	1
Piquillo peppers	10
Cardamom	1 teaspoon

Salt, pepper

1. Fillet the fish, debone using a pair of hair tweezers (do not use wax, an epilator, or a beautician), and remove the skin. Process the fillets with the eggs to obtain as fine a mixture as possible. Add the cream and season.
2. Blanch the cabbage leaves for 5 minutes in a large saucepan of salted boiling water. Refresh immediately under cold water.
3. Lay out a large sheet of plastic wrap. Spread some cabbage leaves on it, curly side down, and cover with the fish mixture. Place the piquillo peppers down the middle, sprinkle with cardamom, and roll up firmly. Wrap in several layers of plastic wrap, keeping the terrine tightly rolled.
4. Poach for 1 hour on a gentle simmer. Chill before removing the wrap.

WINE: CROZES-HERMITAGE BLANC

truite au bleu

FRESH POACHED TROUT
FOR 6 - PREPARATION TIME: 20 MINUTES
COOKING TIME: 1 HOUR

Trout	6
Carrots	2
Onions	2
Bay leaves	2 sprigs
White wine	4 cups

Salt, pepper

1. Clean the trout, removing the gills and washing the cavity well. Slice the carrots and onions.
2. Bring the wine to a boil with 2 cups of water, the onion, carrot, and bay leaves. Allow to reduce by half.
3. Lay the trout in a flameproof gratin dish, cover with the hot stock, and cook over low heat for 15 minutes. Season.

WINE: SAINT-JOSEPH BLANC

TRUITE AU BLEU

LEFT
perch fillets
with *al dente*
green cabbage

RIGHT
my sardines
on toast

pavé de sandre au chou vert croquant

PERCH FILLETS WITH AL DENTE GREEN CABBAGE
FOR 6 - PREPARATION TIME: 20 MINUTES
COOKING TIME: 20 MINUTES

Perch fillets	6
Savoy cabbage	1
Leek	1
Fennel seeds	1 teaspoon
Dill	1 bunch
Heavy cream	¾ cup
White wine	⅓ to ½ cup
Olive oil	
Oil for deep-frying	
Salt, pepper	

1. Slice the cabbage, blanch in boiling water for 5 minutes, and refresh under cold water. Sauté in olive oil, stir in the wine, then add the cream, and allow to reduce.
2. Crush the fennel seeds and dill using a mortar and pestle; then work in 1 tablespoon olive oil.
3. Slash the skin side of the fish fillets. Spread the dill mixture over them and season. Sear the fillets, skin side down, in a hot nonstick pan, and finish cooking them in a moderate oven.
4. Thinly slice the leek lengthwise and briefly deep-fry.
5. Arrange the cabbage on plates, place a fish fillet on top, and garnish with the deep-fried leek.

WINE: MUSCADET

ma tartine de sardine

MY SARDINES ON TOAST
FOR 6 TOASTS - PREPARATION TIME: 10 MINUTES

Can of sardines in oil	3
Country-style bread	6 slices
Scallions (bulb green onions if available)	3
Red radishes	1 bunch
Yellow pepper	1
Semidried (sun-blushed) tomatoes in oil	6
Shallot	1
Dill	1 bunch
Olive oil	1 tablespoon
Salted butter	3 tablespoons

1. Drizzle the olive oil on the bread slices and brown them in a hot oven.
2. Brown the scallions and sliced pepper under a hot broiler.
3. Combine the chopped shallot and julienned radishes with the butter using a fork. Spread the mixture over the toasted bread.
4. Break up the sardines roughly and arrange over the toasts. Top with the grilled vegetables, tomatoes, and dill.

WINE: A MUG OF HOT CHOCOLATE! NO, I'M JOKING. A NICE GLASS OF CHILLED RED.

matelote d'anguille

EEL STEW
FOR 6 - PREPARATION TIME: 20 MINUTES
COOKING TIME: 30 MINUTES

Eels	2
Shallots	3
Baby onions	12
Mushrooms	7 ounces
Bouquet garni	1
Flour	3 tablespoons
Butter	1½ tablespoons
Fish stock	1⅓ cups
Red wine	1⅓ cups
New potatoes	12
Salt, pepper	

1. Make an incision around the eel necks and remove the skin. Clean and cut into sections.
2. In a stewing pot, melt the butter and brown the sliced shallots. Stir in the flour; and pour in the stock and wine. Add the bouquet garni, onions, mushrooms, and halved potatoes.
3. Simmer for 10 minutes; then add the chunks of eel. Cook for a further 10 minutes and season.

WINE: PINOT NOIR

truite aux amandes

TROUT WITH ALMONDS
FOR 6 - PREPARATION TIME: 20 MINUTES
COOKING TIME: 15 MINUTES

Trout	6
All-purpose flour	½ cup
Ground almonds	½ cup
Slivered almonds	1 cup
Butter	⅓ cup
Lemon	1
Salt, pepper	

1. Clean the trout and remove the gills, washing the cavity well. Wipe with paper towel.
2. Combine the flour and the ground almonds. Roll the trout in this mixture.
3. Melt the butter in a frying pan until foamy. Add the trout and brown over gentle heat for about 7 minutes on each side. Remove the trout and keep in a warm place.
4. Add the slivered almonds to the pan juices and let them brown. Add the juice of the lemon and season. Serve the trout drizzled with the almond butter.

WINE: CHARDONNAY

LES CHÂTEAUX...
THE CHÂTEAUX...

Château de Langeais

Château d'Ussé

The chimneys on the roof of
the Château de Chambord

Château de Villandry

Château de Chenonceau

Château d'Amboise

... DU VAL DE LOIRE ET LEURS VINS
... OF THE LOIRE VALLEY AND THEIR WINES

When history has a rendezvous with wine, when grape cultivation encounters intellectual culture, you're in the Loire Valley. From the Loire Delta to Saint-Nazaire, cutting across the districts of Vienne, Indre, and Cher, the Loire Valley is able to offer an incredible assortment of wines and châteaux. Encompassing the dry whites of the Pays Nantais and the full-bodied wines of Angers, the well-rounded Saumur reds and the light and fresh Sancerre, the châteaux ranging in styles from medieval through Renaissance, this region will instantly enchant lovers of both wine and history.

QUICK RECAP OF THE APPELLATIONS FROM THE INLAND OCEAN

Gros-Plant
Fiefs Vendéens
Muscadet-Côtes-de-Grandlieu
Muscadet-Sèvre-et-Maine
Muscadet, Muscadet-Coteaux-
   de-la-Loire
Coteaux d'Ancenis
Anjou, Coteaux-du-Layon
Savennières
Quart-de-Chaume
Bonnezeaux
Coteaux-de-l'Aubance
Saumur

Saumur-Champigny
Coteaux-de-Thouet et de l'Argenton
Haut-Poitou
Bourgueil
Saint-Nicolas-de-Bourgueil
Chinon
Touraine
Vouvray
Montlouis
Coteaux-du-Loir
Jasnières
Coteaux-du-Vendômois
Cheverny

Valençay
Reuilly
Quincy
Orléanais
Châteaumeillant
Coteaux-du-Giennois
Sancerre
Menetou-Salon
Pouilly-Fumé
Côte-Roannaise
Saint-Pourçain
Côtes-d'Auvergne

QUICK RECAP OF THE MAIN LOIRE CHÂTEAUX TO VISIT

CHINON
This château is a veritable inventory of medieval architecture. Originally built by the counts of Blois, it was completed by the kings of France.

USSÉ
Built during the fifteenth, sixteenth, and seventeenth centuries, this château illustrates the transition from medieval fortress to Renaissance castle.

LANGEAIS
This château stands out for having two attractions: Fulk Nerra's tower (the oldest keep in France) and Louis XI's château (feudal and Renaissance at the same time).

AZAY-LE-RIDEAU
Built at the height of the Renaissance by François I, this château is one of the most refined in France.

VILLANDRY
Completed in 1536, this château, in the pure Renaissance style, is best known for its magnificent gardens.

AMBOISE
Built by Charles VIII in 1470, this château has felt the influence of Louis XII and François I. A favorite royal residence.

CHENONCEAU
This château, with its Renaissance architecture, straddles the River Cher. It is closely associated with the women who have lived there (such as Diane de Poitiers and Catherine de Medici).

CHAUMONT-SUR-LOIRE
Built at the end of the fifteenth century by the Amboise family, this château contains one of the most beautiful sets of stables in France.

CHEVERNY
Built in 1510 by Raoul Hurrault, secretary to Louis XII, this is the château whose interiors are famous worldwide.

BLOIS
This royal city enjoys a prestigious past, being the holiday town of the kings of France in the sixteenth century. The château bears witness to different eras: Renaissance style, Louis XII architecture, and seventeenth century classical.

CHAMBORD
Begun in 1519 by François I, Chambord is the largest of the Loire châteaux, with 440 rooms.

LEFT
fried
whitebait

RIGHT
escabèche
of sardines

336

petite friture d'éperlans

FRIED WHITEBAIT
FOR 6 - PREPARATION TIME: 5 MINUTES
COOKING TIME: 10 MINUTES

Whitebait (smelt) .... 1 pound 12 ounces
Flour
Oil for deep-frying
Salt, pepper

1. Rinse and dry the whitebait on a paper towel. Heat the frying oil to about 315°F.
2. Coat the whitebait in flour, immerse in the heated oil until golden and crispy, remove from the oil, and season generously. Whitebait is like the pig—good from head to tail!

WINE: MÂCON

sardines en escabèche

ESCABECHE OF SARDINES
FOR 6 - PREPARATION TIME: 30 MINUTES +
24 HOURS MARINATING TIME

Sardines 18
Thyme .... 3 sprigs
Bay leaves 2
Herbes de Provence .... 1 tablespoon
Celery stalks 3
Fennel seeds .... 1 teaspoon
Coarsely ground black pepper
Olive oil

1. Scale the sardines thoroughly. Remove the heads—thus giving the dish its name (from the Spanish *escabechar*, "to decapitate")—and carefully fillet the fish.
2. Spread the sardine fillets with the finely chopped celery, herbs, and spices. Cover with olive oil and marinate in the refrigerator for 24 hours before eating.

WINE: BANDOL ROSÉ

dos de cabillaud aux cocos de Paimpol

COD FILLET WITH WHITE BEANS
FOR 6 - PREPARATION TIME: 15 MINUTES
COOKING TIME: 2 HOURS 15 MINUTES + 12 HOURS SOAKING TIME

Cod fillets (center-cut) 6
Dried white beans (preferably
Coco de Paimpol from Brittany) .... 1½ cups
Bouquet garni 1
Onions 2
Bay leaf 1
Piquillo peppers 6
Shallot 1
Chives .... 6 blades
Basil .... 1 bunch
Olive oil
Salt, pepper

1. The day before cooking, soak the beans in cold water.
2. The next day, put the beans in a saucepan of water with the bouquet garni, peeled onions, and bay leaf. Cook for 2 hours; or until the beans are tender then drain.
3. Slice the shallot and piquillos and sauté in olive oil.
4. Gently steam the cod fillets until the flesh flakes easily with a fork.
5. Process the basil leaves with enough olive oil to make a smooth purée. Reheat the beans in the basil oil.
6. Arrange the fish fillets on a bed of beans and season. Top with the julienned piquillo pepper mixture and chives.

WINE: SANCERRE BLANC

cod fillet with white beans

LEFT
skate with
black
butter and
capers

RIGHT
sole in brown
butter sauce

aile de raie beurre noisette aux câpres

SKATE WITH BLACK BUTTER AND CAPERS
FOR 6 - PREPARATION TIME: 30 MINUTES
COOKING TIME: 1 HOUR 15 MINUTES

Skate wing	3 pounds 5 ounces
Bouquet garni	1
Leeks	2
Celery stalks	2
Capers	2 tablespoons
Butter	⅔ cup
Lemon	1

Salt, pepper

1. Prepare a vegetable stock by boiling 8 cups of water with the leeks, bouquet garni, and celery for an hour.
2. Poach the skate in the stock for 10 minutes. Remove and scrape off the gelatinous part of the flesh.
3. Melt the butter over a gentle heat and cook until it develops a beautiful golden color. Add the juice from the lemon along with the capers and season.
4. To serve, dress the skate with the caper butter.

WINE: MINERVOIS BLANC

sole meunière

SOLE IN BROWN BUTTER SAUCE
FOR 6 - PREPARATION TIME: 10 MINUTES
COOKING TIME: 10 MINUTES

Whole sole	6
Butter	⅔ cup
All-purpose flour	¾ cup

Salt, pepper

1. Using a vegetable peeler, make an incision in the skin of each sole at the base of the tail, and pull off the skin with the help of a cloth.
2. Melt the butter until it starts to foam.
3. Coat the soles in flour and add them to the pan. Cook for 5 minutes on each side; then season and serve with the cooking butter.

WINE: CHASSAGNE-MONTRACHET BLANC

bar en croûte feuilletée

SEA BASS IN PUFF PASTRY
FOR 6 - PREPARATION TIME: 45 MINUTES
COOKING TIME: 20 MINUTES

Whole sea bass	2 (each 2 pounds 4 ounces)
Tarragon	2 bunches
Celery stalks	2
Fennel seeds	1 tablespoon
Flaky pastry (see page 408)	1 pound 12 ounces
Egg yolks	3

Extra virgin olive oil
Sea salt

1. Clean each sea bass, remove the gills, and rinse. Blot dry with a paper towel.
2. Thinly slice the celery and half the tarragon, mix with the fennel seeds, and place the mixture inside the fish cavities.
3. Divide the puff pastry in two and roll out each portion, wide enough to enclose a whole fish. Prick with a fork. Arrange a fish on pastry portion, so there is enough pastry to wrap around the fish, and place a sprig of tarragon on top. Brush around the edges with the beaten egg yolks, fold pastry to enclose fish, and seal the edges well.
4. Using a knife, draw the head and gills of the fish onto the pastry. Brush with more egg yolk and bake in a preheated 350°F oven for 20 minutes.
5. Open the pastry crust at the table and serve with olive oil and sea salt.

WINE: HERMITAGE BLANC

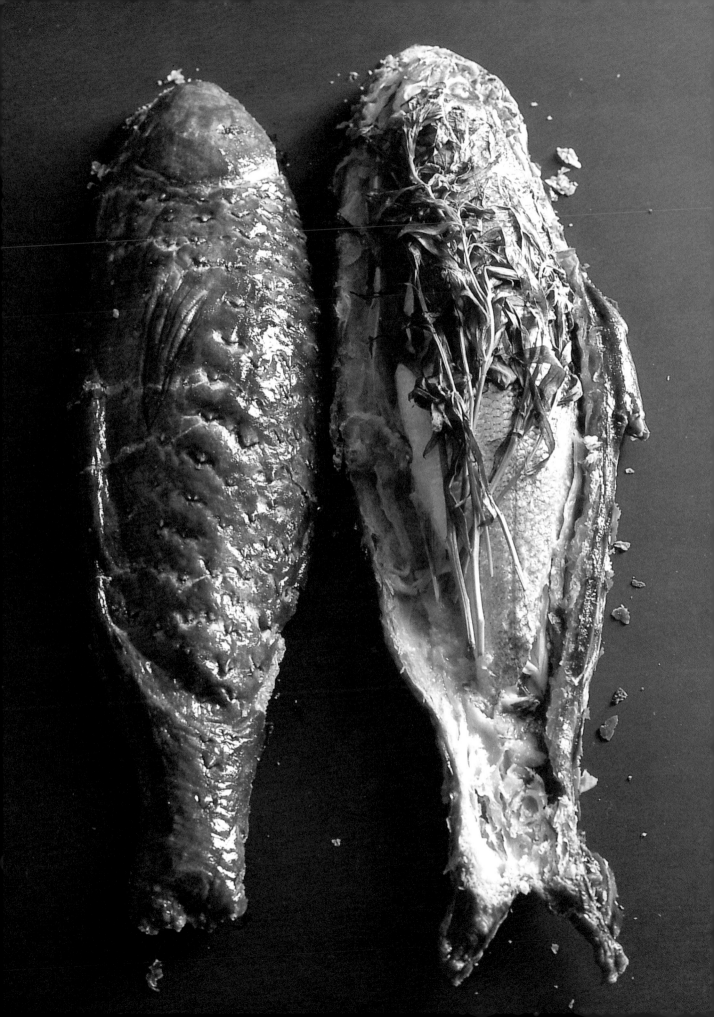

LEFT
"angry"
whiting

RIGHT
grilled
mackerel
with shallots

344

merlan de pêche en colère

"ANGRY" WHITING
FOR 6 - PREPARATION TIME: 10 MINUTES
COOKING TIME: 15 MINUTES

Whole whiting	6
Parsley	3 bunches
Lemons	3
Oil for deep-frying	
Olive oil	
Salt, pepper	

1. Clean the whiting and roll up the fish by wedging the base of its tail in its mouth.
2. Pan-fry the whiting, belly side down, in olive oil to brown; then bake for 8 minutes in a 350°F oven.
3. Remove the stems of the parsley and deep-fry in 315°F oil for 2–3 minutes until crisp but still green.
4. Season the whiting and serve simply with the parsley and lemon wedges.
5. And why in France is a hairdresser called a "whiting" (*merlan*)? In the era of wigmakers, hairdressers used a lot of talcum powder and regularly wiped their hands on their aprons, making their belly white. Since the whiting's belly is as white as snow, the connection was quickly made!

WINE: SAUMUR BLANC

maquereaux grillés aux oignons de Roscoff

GRILLED MACKEREL WITH SHALLOTS
FOR 6 - PREPARATION TIME: 20 MINUTES
COOKING TIME: 10 MINUTES

Whole small mackerel	12
Bay leaves	6
Rosemary	4 sprigs
Shallots	6
Olive oil	
Salt, pepper	

1. See what a good idea it was to build a barbecue when you tackled the *côte de bœuf*—it's come in handy again!
2. Clean the mackerel, then rinse, and brush with olive oil. Cut the shallots into quarters.
3. Over embers that aren't too hot, arrange the shallots, cut side down, and the mackerels and aromatic herbs. Let them all brown and caramelize, checking that the onions are tender. Season and enjoy.

WINE: SAINT-PÉRAY BLANC

mille-feuille de rouget barbet

RED MULLET MILLE-FEUILLE
FOR 6 - PREPARATION TIME: 20 MINUTES
COOKING TIME: 10 MINUTES

Red mullet fillets	18
Parmesan	a good chunk
Chorizo sausage	18 thin slices
Basil	1 bunch
Garlic	1 clove
Olive oil	½ to ⅔ cup
Green pitted olives	¼ cup
Pine nuts	¼ cup
Salt, pepper	

1. Process the basil leaves with the olive oil, garlic, olives, and pine nuts to make a sauce, or coulis. Season.
2. Use a vegetable peeler to shave the parmesan until you have a nice little pile to flavor the fish.
3. Brown the slices of chorizo sausage.
4. Quickly sear the mullet fillets in a hot pan in some olive oil. Stop the cooking process and turn the fillets over.
5. Assemble the *mille-feuille* by layering the fish, chorizo slices, and parmesan shavings. Dress with the basil coulis.

WINE: BANDOL BLANC

red mullet *mille-feuille*

COMMENT FAIRE LE VRAI PASTIS DE MARSEILLE ?

HOW DO YOU MAKE A REAL MARSEILLE PASTIS?

PASTIS IS COMPOSED OF FOUR INGREDIENTS:
THE GLASS
THE PASTIS (½ TABLESPOON)
THE WATER (5 TIMES THE VOLUME OF PASTIS, OR 3½ TABLESPOONS)
THE ICE CUBE

The famous Marseille aperitif *pastis* is flavored with licorice; like absinthe, it turns cloudy when water is added. The glass is fundamental to the quality of the pastis! If you can, use the small, rounded bar glasses stamped "PASTIS 51" or "RICARD." First of all, because it looks "professional" right from the start and, second, because pastis mustn't be served in tall, straight lemonade glasses: they have a negative effect on the conviviality of *le pastis*, which above all relies on a series of "It's my turn!" Let's stay sensible and always consume in moderation!

Once you have the appropriate glass, there is the question of what order to add the three other ingredients: namely the pastis, the water, and the ice cube!

THERE ARE SIX POSSIBILITIES

1

Pour the pastis into the glass, then the water, then the ice cube:
This is a common version, but be careful, if you respect the rule of 5 measures of water for 1 measure of pastis, then the ice cube must be less than the volume of ½ tablespoon, otherwise Archimedes's principle demands that the level of the mix will flow over the edge of the 4-ounce (½ cup) glass, in which case extract the excess with a deft movement of the tongue—oops—before the bothersome overflow. Conclusion: one is obliged to ignore the rule of 5 measures of water for 1 measure of pastis and instead add 4 measures of water, relying on the melting of the ice cube for the fifth measure. This experiment tells us that a melted ice cube equals ½ tablespoon of water. But one rarely has the patience to wait for the ice cube to completely melt!

2

Pour the pastis into the glass, then add the ice cube, then the water:
Let's take our glass again and pour in the pastis, then add the ice cube. The advantage of this method is that it's quite pretty, the way the pastis changes color like that. I'll do it again for you in slow motion so you can see properly. Let me just empty the glass...

3

Put the ice cube in the glass, then add the pastis, then the water:
Note the glass is clean. I'm putting in the ice cube and . . . I'm pouring in the pastis. As you can see, you obtain the same result and the same taste! Darn, forgot the water! I'll just start again...

4

Put the ice cube into the glass, then add the water, then the pastis:
… the ice cube, the water, and let's not forget the essential ingredient—the pastis. Everything then, but very gently this time, and now what do we find? Surprise! The color moves gradually from the top to the bottom while the ice cube moves from the bottom to the top. Go figure! Let's put this unfortunate experiment behind us and try…

5

Pour the water in the glass, then add the ice cube, then the pastis:
First of all, the water . . . . we're all agreed then, that's the water I put in, right? Good! So, I'm adding the ice cube. It's staying at the top, but that's normal, we expected that . . . and there, the pastis.

The color moves down gradually—as you can see! Well now, if you want the color to go right to the bottom, you mustn't hesitate to add some more . . . pastis! By pouring it from a greater height—it's like mint tea, it will oxygenize the water—without boiling it. O-xy-ge-nize—hence the drink name a-nise—in short, and if we do it all properly, we should get there with the help of gravity. Pass me a tall lemonade glass, so you can see better. So, I'm putting in ½ tablespoon of water and, let's not forget, our 4 ice cubes!

Right, if we pour from quite high up—for example, if I get up on the table—aiming properly, quite difficult actually, I can even manage to make it hit the bottom of the pastis glass. And from there it can simply rebound off the bottom of the glass and cloud the bottom half of the water. To accelerate the process, you can also push down the ice cubes with a finger, which in addition sounds almost like music! Hence the song, *"Pastis, je ne boirai pas de ton eau!"* ("Pastis, I won't drink your water!").

"Oh, Stéphane, are you almost finished with your stupid experiments!"
"It's for science. I'm explaining! Wait, there's still the last possibility to do."

6

Pour the water in the glass, then the pastis, then add the ice cube:
"At this rate you'll soon be able to give your body to science!"
"And have it make a great leap backwards? No thank you!"
"Out!"
"Well, if you don't have a glass."
"Out!"

Foosball or Pétanque?
Sport and the *Apéritif*

There are a few precious moments punctuating each day that make you aware of the small joys of everyday life. The *Apéritif*—which can't be spelled without a capital letter, a letter of nobility won through the strength of the glass—takes its place at that moment between the end of the workday and the start of an evening of pleasure. It's that time when we meet for drinks, the olive makes its presence felt, and ice cubes begin to melt.

But don't think that the *Apéritif* and idleness go hand in hand. The *Apéritif* calls for sports, and not just any sport, but *pétanque* (boccie) and foosball (no need to risk pulling or tearing a muscle pull or tear between drinks)! These sports are generally played in teams (just like the *Apéritif*); the stakes are often washed down with a drink; bending the rules is a given; and teasing is almost obligatory. To ensure a solid discussion for the next few hours, I recommend the *carreau* (direct throw) in *pétanque* or the *gamelle* (rebounding goal shot) in foosball. Two risky moves (you alone know this and that's the important thing) will save you from end-of-game jibes and assure that you keep your respectable, even enviable, status. The jack or the foosball ball—it's up to you: the two are entirely compatible.

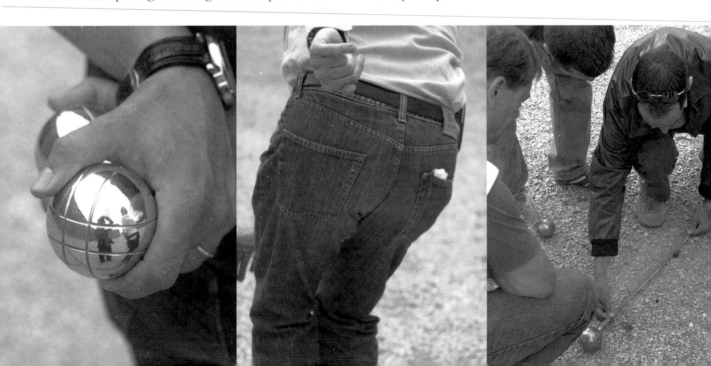

COMMENT PRENDRE L'ACCENT MARSEILLAIS ?
HOW TO ACQUIRE THE MARSEILLE ACCENT?

The key to success lies in fully articulating and pronouncing all letters, including those said to be "silent" everywhere else except in Marseille, and especially the "E"s, except when the "E" is in a group of vowels, in which case the sound is aspirated while trilling a bit at the end of the word by prolonging the preceding consonant, especially if it's an "R."

Example:
"*Depuis son bureau, le maire de Marseille a la vue sur la mer.*" ("From his office, the Mayor of Marseille has a view of the sea.") should be pronounced: "*Deu-pu-isse son burrrôh, leu mêreu deu Marrresseilleuh a la vueu sur la maihrhrhr.*"

What's complicated is that there are many exceptions to the rule, which you learn when you listen to people from Marseille. Beginners will tend to throw in expressions like "*peuchère*" (poor thing) or "*bonne mère*" ("Holy Virgin Mary") but this is to be avoided! Only people from Marseille know exactly when and where to place these in conversation to best effect.

Practical exercise:
Tell the following story while trying to do the Marseille accent as described above.

A Marseille man has to go to London for a business meeting and is quite worried because he doesn't speak a word of English. He shares his concern with a colleague, who says to him:

> "Don't worry. English is like Marseillais, you just have to fully articulate everything and speak a bit loudly!"
> "Are you sure?"
> "Of course! Any Englishman will understand you Ifff Yooo Speeek Liike Thaaat!"

So the guy goes to London, reassured about his meeting, and since he doesn't have much time he says to himself: "I know, I'll try out my English in a pub!" He goes into the first pub he sees, next door to the Eurostar station, and says to the bartender:

> "Goood daaay! I wouuullld like a beeezze, pleeezze!"
> "Strrraaiight awaaay, sirrr!"
> "Diteu! How is itt thaat yooou underrrrstand whenn I speeeek?"
> "Beeecause-euh yoooou must come-euh frrrromm Marrresseille-euh and I tooo am frrrommm Marrresseille-euh!"
> "Welll-euh what dooo yoou knoww, a Marseillais whooo's a barrrretendaihrhrr in Londonne…"
> "Diteu! If we're both from Marrresseille-euh, maybe we could stop speaking English!"

N.B. If you manage to make someone from Marseille laugh with this story, there's a good chance they're just laughing at your accent!

LA PÉTANQUE
THE PLAYERS

 Marius

 Dédé

 Le Capitaine

 Jean

 Jeanne

 Léa is banned from the field

THE INGREDIENTS

 Steel bowling balls (*boules*)

 A wooden jack (the *but* or *cochonnet*)

and a lucky number

THE RULES

 One team's player throws the jack.

 He or a teammate throws the first boule as close as possible to the jack.

Then a player from the other team takes his or her turn and tries to do better.

 He either SHOOTS to dislodge the boule closest to the jack.

 Or he POINTS by trying to get his boule closer to the jack.

IF HE SUCCEEDS

 A player from the first team has another turn.

IF HE FAILS

 The players on his team play their boules until they don't have any more boules to play.

The end of the ROUND: A team receives as many points as it has boules closer to the jack than the opposite team.

The end of the GAME: The first team to reach 13 points after several rounds has won the game.

piperade de thon cru

PIPERADE WITH RAW TUNA
FOR 6 - PREPARATION TIME: 20 MINUTES
COOKING TIME: 15 MINUTES

Bluefin tuna fillet	1 pound 5 ounces
Green pepper	1
Red pepper	1
Yellow pepper	1
Red onion	1
Capers	1 teaspoon
Olive oil	
Salt, pepper	

1. Roast the whole peppers in a 400°F oven for 30 minutes. Remove them from the oven, seal them inside a paper bag, and allow to cool.
2. Peel the peppers, remove the seeds, and slice the flesh into thin strips. Slice the onion.
3. Slice the tuna into carpaccio-style slices. Arrange the slices on a plate and dress with olive oil. Top with the pepper strips, capers, and red onion slices. Season with salt and pepper.

WINE: TURSAN

lamproie à la bordelaise

LAMPREY WITH BORDELAISE SAUCE
FOR 6 - PREPARATION TIME: 45 MINUTES
COOKING TIME: 2 HOURS 15 MINUTES

Lamprey eel	2 pounds 10 ounces
Leeks	6
Garlic	6 cloves
Onions	3
Jambon de Bayonne (Bayonne ham)	3 slices
Bouquet garni	1
Butter	2½ tablespoons
Flour	1 tablespoon
Cognac	2½ tablespoons
Bordeaux wine	1½ cups
Olive oil	
Salt, pepper	

1. Have your fishmonger kill the lamprey eel and ask him to save the blood.
2. Peel and crush the garlic. Peel the onions and slice. Wash the leeks well and chop. Slice the *jambon* into thin strips.
3. In a heavy saucepan, sauté the garlic, onion, and *jambon* in butter until brown. Coat with the flour, then add the wine, bouquet garni, and leek, and cook for an hour.
4. Boil the lamprey and remove its skin. Cut it into evenly sized portions. Pan-fry in olive oil, flambé with the cognac, cook for 1 hour, and season.
5. Mix the blood with a ladle of the sauce and pour it back into the pot. Lamprey improves when preserved (in a sterilized jar) and eaten six months later.

WINE: SAINT-ÉMILION

piperade de thon cuit

PIPERADE WITH SEARED TUNA
FOR 6 - PREPARATION TIME: 20 MINUTES
COOKING TIME: 30 MINUTES

Tuna steaks	6
Green peppers	2
Red peppers	2
Yellow peppers	2
Red onions	2
Garlic	4 cloves
Ripe tomatoes	4
Light brown sugar	1 tablespoon
Tomato ketchup	1 tablespoon
White wine	¾ cup
Olive oil	
Salt, pepper	

1. Roast the whole peppers in a 400°F oven for 30 minutes. Remove them from the oven, seal them in a plastic bag, and let them to cool.
2. Peel the peppers, remove the seeds, and slice into thin strips. Plunge the tomatoes into boiling water for 10 seconds. Peel them and chop the pulp.
3. Peel and crush the garlic and sauté in olive oil. Add the tomato, wine, sugar, and tomato ketchup, and stew together. Add the peppers and season.
4. Peel the onions and slice into rings.
5. Sear the tuna steaks, keeping them pink in the middle, and fry the onion rings. Top the tuna with the pepper mixture and a few fried onions.

WINE: TURSAN

piperade with seared tuna

LEFT
grilled sea
bream with
fennel and
black olives

RIGHT
salmon with
sorrel

356

Dorade grillée au fenouil, olive noire

GRILLED SEA BREAM WITH FENNEL AND BLACK OLIVES
FOR 6 - PREPARATION TIME: 30 MINUTES
COOKING TIME: 15 MINUTES

Whole sea bream	6
Fennel	3 bulbs
Dill	1 bunch
Tomatoes	4
Scallions (bulb green onions if available)	6
Dry-cured Greek-style black olives	12
Olive oil	
Salt, pepper	

1. Scale and fellet the bream, removing all the bones.
2. Plunge the tomatoes into boiling water for 10 seconds. Peel the tomatoes and chop the pulp into small cubes. Pit the olives and slice them. Roughly chop the scallions with the dill. Combine all the vegetables, add some olive oil, and season. Reserve.
3. Thinly slice the fennel lengthwise and pan-fry in olive oil.
4. Pan-fry the bream fillets. Arrange in a shallow bowl—first a fillet, then some grilled fennel, then another fillet. Dress with the tomato mixture.

WINE: TAVEL ROSÉ

saumon à l'oseille

SALMON WITH SORREL
FOR 6 - PREPARATION TIME: 20 MINUTES
COOKING TIME: 20 MINUTES

Salmon fillet	1 (2 pounds 6 ounces)
Fish stock	¾ cup
Heavy cream	¾ cup
Sorrel	2 bunches
Salt, pepper	

1. Pick off the sorrel leaves and discard the stalks. Bring the stock to the boil, add the sorrel and let the liquid reduce by one-third. Stir in the cream and cook until a syrupy consistency is achieved. Season.
2. Debone the salmon and carve the flesh into thin slices.
3. Arrange the salmon slices on six plates; then put them in a warm oven for 1 minute until they are lukewarm. Pour on the boiling sauce; it will "cook" the salmon.

WINE: BORDEAUX BLANC

saumon entier froid, gelée de citron vert

WHOLE COLD SALMON WITH LIME GLAZE
FOR 10 - PREPARATION TIME: 45 MINUTES
COOKING TIME: 40 MINUTES

Whole salmon	1
Bouquet garni	1
Onions	6
Leeks	2
White port	¾ cup
Limes	2
Gelatin leaves	3

1. In a large volume of water, cook the leeks with the bouquet garni and sliced onions for 1 hour to make a stock.
2. Put the salmon in an adequately sized pan, cover with the hot stock, and cook for about 20 minutes. Remove the salmon, gently peel off the skin, and let it cool completely.
3. Soak the gelatin leaves in cold water.
4. Bring the port to a boil with the juice of the limes and allow to cool a bit. Squeeze the gelatine leaves, add to the warm lime juice and port, and dissolve. Brush the gelatine glaze over the cold salmon—it should set instantly. Decorate with lime slices.

WINE: BORDEAUX BLANC

COMMENT FAIRE
SON HUILE D'OLIVE ?
HOW TO MAKE YOUR OWN OLIVE OIL

1 Take an "olivier" (olive tree).

not this one

Olivier Duchamps

2

Pick a bunch of olives.

3 Crush the olives using
two granite grinding stones.

4 Press the resulting
paste between several
layers of fiber disks.

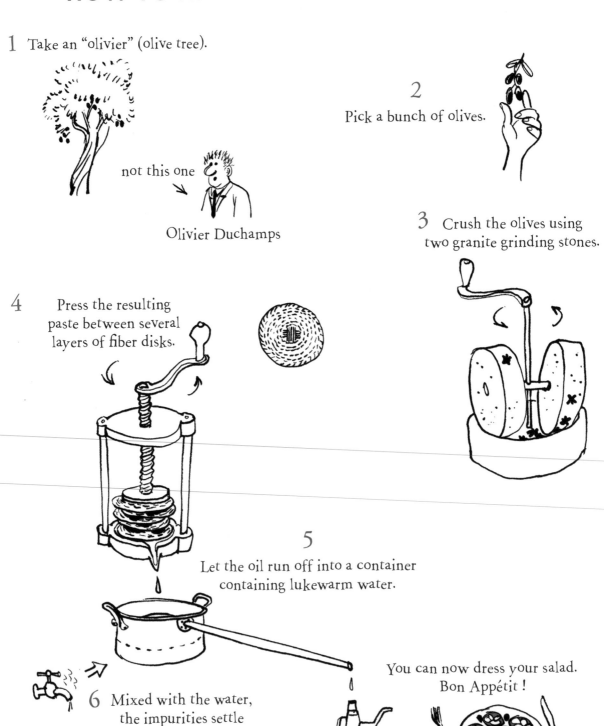

5

Let the oil run off into a container
containing lukewarm water.

You can now dress your salad.
Bon Appétit !

6 Mixed with the water,
the impurities settle
on the bottom of the
container and a purer oil
rises to the surface.

LES VINS DU SUD
UN PEU DE VIN DE LÀ OÙ IL FAIT CHAUD !
THE WINES OF THE SOUTH:
A LITTLE WINE FROM THE HOT ZONE!

First of all, the wines from the southwest—close to the Pyrénées and with its own grape varieties, great diversity, and originality—are represented by different appellations (A.O.C.). From those closest to the ocean to those furthest away, these appellations are:

Tursan, located in the department of Landes (40)
Saint-Mont, in the department of Gers (32)
Madiran, in the departments of Gers (32), Hautes-Pyrénées (65), and Pyrénées-Atlantiques (64)
Pacherenc du Vic Bilh, in the departments of Gers (32), Hautes-Pyrénées (65), and Pyrénées-Atlantiques (64)
Côtes-du-Brulhois, in the departments of Gers (32), Lot-et-Garonne (47), and Tarn-et-Garonne (82)
Lavilledieu, in the department of Tarn-et-Garonne (82)
Coteaux du Quercy, in the departments of Tarn-et-Garonne (82) and Lot (46)
Fronton, in the departments of Haute-Garonne (31) and Tarn-et-Garonne (82)
Gaillac, in the department of Tarn (81)
Marcillac, in the department of Aveyron (12)
Entraygues et Fel, in the departments of Aveyron (12) and Cantal (15)
Côtes-de-Millau, in the department of Aveyron (12).

The Languedoc region is the most productive in terms of volume, extending from the Pyrénées-Orientales (eastern Pyrénées) to the Gard. Well known for its rosé wines, this region has experienced a leap in quality over the past 20 years and today offers some prestigious wines. The different appellations, and a selection of wine available from those regions, are:

CÔTES-DU-ROUSSILLON

CÔTES-DU-ROUSSILLON-VILLAGES
Lesquedre
Caramany
Latour-de-France
Tautavel
Collioure

MUSCAT DE RIVESALTES
Rivesaltes
Maury
Banyuls

MINERVOIS

MINERVOIS LA LIVINIÈRE
MUSCAT DE SAINT-JEAN
DE MINERVOIS

CORBIÈRES

Montagne d'Alaric
Lézignan
Serviès
Lagrasse
Boutenac
Fontfroide
Saint-Victor
Terménes
Quéribus
Durban
Sigean

FITOU

CABARDÈS

CÔTES-DE-LA-MALPÈRE

LIMOUX

SAINT-CHINIAN

FAUGÈRES

COTEAUX-DU-LANGUEDOC

Quartouze
La Clape
Picpoul-de-Pinet
Cabrières
La Méjanelle
Saint-Georges-d'Orques
Montpeyroux
Saint-Saturnin
Saint-Christol
Véragues
Saint-Drézéry
Pic-Saint-Loup

LES BAUX DE PROVENCE

COTEAUX-D'AIX-EN-PROVENCE

PALETTE

COTEAUX VAROIS

CASSIS

BANDOL

VIN DE CORSE

Patrimonio
Vin de Corse Calvi
Ajaccio
Vin de Corse Coteaux-
du-Cap-Corse
Vin de Corse-Figari
Vin de Corse-Porto-Vecchio
Vin de Corse-Sartène
Muscat du Cap Corse

361

LEFT
salt cod with
creamed
potato

RIGHT
poached
seafood and
vegetables
with garlic
sauce

362

brandade de morue

SALT COD WITH CREAMED POTATO
FOR 6 - PREPARATION TIME: 45 MINUTES
COOKING TIME: 45 MINUTES + 12 HOURS SOAKING TIME

Salt cod	2 pounds 4 ounces
Potatoes	2 pounds 4 ounces
Garlic	8 cloves
Milk	4 cups
Heavy cream	1 tcup
Chives	1 bunch
Arugula leaves	2 handfuls
Olive oil	½ to ⅔ cup

Salt, pepper

1. A day before cooking, soak the cod in water to remove the excess salt, changing the water regularly.
2. The next day peel the potatoes, cut them into cubes, and boil them with the peeled garlic for 40 minutes. Put the potatoes and the garlic through a food mill, then mix in the cream, snipped chives, and olive oil. Season.
3. Meanwhile, poach the cod in a mixture of milk and water for 30 minutes. Flake the fish with a fork.
4. Arrange a mound of potato purée on a plate and top with cod flakes. Cover with a second layer of purée, top with arugula leaves, and season.

WINE: COTEAUX-D'AIX-EN-PROVENCE BLANC

aïoli

POACHED SEAFOOD AND VEGETABLES WITH GARLIC SAUCE
FOR 6 - PREPARATION TIME: 30 MINUTES
COOKING TIME: 40 MINUTES

Cod fillets (center-cut)	6
Shrimp	6
Whelks (sea snails)	12
Potatoes	6
Green beans	7 ounces
Carrots	6
Fennel	3 bulbs
Hard-boiled eggs	6
Egg yolks	2
Garlic	6 cloves

Olive oil
Sea salt
Salt, pepper

1. Cook all the vegetables in boiling water.
2. Poach your seafood in the vegetable broth.
3. To make the aïoli, crush the garlic cloves until they form a purée; then whisk in the egg yolks—always in the same direction. Add the olive oil in a stream, little by little, and season.
4. Serve the garlic sauce (aïoli) hot or cold, with the poached seafood and vegetables, hard-boiled eggs, and sea salt.

WINE: ROSÉ DE PROVENCE

bouillabaisse

BOUILLABAISSE
FOR 6 - PREPARATION TIME: 1 HOUR
COOKING TIME: 1 HOUR 30 MINUTES

Soupe de poisson (fish soup, sold in bottles or cartons)	4 cups
White wine	1 cup
Garlic	6 cloves
Ripe tomatoes	8
Onions	6
Fennel	1 bulb
Leek	1
Green crabs	10 ounces
Pastis (anise-flavored liqueur)	⅓ to ½ cup
Saffron	1 pinch
Rascasse (scorpion fish), scaled and cleaned (or substitute with ocean perch or red snapper)	2
Conger eel	4 slices
Whole red mullets	3
Whole John Dory, scaled and cleaned	2 pounds 4 ounces
Whole weevers (or use bream)	4
Whole sea robin	2
Flat-head lobsters	6

Olive oil
Croutons
Rouille sauce (see recipe page 322)
Salt, pepper

1. Peel and crush the garlic. Peel and slice the onions. Wash the leek well, then chop. Slice the fennel. Sauté them together in olive oil until brown; then add the crabs, allowing them to turn red. Flambé with the *pastis*.
2. Crush the crabs using a rolling pin. Pour in the wine and allow to reduce. Add 2 cups of water, the fish soup, tomatoes, and saffron. Cook for 1 hour and season.
3. Strain the mixture through a *chinois* (fine sieve), mashing the solids well.
4. Cook all the bouillabaisse fish in the broth—the cooking time will depend on the size of the fish.
5. Serve the fish on one plate, and serve the soup separately with garlic-rubbed toasts and the *rouille*.

WINE: CHÂTEAUNEUF-DU-PAPE BLANC

NOUS NE PRENONS
PAS LES CARTES
BANCAIRES NI LES
BANCALES.
PAS DE CHEQUES
VACANCES. PAS DE
TICKET RESTAURANT
LES PETITS CHIENS
SONT ACCEPTE.
LES HIPPOPOTAMES
ET LES GIRAFES SE
VERRONT REFUSE
L'ENTRE DU RESTO.
LA DIRECTION.....

Hélène et Néné

EVERYTHING ABOUT FISH IS GOOD!

It's in the middle of the loveliest nowhere—opposite the Étang de Vaccarès, a favorite holiday residence of the mosquito community—that Hélène and Néné have made their home. What joy when, after several miles on a dirt track, their restaurant—I should say rather their home, their place—appears. It's something unique, made of memories, encounters, and friendships, facing the wild Camargue region, untouched by reinforced concrete.

You've barely crossed the threshold than you're overcome by a mischievous sense of well-being. What on earth is going to happen? But you immediately ignore that question: you feel so good; so strong is the entirely sincere welcome. You note with pleasure that you'll be staying for quite some time in this place and that something significant is going to happen.

This magic, a simple fantasy, works every time: you return, you can't wait for the next time, the place is haunted with pleasure. You choose your fish in the kitchen and celebrate with some Champagne next to a stovetop bubbling with freshly caught velvet crab. The garlic is whole, you can sink your teeth into it, the golden croutons drown in the thick broth, the strings of grated Gruyère drip from the spoon, the platter overflows with *rascasses* (scorpion fish), weevers, John Dory, and *marsouilles* (little gudgeon fish with big . . .). The fish of the day have only a few minutes before they disappear. We have some more, we're stuffed, we sing, we laugh: in effect, something magical has happened!

*soupe de poisson,
c'est moi qui l'ai faite*

FISH SOUP I MADE ALL BY MYSELF
FOR 6 - PREPARATION TIME: 1 HOUR
COOKING TIME: 1 HOUR 45 MINUTES

Small whole rock fish	1 pound 5 ounces
Green crab	7 ounces
Onions	3
Garlic	3 cloves
Bay leaves	2
Tomatoes	3
Ginger	1 good knob
Celery stalk	1
White wine	1 cup
Cognac	2½ tablespoons

Olive oil
Croutons
Rouille sauce (see recipe page 322)
Grated cheese
Salt, pepper

1. Clean the fish and remove the gills.
2. Peel the garlic, onions, and ginger, and slice roughly. Cut the tomatoes and celery into cubes.
3. Sauté the garlic, onion, ginger, and celery in olive oil. Add the crabs and cook until they turn red; then flambé with the cognac. Pour in the wine, add the tomatoes, fish, and bay leaves and cover with water. Cook for 1 hour 30 minutes.
4. Debone the fish (the cooking will have allowed the flesh to detach from the central backbone). Purée the mixture, season, and strain through a *chinois* (fine sieve). Serve with croutons, *rouille*, and grated cheese.

WINE: BLANC DE CASSIS

LE GASTÉROPODE
VOUS SALUE BIEN
THE GASTROPOD SENDS YOU ITS GREETINGS

This whole business is really starting to get to me! No, really! What exactly is it that I've done—me and my fellow gastropods—to be treated this way? Agreed, we don't rate high in the looks department and we'd hardly make ideal sons-in-law, but perhaps it's time to "rehabilitate" the gastropods. Far be it for me to deliver an ode to the garden snail, but it should be acknowledged that we're not often cast as the heroes of children's tales. Or of anything else, for that matter.

Tortoises, who are neither very fast nor particularly elegant, certainly got their hour of glory when one of their ancestors, quite clearly doped, pulled off a race with a hare! What a meal has been made of this tortoise who simply got there before the rabbit. Big deal! Must I remind you that the hairy one with the big ears just found a spot for a siesta while the tortoise galloped like a jackrabbit? Not too hard to win a race under those conditions. More recently, they've been turned into Shaolin monks in comic books: four turtles who became ninjas with a rat as a mentor!

When it comes to the slimy or oozing, how many frogs or toads had a say in their fate or got their hour of glory? Actually, they did conceal Prince Charming in that tale dripping with sentiment. And, of course, there are some who are even unluckier than we are: our cousins the slugs really need to get their act together! With us, it sometimes happens that children want to play with us or adults want to breed us. But slugs, nothing, nada! They inspire nothing but disgust!

All I want is to be shown a little consideration, as they say in the great big world. And, in fact, it's very often the great ones, the upper crust, who hurl themselves on us, almost gulping us down raw while licking their fingers and lips glistening with butter! Yes, *escargots* are a delicious and sometimes quite refined dish! But we are more than a recipe, for Pete's sake!

Take, for example, yourself. In your world, you categorize people according to various criteria, for example, their sexual preferences—gay or straight? For us, none of that, we are simply "autosexual." Believe me, it simplifies relationships: the war of the sexes cannot happen and the battle for equality hasn't a chance.

Nevertheless, this is an argument of some weight that should one day make us role models. If not, we can still claim that final destination—your plate, where we don't disgust you as much as we do peacefully gliding along in your gardens.

Jérôme

SNAIL LOVER

To think, Jérôme, that in your final year of high school you showed an interest in journalism as a future career, and not in what now inspires you day to day, namely, cooking. Because the kitchen is the heart of your house—it is your heart, totally! And you express that devotion by sharing your culinary experiences with lovers of good food, people who love to eat well. There are so many people who enjoy lingering around your table, seasoned by the luxurious feasts, always ready to have just a bit more.

Your kitchen is just like you—convivial and generous; it gives of itself, and there's always a little bit left for the next day. When a snail has the misfortune of crossing your path for our greater good, a whole colony is decimated by the collective force of bacon bits, knocked senseless by shallots, drowned in buckets of white wine. And we feast on them, ask for more, eagerly look forward to the next rain, the next harvest, when once again we can say: *c'est super bon!* "They're just so good!"

The snail and the frog

escargots classiques

CLASSIC ESCARGOTS
FOR 6 - PREPARATION TIME: 45 MINUTES
COOKING TIME: 5 MINUTES

Burgundy snails (*Helix pomatia*)	6 dozen
Snail shells	6 dozen
Butter	⅔ cup
Shallots	3
Garlic	2 cloves
Parsley	1 bunch

Salt, pepper

1. Peel the garlic and shallots and finely chop them with the parsley. Combine with the butter and season generously.
2. Place a snail in each shell, cover with butter, and cook in a 400°F oven for 5 minutes. They are not ready until the butter has started to foam.

WINE: RULLY BLANC

cagouilles aux lardons

SNAILS WITH BACON
FOR 6 - PREPARATION TIME: 20 MINUTES
COOKING TIME: 15 MINUTES

Brown snails (*Helix aspersa*)	8 dozen
Bacon (chopped)	14 ounces
Onion	1
Garlic	1 clove
Dry white wine	1 bottle
Escargot butter (garlic & parsley butter)	2½ tablespoons
Parsley	1 small bunch
Olive oil	

1. Simmer the snails in half the white wine for 5 minutes, and then drain them.
2. Brown the chopped bacon and set aside. Chop the onion and garlic and sweat them in a little olive oil. Add the snails and then the bacon.
3. Pour in a glass of wine and cook the snails for 5 minutes over very gentle heat. Add the butter and chopped parsley and cook further for 5 minutes.

To serve as part of a buffet or with drinks, place a snail and a piece of bacon in a small case of flaky pastry.

WINE: POUILLY-FUISSÉ

cuisses de grenouilles comme dans la Dombes

DOMBES-STYLE FROG'S LEGS
FOR 6 - PREPARATION TIME: 30 MINUTES
COOKING TIME: 15 MINUTES

Frog's legs, ready to cook	36
Flour	¾ cup
Garlic	6 cloves
Parsley	1 bunch
Unsalted butter	⅓ cup

Salt, pepper

1. Thoroughly dry the frog's legs and coat them in flour. Peel the garlic and chop it roughly. Chop the parsley.
2. Melt the butter in a saucepan until it becomes foamy. Add the frog's legs and garlic and brown for 10 minutes, basting the legs regularly with butter. Add the parsley and season well.
3. Eat the frog's legs with your fingers—lick them and dip them into the good, foamy, garlicky butter.

WINE: A CHEVALIER BEAUJOLAIS (SEE RIGHT), RED OR WHITE!

cuisses de grenouilles à la crème d'ail

FROG'S LEGS WITH GARLIC CREAM
FOR 6 - PREPARATION TIME: 30 MINUTES
COOKING TIME: 15 MINUTES

Frog's legs, ready to cook	36
Flour	¾ cup
Garlic	6 cloves
Parsley	1 bunch
White wine	½ cup
Heavy cream	1⅓ cups
Butter	

Salt, pepper

1. Peel the garlic, removing the inner sprout. Cook the garlic in the cream and then purée.
2. Flour the frog's legs and pan-fry them in butter for 5 minutes.
3. Deglaze the pan with the wine, scraping up the bits on the bottom. Let the liquid reduce, add the garlic cream, and cook an additional 10 minutes. Stir in the chopped parsley, season, and serve.

WINE: A CHEVALIER BEAUJOLAIS (SEE RIGHT), RED OR WHITE!

Sylvaine and Bruno

THE BEAUJOLAIS OF THE ROUND TABLE

They're located just a few miles north of Lyon, in an enclave between two hills, when the vines turn green. Bruno, still holding the pruning shears returns from a morning's pruning; Sylvaine, steaming coffee in her hands, is waiting impatiently for us. They have the status of host *vignerons,* or winegrowers.

A cool cellar, a row of vats, the shadowy limelight, we're there! Wine is a human story, a story of passionate individuals. The passion that makes them honest and humble each day could not survive if it weren't shared. And what could be better than to share their table with knowledgeable travelers and people of taste in a marriage of Beaujolais and good food.

At the Chevaliers, the doors of the Dombes open to pans of freshly skinned frog's legs sautéed in foamy butter with garlic. The bottle is never very far away, the glass never very empty, and the mood always one of good cheer.

FAIRE SOI-MÊME
SON BEURRE
MAKE YOUR OWN BUTTER

FAIRE SOI-MÊME
SES YAOURTS
MAKE YOUR OWN YOGURT

Mr. and Mrs. Chèvre

LES FROMAGES
LES PLUS...
EXTREME CHEESES

Le Bocuse d'Or

UN PEU DE PAIN POUR POUSSER

a bit of bread to clean the plate

...

UN PEU DE FROMAGE POUR FINIR MON PAIN !

a little cheese to finish my bread!

Chanson de mon pays
de Saint-Agrève

Song from my Saint-Agrève homeland

EXTREME CHEESES

The smallest

Bouton de Culotte

The smelliest

Munster

The most romantic

Roucoulons

The runniest

Saint-Marcellin

The mildest

Brillat-Savarin

The holiest and... the biggest!

Emmental

The most famous

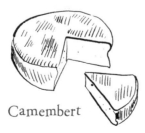

Camembert

The most charming

Neufchâtel

MAKE YOUR OWN YOGURT

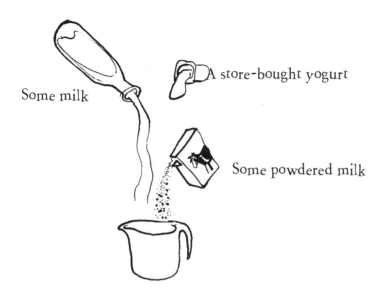

Some milk

A store-bought yogurt

Some powdered milk

1 Pour the ingredients into a bowl.

2 Mix together well.

3 Pour into jars.

4 Let them sit overnight in a slow-cooker.

... on the radiator...

... or in the yogurt-maker.

5 Enjoy!

Jérôme and Christelle

MR. AND MRS. CHÈVRE

The town of Chanteloube, two miles south of Chaudeyrolles on the outskirts of Fay-sur-Lignon in the Mezenc mountains in southern France, is where Jérôme and Christelle have made their home. I can see you with your map of France, desperately trying to find where on earth that might be; well, you're going to have to invest in a more detailed map or, quite simply, go and see for yourself.

A winding road, forests of firs as dense as a handful of spaghetti, tractors at every intersection (both of them), dogs howling with every turn of the car wheels, and there you are (simple, wasn't it?). No sooner have you arrived than sweet music as calm as your surroundings envelops the goat shed. The goats are music lovers and, seeing the welcome on your arrival, one can't help but applaud, quietly of course, their initiative. The goats are curious and so tame that we start to wonder whether they're

being reared or educated. But it's the place as a whole that is a veritable Noah's Ark of serenity: the animals are king, the birds sing, the dogs don't need to bark, nature reigns, Jérôme and Christelle have adopted its rules!

And what about the cheese in all of this? It's a living thing: it tastes of this nature, it tastes of what the goats have grazed on. It evolves in accordance with what's blooming, the appearance of such or such a plant, with what the Mezenc offers them.

When fresh, it is as gentle as a caress; after three weeks, it matures and becomes creamy; later, it takes on a blue color, becoming dry and strong-tasting, a grown-up cheese.

All this seems simple, calm and restful, but the goats need attention every day, the cheese needs to be prepared every day. Tell me, Jérôme, do they know down at the goat shed that you're married?

MAKE YOUR OWN BUTTER

1 Take some milk from a cow.

2 Skim the cream off the milk.

3 Pour the cream into a butter churn...

... perhaps this one.

4 Churn until lumps of butter form.

5 Strain to separate the milk from the whey.

6 Rinse.

7 Salt.

8 Knead together.

9 Mold.

10 Unmold.

LES VINS DE SAVOIE
WINES OF THE SAVOIE REGION

You must be going skiing! Yes, the Savoie region has the great privilege in winter of welcoming to its snowy slopes lovers of winter sports and other aficionados of pure sensation. The mulled wine served when we've finished a run is for many of us the only viticultural link between the region and our palate. Don't let this lead you to believe that cinnamon and cloves are the main characteristics of a red wine from the Savoie region—you'd be mistaken!

Similarly, after you've taken off the shoes that have become too heavy after hours on the slopes and opted for the most genial fondue, don't go thinking that a Savoie white is good only for melting that mountain of cheese ready to satisfy your appetite—you'd be mistaken!

The wines from the Savoie region represent one of the smallest wine productions in France. This region encompasses four departments: Savoie, Isère, Haute-Savoie, and Ain. Its products consist of both red wine varieties—Gamay, Mondeuse, Pinot Noir, Persan, Cabernet Franc, and Cabernet Sauvignon—and white wine varieties—Aligoté, Altesse, Jacquère, Chardonnay, Veltliner Rouge Précoce, Mondeuse Blanche, Gringet, Roussette d'Ayze, and Chasselas.

This large number of grape varieties, a rich soil, and the sunny mountain hillsides provide a good winegrower with a rich palette from which to successfully make a fine wine. You just have to visit the cellars, seek out the vintners, and, above all, taste the wines to discover some truly wonderful things among the 22 *crus* (high-quality growths) offered in the Savoie.

LEFT
savoie-style
fondue

RIGHT
potato gratin
with
reblochon
cheese

fondue savoyarde

SAVOIE-STYLE FONDUE
SERVES 6 - PREPARATION TIME: 20 MINUTES
COOKING TIME: 20 MINUTES

Emmental cheese	10 ounces
Comté cheese	10 ounces
Beaufort cheese	10 ounces
Garlic	2 cloves
Savoie white wine	1¾ cups
Kirsch	2½ tablespoons
Potato starch	1 teaspoon
Eggs	2
Stale baguettes	2

1. Cut up the baguettes for dipping. Rub your fondue pot with some of the garlic, chop the rest, and throw it in. Cut the cheeses into small cubes.
2. Add the wine to the pot and place it on the burner. Bring to a boil and gradully stir in the cheese with a wooden spoon.
3. Blend the potato starch wth the Kirsch and add to the pot.
4. When the pot is almost empty, break two eggs into the bottom and let them cook, stirring often.

WINE: APREMONT OR CHIGNIN BERGERON

tartiflette

POTATO GRATIN WITH REBLOCHON CHEESE
SERVES 6 - PREPARATION TIME: 20 MINUTES
COOKING TIME: 45 MINUTES

Reblochon cheese	1
Potatoes	2 pounds 4 ounces
Onions	5
Grated nutmeg	1 pinch
Heavy cream	1¼ cups
Olive oil	
Salt, pepper	

1. Peel the potatoes and slice them thinly. Then boil them in a large quantity of salted water until barely cooked, keeping them firm.
2. Slice the onions thinly and soften them in olive oil.
3. In a gratin dish, place alternate layers of potato and onions. Season with salt, pepper, and nutmeg; then pour the cream on top.
4. Cut the Reblochon cheese, with its rind, into thin slices and cover the gratin with them. Bake in a 350°F oven for 30 minutes.

WINE: MONDEUSE

picodon rôti au lard

PICODON CHEESES ROASTED WITH BACON
SERVES 6 - PREPARATION TIME: 15 MINUTES
COOKING TIME: 10 MINUTES

Picodon cheeses (small round goat's cheese)	6
Bacon slices	12
Rosemary	6 sprigs
Olive oil	
Cracked pepper	

1. Lay out two slices of bacon in a cross shape. Place a goat's cheese in the middle and season with pepper. Fold the bacon slices over the cheese and pierce with a sprig of rosemary to hold them in place. Repeat to make six parcels.
2. Brush them lightly with oil, place them in a baking dish, and bake in a 400°F oven for 10 minutes.

WINE: SAINT-JOSEPH RED

LES OUTILS
THE TOOLS

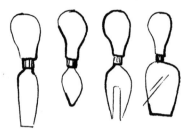

Set of cheese knives

Cheese lyre

Cheese
knife

Cheese
plane

Wire cheese slicer

Cheese grater

Girolle cheese scraper

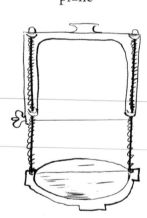

Cheese guillotine

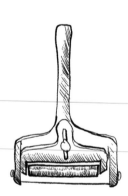

Adjustable cheese slicer

Trap with Gruyère

Melon-baller for making holes

LA DÉCOUPE
THE CARVE-UP

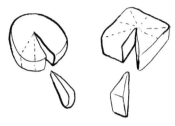

Camembert, Pont-l'Évêque...

Valençay, Pouligny-St-Pierre...

Comté, Ossau-Iraty...

Blue cheeses, Roquefort...

Sainte-Maure, Rouleau de Provence...

Cabécou, small chèvre cheeses...

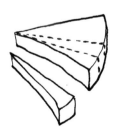

Brie or Coulommiers...

Vacherin or Époisses...

Babybel

Song from my
Saint-Agrève homeland

Music: "La Mazurka sous les pins" (a Provençal dance)
Lyrics to this tune written by Father Xavier Belin

Du grand bel vé dè re qu'est le mont Chi niac On voit St A-

grè ve tout près de son lac. Les gran des prai ri es lui font un ta-

pis. De plan tes fleu ri es comme en pa ra dis. Mon pa ys de St A-

grè ve est le plus jo li can ton. On s'y re pose on y re ve. Quand

vient la bel le sai son mon pa ys de St A grè ve est le plus jo li can-

ton, on s'y re pose on y re ve quand vient la bel le sai son.

Verse nº 1	Verse nº 2	Verse nº 3
Du grand belvédère	*Ses terres fertiles,*	*Nous avons encore*
Qu'est le Mont Chiniac	*Allez cultiver,*	*De grandes forêts*
On voit Saint-Agrève,	*Paysans habiles*	*De sapins sonores*
Tout près de son lac.	*À les exploiter*	*Avec des genets.*
Les grandes prairies,	*Car la providence*	*La petite airelle*
Lui font un tapis,	*A fait ses lieux*	*Le beau framboisier,*
De plantes fleuries	*Grenier d'abaondance*	*Et l'humble prunelle,*
Comme en paradis	*Et le soleil radieux.*	*Le fruit du hallier.*

Verse nº 4	Verse nº 5	Chorus
Quand le dur nivose	*Si la canicule*	*Mon pays de Saint-Agrève*
Prend son manteau blanc,	*Vous fait éponger,*	*Est le plus joli canton*
Dans la maison close	*Allez sans scrupule*	*On s'y repose, on y rêve*
Nos membres tremblants,	*Vous revigorer*	*Quand vient la belle saison*
Retrouvent la vie	*Au pays du rêve*	*Mon pays de Saint-Agrève*
Près d'un feu ardent,	*Où l'air est si pur,*	*Est le plus joli canton,*
Quelle poésie !	*J'ai dit : Saint-Agrève,*	*On s'y repose, on y rêve*
Quel charme prenant.	*Le conseil est sur.*	*Quand vient la belle saison.*

LE BOCUSE D'OR

The *Bocuse d'Or* today represents the World Cup of gastronomy. It is a veritable culinary jousting match colored by a South American-style fervor that the happy finalists will experience. (The stadiums are worthy of the greatest sporting competitions). Every other year since 1987, Paul Bocuse, the founder of the event and president of the competition, has announced the much-anticipated list of medal winners of this trench warfare.

	Gold medal	Silver medal	Bronze medal
2007	Fabrice Desvignes (France)	Ramsus Kofoed (Denmark)	Frank Giovannini (Switzerland)
2005	Serge Vierra (France)	Tom Victor Gausdal (Norway)	Ramsus Kofoed (Denmark)
2003	Charles Tjessem (Norway)	Franck Putelat (France)	Claus Weitbrecht (Germany)
2001	François Adamski (France)	Henrik Norström (Sweden)	Hakon Mar Orvarsson (Iceland)
1999	Terje Ness (Norway)	Yannick Alleno (France)	Ferdy Debecker (Belgium)
1997	Mathias Dalhgren (Sweden)	Roland Debuyst (Belgium)	Odd Ivar Solvold (Norway)
1995	Régis Marcon (France)	Melker Andersson (Sweden)	Patrick Jaros (Germany)
1993	Bent Stiansen (Norway)	Jens Peter Kolbelck (Denmark)	Guy Van Cauteren (Belgium)
1991	Michel Roth (France)	Lars Erik Underthun (Norway)	Gert Jan Raven (Netherlands)
1989	Léa Linster (Luxembourg)	Pierre Paulus (Belgium)	William Wai (Singapore)
1987	Jacky Fréon (France)	Michel Addons (Belgium)	Hans Hass (Germany)

Marcel and Marie-Cécile

COW-TOW

Eighty cows to be milked morning and evening, eighty cows to take out as soon as the grass allows, eighty cows to bring in again as soon as evening falls, eighty cows demanding constant attention—servicing, calving, feeding, hay to cut and store, barns to clean. Huff and puff, take a breather, start again. Endless days dictated by the rhythm of the seasons and the agonies of bad weather. These are the parameters that every day transform milk production into a feat of human prowess.

Marcel and Marie-Cécile have chosen to live and breathe milk, and, believe me, it's not easy! No time for vacation, no room for free time: farmers are always working; they are inseparable from their animals. It's something to see—expert observers talking endlessly about Royale, the gentle one; Tartine, the stubborn one; Salade, the greedy one. Eighty cows, eighty first names, and so much proof of their love. The cows

are named because they are beings in their own right; they're not simply cash cows, but part of the family. You don't want to run into Marie-Cécile or Marcel when one of the animals unfortunately meets its end—the farm is in mourning, smiles are put away, and it's a time for remembrance.

For Marcel and Marie-Cécile, cows are their passion, their reason for living, and milk their mode of existence. But it so happens that nowadays they are also making their debut as pig farmers, bringing up Howard the pig, the newest arrival on the farm. Howard lives next door to the deluxe hen house, proud of his new family, and so close to it that each day the inevitable mutation into sausages and hams, the usual lot of his fellow creatures, becomes a more distant prospect. Careful, lovers of cows, poultry, and pigs, your farm may soon be X-rated!

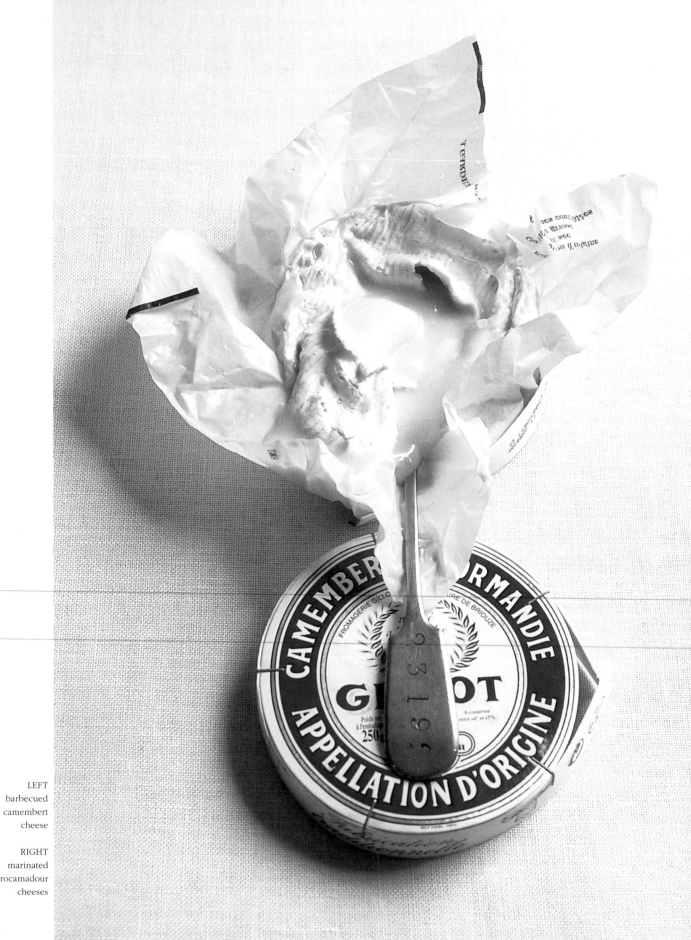

camembert au barbecue

BARBECUED CAMEMBERT CHEESE
SERVES 6 - PREPARATION TIME: 30 MINUTES
COOKING TIME: 8 MINUTES + 30 MINUTES SOAKING TIME

Camembert cheeses..2

1. Take the cheeses out of their wooden boxes and soak the boxes in salted water for 30 minutes.
2. Put the cheeses back in the boxes, wrap them in foil, and place them on hot barbecue coals for 8 minutes.
3. Serve with a spoon.

WINE: A GOOD RED (CAMEMBERT TRANSFORMS
ALL RED WINES INTO VERITABLE NECTARS!)

rocamadours marinés

MARINATED ROCAMADOUR CHEESES
SERVES 6 - PREPARATION TIME: 10 MINUTES
MARINATING TIME: 2 DAYS

Rocamadour cheeses (small goat's cheeses)......................................12
Garlic.. 2 cloves
Bay leaf...1
Thyme ....2 sprigs
Juniper berries 8
Olive oil

1. Place the cheeses in a jar with the herbs and spices.
Fill the jar with olive oil and leave to marinate for 2 days before eating.

WINE: PULIGNY-MONTRACHET

terrine de roquefort

ROQUEFORT CHEESE TERRINE
SERVES 6 - PREPARATION TIME: 20 MINUTES
REFRIGERATION TIME: 24 HOURS

Roquefort cheese..................................... 1 pound 2 ounces
Butter...¾ cup
Celery stalks...3
Sea salt

1. Finely chop the celery, and combine with the butter and some sea salt.
2. Line the inside of a terrine with plastic wrap. Crush half of the cheese with a fork and press it onto the base of the terrine. Spread the celery butter on top and cover with the remaining Roquefort.
3. Cover the top of the terrine with plastic wrap. Chill for 24 hours and cut into slices before serving.

WINE: BANYULS

BREADS

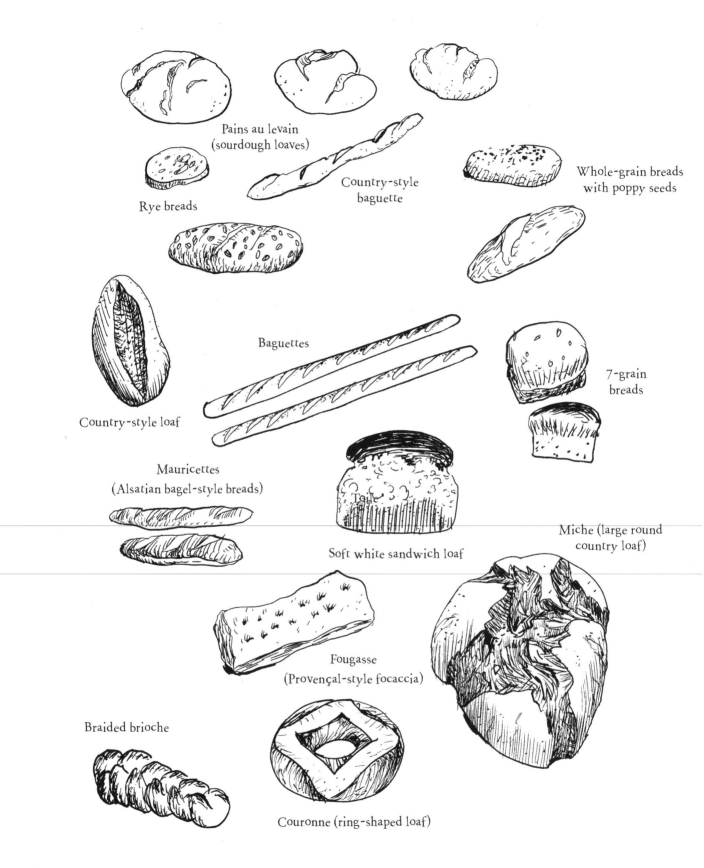

Pains au levain
(sourdough loaves)

Rye breads

Country-style
baguette

Whole-grain breads
with poppy seeds

Baguettes

Country-style loaf

7-grain
breads

Mauricettes
(Alsatian bagel-style breads)

Toast

Miche (large round
country loaf)

Soft white sandwich loaf

Fougasse
(Provençal-style focaccia)

Braided brioche

Couronne (ring-shaped loaf)

FLOURS

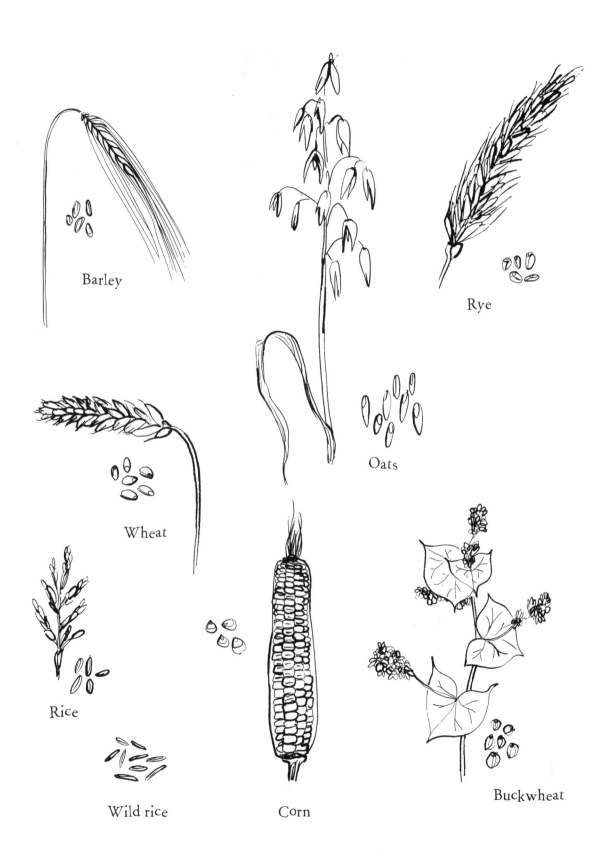

Barley

Oats

Rye

Wheat

Rice

Wild rice

Corn

Buckwheat

399

Olivier

SEXY BAKER

First the kilt, now the apron! It's easy to use the excuse of the bakery heat to flaunt a little maid's apron just long enough or a tad too short to draw the customer's eyes and the eyes of Marie-Jo, already conquered.

No, Olivier, you don't need to resort to this sort of contrivance to empty the pockets of enlightened lovers of good bread and lovely buns.

It's an easy analogy, but so delicious! The news is that hemlines are high in bakery fashion this year! 100°F near the oven, prematurely gray hair, dusted with Type 55 flour, going to bed too late and getting up too early to ensure the perfect crust on a good dough: this is the life of the baker. And today you continue this tradition with a real labor-intensive sourdough, risen to perfection. The shop is lit up at midnight, the T-shirt always white so that you melt into a David Hamilton-like ambience (especially the floury blur and torrid aspect). Bread is not simply nourishment; it exists for its own sake. We could almost say that we cook because of bread, rather than the other way around!

Les cannelés
d'HÉLÈNE
Hélène's cannelés

CHAMPAGNE!

Le roulage des croissants et des
pains au chocolat
Rolling out croissants and chocolate bread

COGNAC
ET ARMAGNAC
COGNAC AND ARMAGNAC

LA TAILLE DES CIGARES
CIGAR SIZES

SUCRE
SUCRÉ
SUCRETTE...

sweet, sweeter, saccharine...

croissants & pains au chocolat

The basic recipe is the same, but can be put together in different ways.

FOR A LARGE FAMILY - PREPARATION TIME: 3 HOURS 30 MINUTES
(INCLUDING RESTING TIME)
COOKING TIME: 15 MINUTES

Bread flour	2 pounds 4 ounces
Salt	2 tablespoons
Sugar	⅔ cup
Yeast	1½ ounces
Water	2¼ cups
Butter	1 pound 5 ounces

Bar of bittersweet chocolate
Egg yolk for brushing

1. Knead the flour, salt, sugar, yeast, and water together for 10 minutes to obtain a smooth dough. Roll the dough into a rectangle, place the butter in the middle, then fold the sides over to enclose the butter. Chill for 30 minutes.
2. As for flaky pastry (see page 408), give the dough two turns: roll the chilled dough into a strip, fold it in three, turn it 90 degrees, roll it out again and fold in three. Chill for another hour, and give it another turn. This process of rolling and folding creates the flaky pastry dough known as *pâte feuilletée* (puff pastry).
3. Roll the dough into the desired shape (croissant or *pain au chocolat*) and leave at room temperature for 2 hours. Add a bar of chocolate if required, brush with the egg yolk, and bake for 15 minutes in a preheated 315°F oven.

MAKING PAIN AU CHOCOLAT

1 Roll out the dough into a large rectangle shape and cut it into smaller rectangles.

2 Place the chocolate on top.

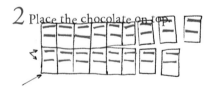

3 Roll the dough back on itself.

Et voilà !

brioche

FOR SEVERAL BRIOCHE - PREPARATION TIME: 45 MINUTES
REFRIGERATION TIME: 12 HOURS
COOKING TIME: ABOUT 20 MINUTES + 13 HOURS RESTING TIME

Bread flour	2 pounds 4 ounces
Sugar	⅔ cup
Salt	2 tablespoons
Yeast	1½ ounces
Butter	1 pound 2 ounces
Eggs	10

Egg yolk for brushing

1. Knead the flour, sugar, salt, and yeast together to obtain a smooth dough. Add the butter and knead until completely incorporated. Chill the dough for 1 hour in the refrigerator.
2. Give the dough a very gentle "folding" knead and chill for a further 12 hours.
3. Divide the brioche dough into the desired shapes and add whatever you like—for example, praline, chocolate, sugar.
4. Allow the brioche to rise at room temperature. Brush each one with beaten egg yolk and bake in a preheated 300°F oven until done. The actual cooking time depends on the size of the brioches.

tresse aux amandes

BRAIDED ALMOND BRIOCHE
FOR SEVERAL PLAITS - PREPARATION TIME: 45 MINUTES
REFRIGERATION TIME: 12 HOURS
COOKING TIME: ABOUT 20 MINUTES

Butter	¾ cup
Sugar	1 cup
Ground almonds	2 cups
Eggs	2

Egg yolk for brushing

1. Melt the butter and combine with the sugar and ground almonds. Add the eggs and mix together to create an almond cream.
2. Divide some brioche dough (see above) into three identically sized sausages. Form them into a braid and cover the intersections with the almond cream.
3. Allow to rise at room temperature. Brush with a beaten egg yolk and bake, as in the recipe for brioche.

LE ROULAGE DES CROISSANTS
ROLLING OUT CROISSANTS

1 Roll out the dough to make a large rectangle.

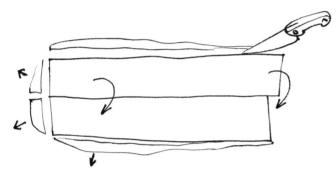

2 Trim any uneven edges; divide the rectangle in two.

3 Place the two rectangles on top of each other.

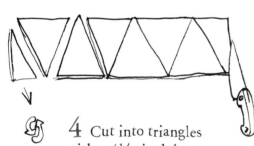

4 Cut into triangles with a 4½-inch base.

5 Make a light incision (½-inch long) in the base of each triangle.

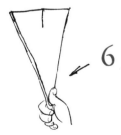

6 7

Roll up the croissants.
Be careful not to roll the dough too tightly.

Et voilà !

CHAMPAGNE!

Half bottle
in case of emergency

Bottle
an essential fridge ingredient

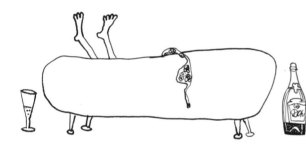

Magnum
(2 bottles) for a romantic evening

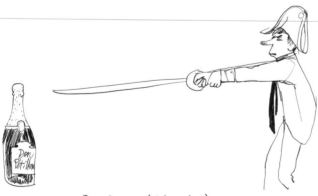

Jeroboam (4 bottles)
for showing off between friends

Salmanazar (12 bottles)
raise the roof!

Balthazar (16 bottles)
if you ever win a Formula 1 Grand Prix

Methuselah (8 bottles)
for Nanna's 80th

Nebuchadnezzar (20 bottles)
as long as it's not corked!

les pâtes à tartes

THE TART PASTRIES

PÂTE SABLÉE/RICH SWEET SHORT-CRUST PASTRY (FOR 1 TART)

All-purpose flour ....2 cups
Ground almonds...½ cup
Butter...½ cup
Superfine sugar... ⅓ cup
Egg 1

1. Mix the softened butter with the sugar and ground almonds; then add the sifted flour little by little.
2. Add the egg to obtain a very smooth dough (add a little water if the dough is too dry). Chill before using.

PÂTE BRISÉE/SHORT-CRUST PASTRY (FOR 1 TART)

All-purpose flour ....2 cups
Butter...½ cup
Egg 1
Heavy cream..2½ tablespoons

1. Sift the flour, make a hollow in the middle, and add the egg, cream, and the softened butter.
2. Knead the mixture together, pushing down hard with the palm of your hand to completely incorporate the flour. Add a little water if necessary.

PÂTE FEUILLETÉE/PUFF PASTRY
(FOR 3 TARTS, CAN BE FROZEN)

All-purpose flour .... 1 pound 2 ounces
Butter..1⅔ cups
Confectioners' sugar

1. Mix the flour with ½ to ⅔ cups of water and 3 tablespoons of the softened butter to make a pliable dough.
2. Knead the remaining butter until it gives up all of its moisture content.
3. Roll the dough into a square ½-inch thick. Roll out the butter into a square shape and place it in the center of the dough, known as the *détrempe*. Fold up the dough like a wallet, enclosing the butter.
4. Roll the dough into a rectangular shape and fold it in three. Chill for 30 minutes and repeat the process in the opposite direction. Do this three times. For a sweet flaky pastry, dust with confectioners' sugar each time you roll out the dough. This process of rolling and folding produces the multilayer flaky, pastry dough known as *pâte feuilletée* (puff pastry).

tarte tatin

UPSIDE-DOWN APPLE TART
FOR 6 - PREPARATION TIME: 30 MINUTES
COOKING TIME: 45 MINUTES

Flaky pastry ....9 ounces
Reine des reinettes (Golden Delicious) apples....................................8
Butter..3 tablespoons
Superfine sugar...½ cup

1. In a pie dish, melt the butter, add sugar, and caramelize on top of the stove.
2. Peel the apples, cut them in two, and remove the core.
3. Arrange the apples in a pie dish, packing them together tightly. Dust with the sugar.
4. Bake in a preheated 350°F oven for 20 minutes. Roll out the flaky pastry to make a pie lid, and place it over the apples. Bake for an additional 20 minutes. Unmold while still hot.

PEAR
Use the same method as in the apple version; just add some almonds to the pears.

BANANA AND PINEAPPLE
After making the caramel, arrange the fruit in the pie dish and cover with the pastry before baking for 20 minutes.

QUINCE
Cook the quinces for 15 minutes in water along with the juice of a lemon; then proceed as in the apple version.

LEFT
alsatian
apple tart

RIGHT
thin french
apple tart

tarte aux pommes alsacienne

ALSATIAN APPLE TART
FOR 6 - PREPARATION TIME: 20 MINUTES
COOKING TIME: 30 MINUTES

Short-crust pastry (see page 408) ....9 ounces
Granny Smith apples 6
Heavy cream ....¾ cup
Milk ....⅓ to ½ cup
Light brown sugar ....½ cup
Vanilla bean 1
Eggs 3

1. Peel the apples, cut into quarters, and core them. Lay out the pastry in a deep pie dish.
2. Whisk the eggs with the cream and milk before whisking in the sugar and vanilla. Pour this mixture over the tart and bake in a preheated 350°F oven for 30 minutes. Don't eat the vanilla bean.

tarte fine aux pommes

THIN FRENCH APPLE TART
FOR 6 - PREPARATION TIME: 30 MINUTES
COOKING TIME: 20 MINUTES

Flaky pastry (see page 408) ....9 ounces
Apples 5
Couscous ....1 tablespoon
Superfine sugar ....½ cup
Butter ....2½ tablespoons

1. Roll out the pastry over ¼ cup of the superfine sugar. Place on a sheet of parchment paper. Prick the pastry with a fork and sprinkle the couscous over the top (it will absorb the juice of the apples).
2. Peel the apples, cut them in half, and remove the cores. Slice the apples very thinly and arrange in a rosette pattern over the pastry.
3. Melt the butter and brush the tart to glaze. Sprinkle with the remaining sugar and bake in a preheated 350°F oven for 20 minutes.

tarte Linzer

LINZER TORTE (JAM TART)
FOR 6 - PREPARATION TIME: 30 MINUTES
COOKING TIME: 20 MINUTES

Rich sweet short-crust pastry (see page 408) ....7 ounces
Ground almonds ....½ cup
Ground cinnamon ....1 tablespoon
Raspberry jam (with seeds) ....⅓ cup

1. Mix the pastry dough with the cinnamon and almonds.
2. Roll out two-thirds of the dough to form a tart base and cover with the raspberry jam.
3. Roll out the remaining dough, cut into strips ½-inch wide, and spread them over the tart in a lattice pattern.
4. Bake in a preheated 350°F oven for 20 minutes; the jam will lightly caramelize.

tarte aux figues

FIG TART
FOR 6 - PREPARATION TIME: 30 MINUTES
COOKING TIME: 30 MINUTES

Flaky pastry (see page 408) ....9 ounces
Fresh figs 10
Ground almonds ....1 cup
Butter ....⅓ cup
Sugar ....½ cup
Egg 1
Sliced almonds ....½ cup

1. Roll out the pastry into a rectangle shape.
2. Melt the butter, mix with the sugar and ground almonds, and add the egg. Spread this cream on top of the pastry.
3. Cut the figs in half, arrange them on the tart base, and sprinkle a few sliced almonds on top.
4. Bake in a preheated 350°F oven for 30 minutes.

tarte aux pralines

PRALINE CREAM TART
FOR 6 - PREPARATION TIME: 15 MINUTES -
COOKING TIME: 15 MINUTES

Rich sweet short-crust pastry (see page 408) ....9 ounces
Pralines rouges (French candied almonds) ....3½ ounces
Heavy cream ....⅓ to ½ cup

1. Roll out the pastry thinly and lay it in a tart pan lined with parchment paper. Bake in a preheated 350°F oven for 15 minutes.
2. Melt the candied almonds in the cream: all the sugar must melt into the cream, leaving only the almonds.
3. Spread this praline cream on top of the pastry; then refrigerate to allow the cream to set.

LEFT
blueberry (or
blackberry)
almond tart

RIGHT
lemon
meringue pie

414

tarte myrtilles et amandes

BLUEBERRY (OR BLACKBERRY) ALMOND TART
FOR 6 - PREPARATION TIME: 20 MINUTES
COOKING TIME: 30 MINUTES

Rich sweet short-crust pastry (see page 408) ....7 ounces
Blueberries (or blackberries) ....1½ cups
Butter...⅓ cup
Sugar...½ cup
Almonds...⅓ cup
Hazelnuts...⅓ cup
Eggs...2
Sliced almonds..⅔ cup

1. Roll out the pastry and lay it in a tart pan.
2. Process the almonds and hazelnuts with the sugar. Stir in the melted butter and mix in the eggs. Add the berries, and mix together gently.
3. Pour the filling into the tart base and sprinkle the sliced almonds over the top. Bake in a preheated 350°F oven for 30 minutes.

tarte citron meringuée

LEMON MERINGUE PIE
FOR 6 - PREPARATION TIME: 30 MINUTES
COOKING TIME: 30 MINUTES + 1 HOUR RESTING TIME

Rich sweet short-crust pastry (see page 408) ....7 ounces
Lemons...3
Superfine sugar... 1 cup
Butter..⅓ cup
Cornstarch ....1½ tablespoons
Eggs..3
Egg whites 3

1. Roll out the short-crust pastry and fit it into a round pie pan. Bake in a preheated 350°F oven for 30 minutes.
2. Meanwhile, remove the zest from one of the lemons, and juice all the lemons. Melt the butter with the lemon juice, lemon zest, and ⅔ cup of the sugar. Cook for 5 minutes.
3. Remove the pan from the heat. Blend the cornstarch and eggs, and stir into the butter mixture. Cover the tart base with the lemon curd and chill for 1 hour.
4. Beat the egg whites into stiff peaks, and beat in the remaining sugar to stabilize them. Using a piping bag, top the pie with the egg-white meringue, swirling it into peaks. Place the pie under a hot broiler for 1 minute to brown the meringue.

tarte au chocolat

CHOCOLATE TART
FOR 6 - PREPARATION TIME: 15 MINUTES
COOKING TIME: 30 MINUTES + 30 MINUTES RESTING TIME

Rich sweet short-crust pastry (see page 408) ....7 ounces
Ground hazelnuts..½ cup
Dark chocolate ....5 ounces
Butter..¼ cup
Heavy cream.. 1 cup
Whiskey ....1 tablespoon

1. Roll out the pastry and fit it into a round tart pan. Sprinkle the ground hazelnuts on top and bake in a preheated 350°F oven for 30 minutes.
2. Melt the chocolate with the cream, butter, and whiskey. Fill the pastry shell with this mixture and chill for at least 30 minutes before serving.

LEFT
linzer cookie

RIGHT
epiphany
pastry cake
with
frangipane

418

cyclope

LINZER COOKIES
FOR 6 - PREPARATION TIME: 20 MINUTES
COOKING TIME: 30 MINUTES

Rich sweet short-crust pastry (see page 408) .... 1 pound 2 ounces
Your choice of jam .... ⅓ cup
Confectioners' sugar .... ¾ cup

1. Roll out the pastry. Cut out circles using a cookie cutter.
Cut out a smaller circle in half of the pastry rounds so that
they're left with a hole in the middle. Bake all the rounds in
a preheated 350°F oven for 30 minutes.
2. Place some jam on the whole pastry rounds. Dust the
other rounds (the ones with a hole in the middle) with
confectioners' sugar and place them on top of the whole
rounds.

galette Des rois

EPIPHANY PASTRY CAKE WITH FRANGIPANE
FOR 6 - PREPARATION TIME: 20 MINUTES
COOKING TIME: 30 MINUTES

Flaky pastry (see page 408) .... 14 ounces
Blanched almonds .... 1 cup
Superfine sugar .... ⅔ cup
Eggs 2
Butter .... ⅔ cup
Almond extract .... a few drops
Egg yolk 1

1. Make an almond cream by processing the almonds with
the sugar. Mix in the butter, eggs, and almond extract.
2. Roll out the pastry into two circles. Spread one of them
with the almond cream, leaving a ½-inch margin around the
edge. Brush the edge with beaten egg yolk, then cover and
seal with the second pastry circle.
3. Using the point of a knife, trace a rosette pattern on top.
Brush with egg yolk and bake in a preheated 350°F oven
for 30 minutes.

meringues

FOR A MERINGUE PARTY
PREPARATION TIME: 10 MINUTES
COOKING TIME: 2 HOURS MINIMUM

Egg whites .... 7 ounces
Superfine sugar .... 1 cup
Confectioners' sugar .... 1⅔ cups

1. Beat the egg whites into stiff peaks using an electric mixer.
Add the superfine sugar and let the mixer run for 5 minutes.
Gently fold in the confectioners' sugar.
2. Shape the meringues however you like, place on a baking
sheet, and bake in a preheated 200°F oven for 2 hours;
depending on the shape and size of your meringues, you
may need to cook them a little longer. They should be
completely dry.

LEFT
cannelés

RIGHT
almond tuiles

cannelés

CANNELÉS
FOR ABOUT 50 CANNELÉS - PREPARATION TIME: 15 MINUTES
COOKING TIME: 1 HOUR + 24 HOURS REFRIGERATION TIME

Milk ....4 cups
Superfine sugar..2¼ cups
Butter.. ⅓ cup
Vanilla bean 1
Egg yolks...4
Rum ....⅓ to ½ cup
All-purpose flour ....2½ cups

1. Heat the milk with the vanilla bean, and melt the butter
into this mixture. Remove from the heat, add the egg yolks,
and mix well. Stir in the sifted flour, sugar, and rum; then
chill for 24 hours. Remove the vanilla bean.
2. Using silicone *cannelé* molds if available, fill two-thirds of
each mold with the chilled milk mixture.
3. Bake in a preheated 400°F oven for 30–45 minutes: the
cannelés are done when they are well caramelized. Unmold
immediately after baking.

tuiles aux amandes

ALMOND TUILES
FOR 20 TUILES - PREPARATION TIME: 10 MINUTES
COOKING TIME: 5 MINUTES

Egg whites 2
All-purpose flour ....¼ cup
Superfine sugar..¼ cup
Butter..2½ tablespoons
Sliced almonds..½ cup

1. Beat the egg whites with the sugar until stiff. Add the
melted butter and flour.
2. Drop spoonfuls of the mixture onto a baking sheet lined
with parchment paper. Sprinkle the sliced almonds on top
and bake in a preheated 400°F oven for 5 minutes.
3. Remove the *tuiles* from the oven and quickly drape them
over a rolling pin to shape them; be gentle since they are
very fragile.

tuiles à l'orange

ORANGE TUILES
FOR 20 TUILES - PREPARATION TIME: 10 MINUTES
COOKING TIME: 10 MINUTES

Superfine sugar...½ cup
All-purpose flour ....⅓ cup
Orange juice ....3½ fluid ounces
Orange 1
Butter...⅓ cup
Ground almonds..⅓ cup

1. Melt the butter and zest the orange. Mix together all of the
ingredients.
2. Drop spoonfuls of the mixture onto a baking sheet lined
with parchment paper. Bake in a preheated 400°F oven for
10 minutes.
3. Remove the *tuiles* from the oven and quickly drape
them over a rolling pin to shape them—be gentle as they
are very fragile.

Hélène

CANNELÉ IN THE BORDELÉ

The *cannelé*, a miniature sweet pudding and specialty of Bordeaux, is one of the safe bets of the Bordeaux cuisine. When it is made by a winegrower, it has an extra little *je ne sais quoi*—indefinable but precious. Is it the setting, a château in the Graves, that enhances the experience of eating a *cannelé?* Or is it the Graves wine tasted at the château that heightens this experience? Any way you look at it, Hélène's *cannelés* are, from every angle, caramel-crisp outside, creamy inside, and Graves all around.

425

MIGNARDISES

sablés cacao

COCOA SHORTBREAD FINGERS
MAKES 30
PREPARATION TIME: 10 MINUTES
COOKING TIME: 10 MINUTES

Rich sweet short-crust pastry
(see page 408) .... 10 ounces
Cocoa powder .... 2 tablespoons
Chopped dark chocolate..................... ⅓ cup

1. Mix the cocoa powder with the
pastry dough and add the chocolate.
2. Roll out the dough and cut into
small rectangles.
3. Arrange on a baking sheet lined with
parchment paper; then chill.
4. Bake in a preheated 350°F oven for
10 minutes.

mendiants

FRUIT AND NUT CHOCOLATE DISCS
MAKES 30
PREPARATION TIME: 15 MINUTES

Dark chocolate .... 10 ounces
Butter.. ½ cup
Candied orange peel.......................30 pieces
Pistachio nuts.. 30
Whole almonds.. 30
Whole hazelnuts... 30

1. Melt the chocolate and the butter in
a double-boiler. Drop small spoonfuls
of the mixture onto a baking sheet
lined with parchment paper.
2. Top each disc with a hazelnut,
pistachio nut, almond, and piece of
orange peel. Chill until set.

sacristains

SWEET PASTRY TWISTS
MAKES 30
PREPARATION TIME: 20 MINUTES
COOKING TIME: 15 MINUTES

Flaky pastry (see page 408)............ 7 ounces
Egg yolks.. 2
Superfine sugar.. ½ cup

1. Roll out the pastry, dusting both
sides with the sugar.
2. Brush with the beaten egg yolks and
dust again with the sugar.
3. Cut into thin strips, and twist each
strip into a coil.
4. Bake in a preheated 315°F oven for
15 minutes.

sablés cannelle

CINNAMON SHORTBREAD BISCUITS
MAKES 30
PREPARATION TIME: 10 MINUTES
COOKING TIME: 10 MINUTES

Rich sweet short-crust pastry
(see page 408) .... 10 ounces
Ground cinnamon ....1 tablespoon
Ground almonds........................1 tablespoon
Whole hazelnuts... 30

1. Combine the cinnamon and almonds
with the pastry dough.
2. Roll out the dough, cut out whatever
shapes take your fancy, and top each
one with a whole hazelnut.
3. Bake in a preheated 350°F oven for
10 minutes.

macarons

MACAROONS
MAKES 30
PREPARATION TIME: 15 MINUTES
COOKING TIME: 15 MINUTES +
10 MINUTES DRYING TIME

Confectioners' sugar ....1¾ cups
Ground almonds.................................1¼ cups
Egg whites ....3½ ounces

1. Mix together the sugar and ground
almonds. Sift the mixture.
2. Beat the egg whites into stiff peaks
and carefully incorporate the sugar-
almond mixture with a rubber spatula.
3. Pipe mounds of identical size onto a
baking sheet lined with parchment
paper. Allow to dry for 10 minutes.
4. Bake in a preheated 315°F oven for
15 minutes. Sandwich together with a
filling of your choice.

madeleines

MINIATURE BUTTER CAKES
MAKES 30
PREPARATION TIME: 10 MINUTES
COOKING TIME: 10 MINUTES +
30 MINUTES RESTING TIME

Eggs...2
All purpose-flour ....1¼ cups
Sugar ....⅔ cup
Butter...½ cup
Vanilla ....1 teaspoon
Yeast...½ sachet
Lemon 1

1. Whisk the eggs with the sugar and
vanilla until the mixture becomes pale
and thick.
2. Add the melted butter, then the flour,
yeast, and zest from a lemon. Fill
two-thirds of each small cake mold.
3. Allow to rest for 30 minutes.
4. Bake in a preheated 400°F oven for
for about 10 minutes.

LEFT
chantilly
cream pastries

RIGHT
paris-brest

428

pâte à choux

CHOUX PASTRY

All-purpose flour	1 pound 2 ounces
Butter	1 cup
Eggs	4

1. Heat ½ cup of water with the butter. Bring to a boil, add the flour all at once, and stir until the mixture detaches from the side of the saucepan.
2. Mix in the eggs one at a time. Rest for 30 minutes before using.

choux chantilly

CHANTILLY CREAM PASTRIES
FOR 10 PASTRIES - PREPARATION TIME: 30 MINUTES
COOKING TIME: 30 MINUTES

Choux pastry	7 ounces
Egg yolks	2
Heavy cream	4 cups
Superfine sugar	1 cup
Confectioners' sugar	½ cup

1. Using a piping bag, pipe about 20 mounds of *choux* pastry onto a baking sheet lined with parchment paper. Brush them with the beaten egg yolks.
2. Bake in a preheated 350°F oven for 20 minutes; then slightly open the oven door and cook for an additional 10 minutes. Allow to cool.
3. Whip the cream into a firm Chantilly; the consistency should be almost buttery. Gently fold in the superfine sugar.
4. Fill the *choux* pastries generously with the Chantilly cream and dust with confectioners' sugar.

paris-brest

PARIS-BREST
FOR 6 - PREPARATION TIME: 30 MINUTES
COOKING TIME: 30 MINUTES

Choux pastry	14 ounces
Pastry cream (see page 456)	10 ounces
Praline (confection of almonds and caramelized sugar)	3½ ounces
Butter	⅓ cup
Sliced almonds	½ cup
Egg yolk	1
Confectioners' sugar	

1. Using a piping bag, prepare a good-sized ring of *choux* pastry on a baking sheet lined with parchment paper. Brush with beaten egg yolk and sprinkle the sliced almonds on top.
2. Bake in a preheated 350°F oven for 20 minutes; then open the oven door slightly and cook for an additional 10 minutes.
3. Combine the pastry cream with the praline and softened butter.
4. Slice the *choux* pastry ring in half horizontally. Spread the bottom half generously with the praline cream, top with the other pastry half, and dust with confectioners' sugar.

beignets confiture

JAM DOUGHNUTS
FOR 20 DOUGHNUTS
PREPARATION TIME: 20 MINUTES + 2 HOURS RESTING TIME
COOKING TIME: 5 MINUTES

All-purpose flour	1 pound 5 ounces
Yeast	2½ ounces
Eggs	5
Butter	⅓ cup
Sugar	¾ cup
Milk	⅓ to ½ cup
Orange-flower water	2½ tablespoons
Rum	2½ tablespoons
Oil for deep-frying	
Jam of your choice	
Sugar for dusting	

1. Heat the milk and blend in the yeast.
2. Sift the flour; then mix in the eggs, sugar, melted butter, milk mixture, rum, and orange-flower water. Let it rise for an hour in a warm (75°F) place.
3. Roll out the dough to ¾-inch thickness. Cut out rounds of about 4 inches in diameter and allow to rise again for an hour.
4. Deep-fry the doughnuts in oil at 315°F for 2–3 minutes on each side. Drain on paper towels and dust with sugar.
5. Fill the center of the doughnut with jam of your choice.

LEFT
chocolate,
coffee, and
vanilla eclairs

RIGHT
mille-feuille

432

éclairs chocolat, café, vanille

CHOCOLATE, COFFEE, AND VANILLA ECLAIRS
FOR 6 - PREPARATION TIME: 20 MINUTES
COOKING TIME: 30 MINUTES

Choux pastry (see page 430)	10 ounces
Pastry cream (see page 456)	14 ounces
Cocoa powder	½ cup
Espresso coffee	⅓ to ½ cup
Glacé icing	3½ ounces
Egg yolks	2

1. Using a pastry bag, pipe *choux* pastry shaped into eclairs onto a baking sheet lined with parchment paper. Brush them with the beaten egg yolks.
2. Bake in a preheated 350°F oven for 20 minutes; then open the oven door slightly and cook further for 10 minutes.
3. Divide the pastry cream into three portions. Gently heat two of them. Mix most of the cocoa powder into one warmed portion, and most of the coffee into the other; keep a little for mixing into the glacé icing.
4. Divide the glacé icing into three portions. Mix the remaining cocoa powder into one portion and the remaining coffee into another.
5. Cut the éclairs horizontally in two. Spread the bottom half of each éclair generously with one of the three types of pastry cream. Dip the tops in the corresponding glacé icing—plain, chocolate, or coffee—and place on top of the pastry cream.

mille-feuille

MILLE-FEUILLE
FOR 6 - PREPARATION TIME: 30 MINUTES
COOKING TIME: 20 MINUTES

Flaky pastry (see page 408)	1 pound 2 ounces
Pastry cream (see page 456)	14 ounces
Chantilly cream (see page 456)	7 ounces
Confectioners' sugar	¾ cup
Gelatin	3 leaves

1. Roll out the pastry into three identical rectangles and dust them with confectioners' sugar. Cover the rectangles with a sheet of parchment paper.
2. Bake between two racks placed ¾-inch apart in a preheated 350°F oven for 20 minutes (the pastry sheets must brown well).
3. Soak the gelatin leaves in cold water.
4. Heat the pastry cream to lukewarm. Add the squeezed gelatin sheets, mix well, and allow to cool. Mix together with the Chantilly cream and spoon into a pastry bag.
5. Pipe the mixture on two of the three pastry rectangles. Stack one rectangle on top of the other; top with the third pastry rectangle and dust again with confectioners' sugar.

saint-honoré

PROFITEROLE CAKE
FOR 6 - PREPARATION TIME: 45 MINUTES
COOKING TIME: 30 MINUTES

Choux pastry (see page 430)	14 ounces
Flaky pastry (see page 408)	5½ ounces
Pastry cream (see page 456)	10 ounces
Egg whites	4
Sugar	1⅓ cups

1. Roll out a circle of flaky pastry and prick it with a fork.
2. Make a ring of *choux* pastry and place it around the flaky pastry. Using a pastry bag also pipe 15 small *choux* mounds to cover the top of the cake.
3. Bake in a preheated 350°F oven for 20 minutes; then open the oven door slightly and cook for an additional 10 minutes.
4. Cook ⅔ cup of the sugar in a little water: dip a fork into the sugar; then into some cold water; when the sugar on the fork reaches the "soft ball" stage, stop the cooking process.
5. Beat the egg whites into stiff peaks, and add the sugar syrup little by little, beating all the time. Gently fold this mixture into the pastry cream. Spoon into a pastry bag with a pointed nozzle and pipe the cream into the *choux* pastries.
6. Prepare a caramel with the remaining sugar. Dip the *choux* pastries in the caramel and arrange them around the crown of the *choux* pastry ring. Fill the center with the rest of the pastry cream or with Chantilly (see p. 456) cream.

bugnes

LYON-STYLE PASTRY STICKS
(OR, HOW TO TRAP BUTTER INSIDE OIL!)

Bugnes are best when they haven't had to wait around
too long! They should be cooked just before the meal
if you want to have them for dessert.

FOR 6 - PREPARATION TIME: 30 MINUTES
COOKING TIME: 5 MINUTES + 6 HOURS RESTING TIME

All-purpose flour	1 pound 2 ounces
Salt	1 teaspoon
Baking powder	2½ teaspoons
Superfine sugar	⅓ cup
Eggs	4
Butter	¾ cup
Peanut oil	4 cups
Milk	2 tablespoons
Dark rum	2 tablespoons

Confectioners' sugar for dusting

1. Melt the butter in a small saucepan with milk, rum, and
1 tablespoon of peanut oil.
2. Mix the flour with the salt, baking powder, and sugar. Mix
in the eggs one at a time, and then the melted butter
mixture. Knead the dough until it detaches from the side of
the bowl; then leave it to rest for 6 hours in the refrigerator.
3. Roll out the dough thinly, and cut out into long sticks.
4. Heat the peanut oil, immerse the dough sticks, and wait
until they rise to the surface. Allow them to brown, turning
them over regularly. Dust with confectioners' sugar.

charlotte aux fraises

STRAWBERRY CHARLOTTE
FOR 6 - PREPARATION TIME: 30 MINUTES
RESTING TIME: 24 HOURS

Strawberries	2⅔ cups
Savoiardi (ladyfingers)	18
Pastry cream (see page 456)	9 ounces
Heavy cream	¾ cup
Superfine sugar	½ cup
Gelatin leaves	4

1. Hull the strawberries and slice half of them into quarters. Purée the rest and strain through a *chinois* (fine sieve).
2. Soak the gelatin leaves in cold water.
3. Gently heat the strawberry coulis and blend in the gelatin. Allow to cool at room temperature.
4. Whip the cream into a firm Chantilly (see page 456) and add the sugar.
5. Combine the strawberry coulis and pastry cream; then add the whipped cream and diced strawberries.
6. Line a charlotte mold with plastic wrap. Arrange the ladyfingers all around and fill with the strawberry cream. Chill for 24 hours before unmolding.

vacherin aux gariguettes

STRAWBERRY VACHERIN
FOR 6 - PREPARATION TIME: 15 MINUTES

Gariguette strawberries (or other very sweet ones)	4 cups
Meringues	6
Chantilly cream (see page 456)	10 ounces
Lemon	1
Strawberry sorbet	

1. Hull the strawberries. Purée half of them with the juice of the lemon and then strain through a *chinois* (fine sieve).
2. Break up the meringues roughly.
3. In clear serving glasses, place a layer of strawberries, a layer of the strained fruit purée, a bit of Chantilly cream, some crushed meringue, and a scoop of sorbet. Finish with another layer of strawberries, purée, and cream.

The basic ingredients of a *vacherin* are always the same: meringues, Chantilly, sorbet. It's just the additions that vary:
• chestnut purée, candied chestnut, ice cream
• roasted peach, apricot coulis, sorbet
• pineapple, coconut milk with rum, sorbet

clafoutis

CLAFOUTIS
FOR 6 - PREPARATION TIME: 10 MINUTES
COOKING TIME: 20 MINUTES

Black cherries (or other fruit)	1 pound 2 ounces
All-purpose flour	1 cup
Eggs	2
Milk	1 cup
Sugar	½ cup
Butter	

1. Put the flour in a bowl and make a hollow in the middle. Mix in the eggs one by one, not allowing the mixture to become lumpy.
2. Add half the sugar, then the milk: the batter should have a pouring consistency.
3. Butter a baking dish and arrange the cherries in it. Pour in the batter and bake in a preheated 350°F oven for 20 minutes.
4. Remove from the oven and immediately dust with the remaining sugar. Serve at room temperature.

gâteau à l'orange

ORANGE SEMOLINA CAKE
FOR 6 - PREPARATION TIME: 20 MINUTES
COOKING TIME: 30 MINUTES

Eggs...4
Oranges..3
Butter..1 cup
Medium-grain semolina.................................¾ cup
All-purpose flour ....1¼ cups
Baking powder ....1½ teaspoons
Sugar ....1⅔ cups

1. Beat the 4 eggs with 1 cup of sugar. Melt the butter in a cake pan and use some of the melted butter to grease the side of the pan.
2. Mix the melted butter into the egg mixture. Then mix in the flour and the semolina, then the baking powder. Finally, mix in the zest and juice of one orange.
3. Pour the batter into the cake pan and then place the pan in the oven (very important to follow this order, or you end up with a puddle at the bottom of the oven and an empty pan!). Bake in a preheated 350°F oven for about 30 minutes.
4. Meanwhile, make a syrup with the remaining sugar along with the zest and juice of the two remaining oranges.
5. Remove the cake from the oven, unmold it immediately and carefully moisten the cake with the syrup. Wait a while before eating: it is better cold.

gâteau de Savoie

SAVOY CAKE (BLOW-AWAY SPONGE)
FOR 6 - PREPARATION TIME: 15 MINUTES
COOKING TIME: 40 MINUTES

Eggs...6
Superfine sugar...1 cup
Vanilla .... 1 teaspoon
All-purpose flour ....⅔ cup
Cornstarch...⅔ cup

1. Separate the egg whites from the yolks. Beat the yolks with the sugar until the mixture is pale and thick. Add the vanilla, flour, and cornstarch.
2. Beat the egg whites into stiff peaks and fold them gently into the rest of the mixture using a spatula. Pour into a nonstick pan and bake at 300°F for 40 minutes.
3. You can use your imagination with this cake: slice it in two, fill it with jam, soak it in rum, or add vanilla cream.

baba au rhum

RUM BABA
FOR 6 - PREPARATION TIME: 20 MINUTES
COOKING TIME: 30 MINUTES + 1 HOUR RESTING TIME

All-purpose flour ....1 cup + extra for the molds
Butter..............................¼ cup + extra for the molds
Honey ....1 tablespoon
Raisins ....½ cup
Rum ....⅓ to ½ cup
Yeast ....¼ ounce
Milk ....⅔ cup
Eggs...3

SYRUP

Orange juice ....¾ cup
Sugar .... 1 cup
Rum .... ⅓ to ½ cup + the rum used for the raisins

1. Heat the rum and soak the raisins in it to plump them up.
2. Mix the yeast and milk.
3. To prepare the dough, whisk the eggs with the honey; then combine with the sifted flour, melted butter, and yeast mixture. Add the soaked and drained raisins, but reserve the rum.
4. Butter and flour your 6 baba molds and fill two-thirds of each with the baba dough. Allow the dough to rise for an hour at room temperature.
5. Bake in a preheated 350°F oven for about 30 minutes. Unmold immediately.
6. Make the syrup by bringing all the ingredients to the boil with 1¾ cups of water. Soak the babas in this syrup and serve with Chantilly cream (see page 456).

kouign-amann

BRETON BUTTER CAKE
FOR 6 - - PREPARATION TIME: 15 MINUTES
COOKING TIME: 40 MINUTES

All-purpose flour	2⅔ cups
Superfine sugar	½ cup
Soft brown sugar	⅔ cup
Yeast	¼ ounce
Salted butter	1 cup
Egg yolks	4
Rum	2 tablespoons

1. Mix together the flour, sugars, and yeast. Grate the butter (just out of the refrigerator), add to the mixture, along with three of the egg yolks, and knead together. The dough will be quite crumbly.

2. Place a sheet of parchment paper in a tart pan that is about 8 inches in diameter and spread the dough over its base. Beat the remaining egg yolk and brush it on the dough. Ridge the dough surface using a fork.

3. Bake in a preheated 400°F oven for about 25 minutes; then lower the temperature to 350°F and continue cooking for 15 minutes. Allow the cake to cool in the oven with the door open.

4. When the cake is lukewarm, wrap it in foil. This cake is better when it is not so fresh—the day after, or the day after that.

Michou

I had been entrusted with a mission: discover Michou's recipe for *kouign-amann* (Breton butter cake). So that's how I came to immerse myself in the mystical and mysterious world of the Breton people. The fear and dread of a chance meeting with a few *korrigans* or *farfadets* (folkloric creatures) recently escaped from the cliffs of Ushant Island was increasingly palpable. How can you tame a land inspired by its steep coastline with these sheer drops and high cliffs, whipped by roiling waves?

How can you tame a land covered with stones standing or supine, pointed or rounded, and crossed by dense forests where the breath of a lurking *Poulpiquet* (an especially ugly *korrigan)* freezes your blood as never before? I had to resist all of these forces to accomplish my mission; I had to ignore the irresistible call of a few malevolent sirens. I had to find the good fairy who could nurture my hope of holding in these trembling hands the magic charm of all desserts. But where?

"Stéphane, are you asleep? Maybe you had a little too much *chouchen* (Breton mead). The *kouign-amann* is ready. Would you like a piece?"

LEFT
cake classique
(light fruit
cake)

RIGHT
semolina cake

446

cake classique

LIGHT FRUIT CAKE
FOR 1 CAKE - PREPARATION TIME: 20 MINUTES
COOKING TIME: 50 MINUTES

Eggs	3
All-purpose flour	1½ cups
Butter	⅔ cup
Superfine sugar	⅔ cup
Confectioners' sugar	½ cup
Baking powder	1½ teaspoons
Rum	2½ tablespoons
Whole candied fruits	7 ounces
Raisins	¾ cup

1. Plump up the raisins in a mixture of rum and hot water.
2. Whisk the eggs with the superfine sugar until the mixture becomes pale and thick. Add the softened butter, sifted flour, and baking powder.
3. Cut the fruit into a large dice, combine with confectioners' sugar (to prevent them from sticking together), and add to the macerated raisin mixture.
4. Butter and flour a pound-cake pan, pour in the mixture, and bake in a preheated 350°F oven for 20 minutes. Lower the oven temperature to 235°F and bake the cake for an additional 30 minutes. Check with a knife to see if it's cooked: the blade will come out clean.

gâteau de semoule

SEMOLINA CAKE
FOR 6 - PREPARATION TIME: 20 MINUTES
COOKING TIME: 40 MINUTES

Medium-grain semolina	2½ cups
Butter	2½ tablespoons
Milk	2 cups
Heavy cream	2 cups
Eggs	4
Sugar	⅔ cup
Raisins	¾ cup
Cointreau	2½ tablespoons
Orange	1

1. Heat the milk with the cream and butter. Mix in the raisins and sugar, and then the semolina in a stream. Cook gently for 20 minutes. Then add the zest of an orange, Cointreau, and the eggs.
2. Coat a nonstick baking pan with butter and superfine sugar. Pour in the cake mixture and cook in a water bath in a preheated 350°F oven for 20 minutes.
3. Allow the cake to rest before unmolding.

quatre-quarts

FRENCH POUND CAKE
FOR 1 CAKE - PREPARATION TIME: 10 MINUTES
COOKING TIME: 45 MINUTES

All-purpose flour	1⅔ cups
Sugar	1 cup
Butter	¾ cup
Eggs	4
Baking powder	2½ teaspoons

1. Whisk the eggs with the sugar until the mixture is pale and thick. Add the softened butter, sifted flour, and baking powder.
2. Bake in a preheated 315°F oven for 45 minutes. This cake is an ideal basic recipe that can be personalized by adding apples, pears, banana, fruit conserves, jam, almonds, hazelnuts…

gâteau roulé

SWISS ROLL
FOR 1 ROLL - PREPARATION TIME: 15 MINUTES
COOKING TIME: 10 MINUTES

All-purpose flour	1 cup
Sugar	1 cup
Vanilla	1 teaspoon
Eggs	4
Baking powder	2½ teaspoons
Sugar for dusting	

1. Separate the egg whites from the yolks. Whisk the yolks with the vanilla and ⅔ cup of the sugar until the mixture becomes pale and thick.
2. Beat the egg whites into stiff peaks.
3. Sift the flour, add baking powder, and mix with the egg yolks. Gently incorporate the beaten egg whites.
4. Spread the cake mixture onto a baking sheet lined with parchment paper. Bake in a preheated 350°F oven for 10 minutes. Turn the cake out onto a clean damp cloth sprinkled with ½ cup sugar. Fill with good things and roll up at once.

NUTELLA AND COOKIES
Mix 1 cup warmed Nutella with 1¼ cups crushed Dutch (*speculaas*) cookies and ½ cup Chantilly cream.

CHESTNUTS
Mix 1 cup sweetened chestnut purée with ½ cup Chantilly cream and 3½ ounces *marron glacé* (candied chestnuts).

BLACK CHERRY AND CHOCOLATE
Combine 3½ ounces dark chocolate, 2 tablespoons melted butter, and ½ cup Heavy cream. Then mix with ⅓ cup black cherry jam.

SUGARED ALMOND AND PRALINE
Make a caramel with ⅔ cup sugar. Add ⅔ cup almonds and let it harden on a piece of oiled parchment paper. Chop finely and mix with 7 ounces Paris-Brest filling (see page 430).

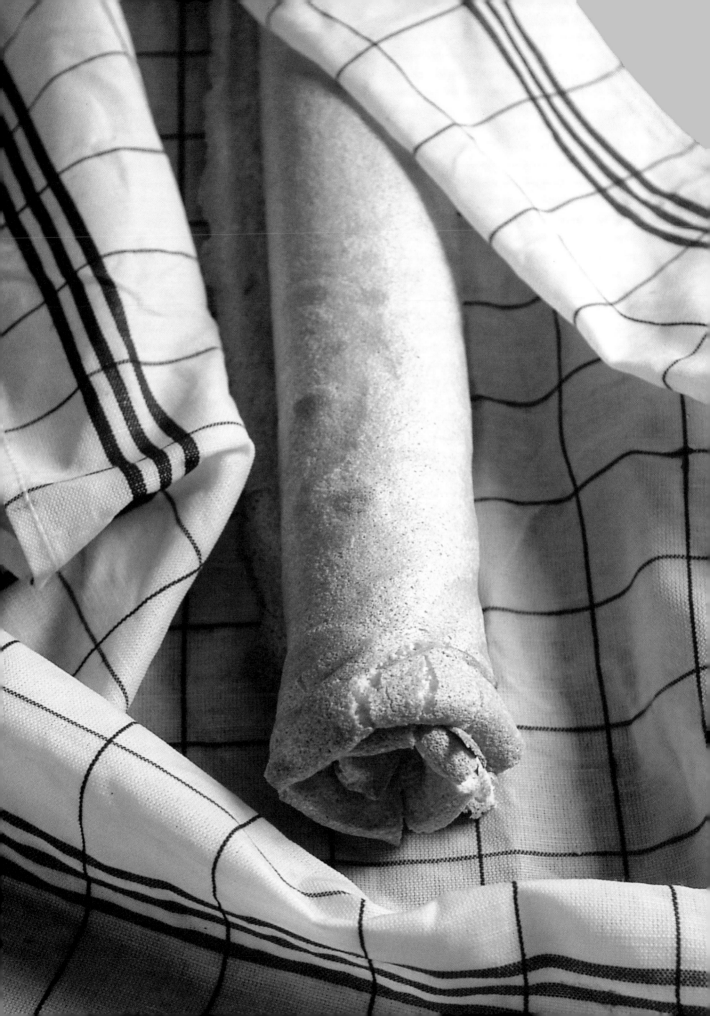

Gérald

It's a mill that first greets you between Biarritz and Arbonne, its stones working to grind the very best grains. Then comes a small shop that releases an aroma to make even the most sinus-congested customer's mouth water. And there they are on the racks, in different sizes, ridged with fork patterns, glazed golden with egg yolk, stuffed with cream or black cherry jam: the famous *gâteaux basques,* traditional basque cakes, within our reach!

A piece of this one, another of that one. The gluttony feeds on itself, intensifies, becomes huge; we are full but never sated. Gérald finally shows us the heart of the mill, the hotbed of creation. Gluttony makes you say such things!

Mountains of baking pans are on display, knocked about by an already well-spent life, their enamel seasoned by the heat of the oven. Hands stir around the cake dough; the buttered pans are filled. There ensues a constant back-and-forth between the oven and the racks, punctuated by a bell chiming the end of the baking. The cakes are done, the oven is still warm—it's Sunday.

gâteau basque

TRADITIONAL BASQUE CAKE
FOR 6 - PREPARATION TIME: 20 MINUTES
COOKING TIME: 30 MINUTES

Eggs..3
Sugar ....¾ cup
All-purpose flour ....2½ cups
Butter...¾ cup
Baking powder ....2½ teaspoons
Light rum...2½ tablespoons
Egg yolks...2
Pastry cream (see page 256)...................................9 ounces
(or black cherry jam)

1. Whisk the eggs along with the sugar until the mixture is pale and thick. Sift the flour and add the baking powder, beaten eggs, rum, and softened butter. Mix to obtain a pliable dough and allow the dough to rest.

2. Divide the dough into two sections and roll out two identical rounds. Spread the pastry cream (which you can flavor with rum) or the black cherry jam on one of them. Cover with the second round and seal the edges by pressing down firmly.

3. Scratch a lattice pattern on top with a fork. Brush with the beaten egg yolks.

4. Bake in a preheated 350°F oven for 30 minutes.

FRUIT COMPOTES

pommes à la cannelle

APPLE AND CINNAMON

Granny Smith apples	8
Light brown sugar	½ cup
Dry hard cider	5 fluid ounces
Ground cinnamon	1 tablespoon
Calvados (apple brandy)	1 tablespoon

1. Peel the apples, cut them in quarters, and remove the cores.
2. In a large heavy-based saucepan, bring the cider to a boil. Add the cinnamon, apples, and sugar, and stew over a gentle heat.
3. Purée and add the Calvados. Serve very cold.

bananes au sirop d'érable

BANANA AND MAPLE SYRUP

Bananas	6
Lemons	2
Orange	1
Maple syrup	⅓ cup

1. Peel the bananas and slice them into rounds.
2. Make the maple syrup into a caramel, add the banana slices and cook for 10 minutes.
3. Stir in juice from the orange and lemons; then purée and serve very cold.

abricots

APRICOT

Fresh apricots	2 pounds 4 ounces
Amaretto liqueur	3½ fluid ounces
Sugar	1 cup
Vanilla pod	1

1. Remove the pits from the apricots. Split the vanilla pod in two and sprinkle the vanilla seeds on the apricots.
2. Cook them gently with the amaretto and sugar. Stew, purée, and serve very cold.

poires et fruits rouges

PEAR AND BERRY

Pears	6
Raspberries	1 pint
Strawberries	1 pint
Bueberries	1 pint
Sugar	⅔ cup
Lemon	1

1. Peel and core the pears, and cut them into quarters.
2. Cook them in a saucepan with a little water; then add the berries, sugar, and juice from the lemon. Stew, purée, and serve chilled.

LES CRÈMES
THE CREAMS

crème anglaise

"ENGLISH CREAM"
PREPARATION TIME: 10 MINUTES

Milk	4 cups
Egg yolks	8
Sugar	1 cup
Vanilla bean	1

1. In a metal bowl, whisk the sugar and egg yolks until the mixture turns pale and thick.
2. Bring the milk to a boil with the split vanilla bean. Pour the milk gradually into the egg mixture while continuing to whisk.
3. Pour the mixture into a clean saucepan and cook very gently on the edge of the heat, stirring constantly. The temperature of the custard mustn't rise above 175°F or the yolks will curdle. The custard is cooked when it coats the back of a spoon.
4. Cool down the custard quickly. Remove the vanilla bean.

Your choice of variations, to be added to the scalded milk:
    2 spoonfuls of instant coffee granules
    2 spoonfuls of cocoa powder
    1 spoonful of pistachio nut paste
    2 tablespoons of caramel

crème pâtissière

PASTRY CREAM
PREPARATION TIME: 15 MINUTES

Milk	4 cups
Eggs	2
Egg yolks	4
Sugar	1 cup
All-purpose flour	⅔ cup
Butter	⅓ cup

1. Whisk the whole eggs, egg yolks, and sugar until the mixture becomes pale and thick. Add the sifted flour and mix well.
2. Bring the milk to a boil with the butter and add to the egg mixture.
3. Pour into a heavy-based saucepan and cook gently over low heat for 10 minutes. Then dust with sugar and chill.

Your choice of variations to add during the cooking process:
    zest and juice of an orange or lemon
    1 spoonful of green tea to infuse with the scalded milk

crème au beurre

BUTTER CREAM

Egg yolks	6
Sugar	1 cup
Butter	1 cup

1. Whisk the egg yolks and sugar together until the mixture becomes pale and thick.
2. Add the softened butter, mix together, and add the flavor of your choice: cocoa powder, coffee, rum, lemon, orange…

crème Chantilly

CHANTILLY CREAM

Heavy cream	2 cups
Sugar	1 cup

1. Whip the cream in a chilled bowl until it develops an almost buttery consistency.
2. Gently incorporate the sugar with a rubber spatula. It is the little crunch of sugar that gives a Chantilly cream its charm.

crème caramel

BAKED CUSTARD WITH CARAMEL SAUCE
FOR SEVERAL SMALL ONES, A FEW MEDIUM-SIZED ONES,
OR ONE VERY LARGE ONE
PREPARATION TIME: 10 MINUTES
COOKING TIME: ABOUT 35 MINUTES

Milk	4 cups
Eggs	5
Egg yolks	2
Vanilla bean	1
Sugar	⅔ cup

FOR THE CARAMEL

Sugar	1 cup
Lemon	½

1. Prepare a pale caramel with the sugar and 2½ tablespoons water. Stop the cooking process by adding the juice of half a lemon. Turn off the heat. Pour a thin layer of the caramel into the ramekins.
2. Whisk the eggs and egg yolks together with the sugar until the mixture becomes pale and thick.
3. Bring the milk to the boil with ⅔ cup split vanilla bean. Pour the milk over the egg mixture and whisk. Remove the vanilla bean. Pour into the ramekins and bake in a water bath in a preheated 400°F oven for about 30 minutes; the *crème* is cooked when the tip of a knife comes out clean.
4. Allow to cool before unmolding.

crème caramel (baked custard with caramel sauce)

CRÈME CARAMEL

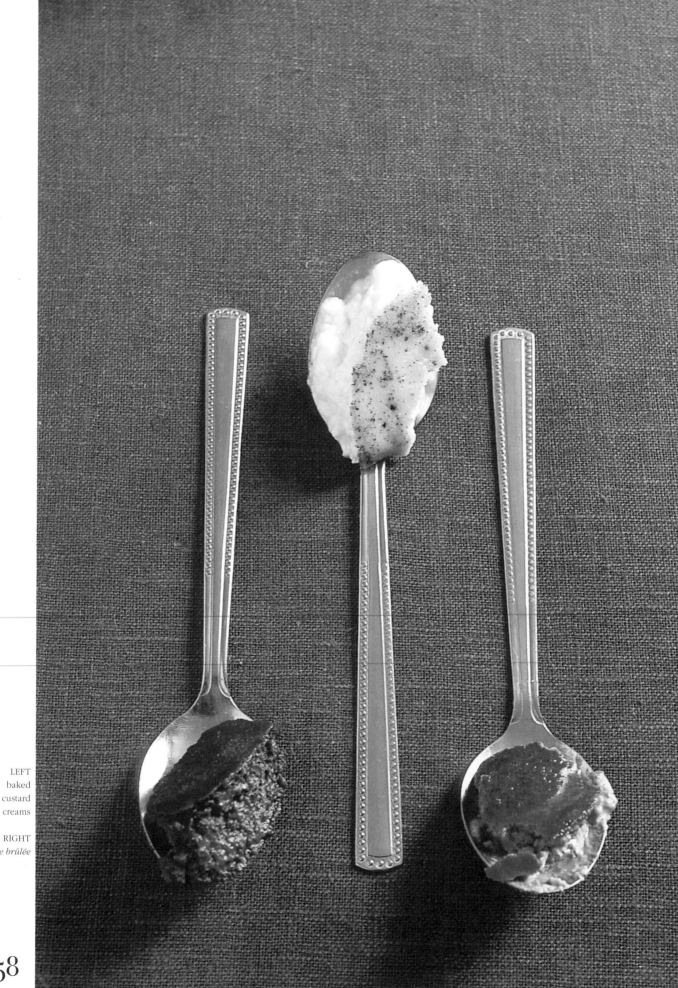

LEFT
baked
custard
creams

RIGHT
crème brûlée

petits pots de crème

BAKED CUSTARD CREAMS
FOR 6 *PETITS POTS* (SMALL RAMEKINS)
PREPARATION TIME: 15 MINUTES - COOKING TIME: 30 MINUTES

CHOCOLATE

Dark chocolate	9 ounces
Heavy cream	1¼ cups
Milk	1¼ cups
Egg yolks	4
Sugar	⅓ cup

1. Whisk the egg yolks and sugar until pale and thick.
2. Heat the milk with the cream. Pour the scalded liquid over the chocolate and mix until it melts; then add the egg yolk mixture.
3. Pour the mixture into ramekins and cook in a water bath in a preheated 350°F oven for 20 minutes.

VANILLA

Cream	2 cups
Milk	2 cups
Eggs	6
Sugar	⅔ cup
Vanilla bean	1

1. Whisk the eggs along with the sugar until pale and thick.
2. Heat the milk with the cream, adding the split vanilla bean.
3. Off the heat, pour the scalded liquid into the egg mixture. Remove the vanilla bean. Pour into ramekins and cook in a water bath in a preheated 350°F oven for 20 minutes.

COFFEE

Milk	3¼ cups
Espresso coffees	3
Rum	2½ tablespoons
Eggs	6
Sugar	1 cup

1. Whisk the eggs with the sugar until pale and thick.
2. Heat the milk with the coffee and rum.
3. Off the heat, pour the scalded liquid into the egg mixture.
4. Pour into ramekins and cook in a water bath in a preheated 350°F oven for 20 minutes.

crème brûlée

CRÈME BRÛLÉE
FOR 8 CRÈME BRÛLÉES
PREPARATION TIME: 10 MINUTES - COOKING TIME: 30 MINUTES

Heavy cream	4 cups
Sugar	⅔ cup
Egg yolks	8
Vanilla bean	1
Light brown sugar	½ cup

1. Whisk together the egg yolks and sugar until pale and thick.
2. Heat the cream and add the split vanilla bean.
3. Off the heat, combine the cream and egg yolk mixture; then pour into the ramekins. Discard the vanilla bean.
4. Cook in a water bath in a preheated 315°F oven for 30 minutes; then allow to cool.
5. Sprinkle the sugar on top. Then caramelize under a hot broiler or using a kitchen blowtorch. Serve immediately.

riz au lait

RICE PUDDING
FOR 6 - PREPARATION TIME: 15 MINUTES
COOKING TIME: 25 MINUTES + 20 MINUTES RESTING TIME

Short-grain rice	1⅓ cups
Milk	4 cups
Sugar	1½ cups
Vanilla bean	1
Chantilly cream (see page 456)	7 ounces
Salted butter	2½ tablespoons
Heavy cream	¾ cup
Almond extract	a few drops

1. Heat the milk with 1 cup of the sugar and the split vanilla pod. Add the rice and almond extract and cook gently for 20 minutes. Leave it to cool and rest for 20 minutes.
2. Chill and mix with a plain Chantilly cream.
3. Prepare a caramel with the remaining sugar and a little water. Stir in the butter and cream.
4. Serve the rice pudding on the caramel sauce.

crêpes

FOR 6 - PREPARATION TIME: 10 MINUTES
COOKING TIME

Eggs..4
All-purpose flour ....1⅔ cups
Milk .... 1 cup
Sugar...1/4 cup
Butter....................................2½ tablespoons

1. Break the eggs into the sifted flour and mix well to get rid
of lumps. Add the milk, sugar, and melted butter. Oil the
frying pan and flip, flip, flip—until exhausted.
2. Serve with jam, sugar, lemon, chocolate, cream, fruit
purée, fresh fruits, syrup, alcohol, and more if you prefer.

Georges

HE HAS THE SPARKLING APPLE...

The soil makes the tree, the tree produces the apple, the worm eats the apple, the apple rots, falls to the ground, and goes back to the soil.

So I meet someone much more cunning who, at a given moment, picks the apple and turns it into cider: a Breton who, one fine day, decided to grow varieties that tended to be forgotten—varieties that, through lack of yield, had forsaken our fields. Georges thinks in a different way: he thinks quality, he thinks of respecting nature, he thinks good.

After you've eaten the apples, now you can drink them!

LEFT
black and
white mousse

RIGHT
flourless
chocolate cake

464

mousse blanc et noir

BLACK AND WHITE MOUSSE
FOR 6 - PREPARATION TIME: 20 MINUTES

WHITE MOUSSE

White chocolate	7 ounces
Eggs	3
Sugar	¼ cup
Chantilly cream (see page 456)	½ portion

1. Beat the eggs with the sugar until very pale and thick.
2. Melt the chocolate in a double-boiler. Cool until lukewarm and mix with the egg mixture.
3. Mix with the Chantilly cream and serve immediately.

BLACK MOUSSE

Dark chocolate	7 ounces
Butter	⅓ cup
Eggs	4
Sugar	2 tablespoons

1. Melt the chcolate in a double-boiler with the butter.
2. Beat the egg whites into stiff peaks, and beat in the sugar. Blend the egg yolks and chocolate.
3. Incorporate the beaten egg whites using a rubber spatula and serve immediately.

fondant au chocolat

FLOURLESS CHOCOLATE CAKE
FOR 6 - PREPARATION TIME: 20 MINUTES
COOKING TIME: 15–30 MINUTES

Chocolate	10 ounces
Butter	¾ cup
Eggs	5
Sugar	¾ cup
Ground almonds	¾ cup
Cornstarch	3 tablespoons

1. Melt the chocolate and the butter in a double-boiler. Stir in the ground almonds.
2. Whisk the egg yolks and sugar until pale and thick and add to the chocolate mixture.
3. Beat the egg whites into peaks and gently incorporate them into the chocolate mixture using a rubber spatula.
4. Coat a baking pan with butter and cornstarch. Pour the mixture into the pan and bake in a preheated 350°F oven for 15–30 minutes, until it reaches the desired consistency.
5. Chill and then unmold.

opéra

LAYERED CAKE
FOR 6 - PREPARATION TIME: 30 MINUTES
COOKING TIME: 20 MINUTES

BISCUIT

Eggs	5
Egg whites	5
Sugar	¾ cup
Ground almonds	1¾ cups
All-purpose flour	½ cup

1. Beat the 5 whole eggs with the sugar until the mixture is pale and thick. Incorporate the flour and ground almonds.
2. Beat the egg whites into peaks and gently fold them into the egg and almond mixture using a rubber spatula.
3. Spread the mixture over a baking sheet lined with parchment paper and bake in a preheated 350°F oven for about 10 minutes. Allow to cool.

GANACHE

Chocolate	9 ounces
Heavy cream	⅔ cup
Milk	⅓ to ½ cup

Melt the chocolate in a double-boiler; then add the milk and cream, and mix well.

COFFEE CREAM

Sugar	1 cup
Butter	1⅓ cups
Coffee extract	a few drops
Egg yolks	2

1. Cook the sugar to the "soft ball" stage: dip a fork into the sugar, then into some cold water; and when the sugar on the fork forms a soft ball, stop the cooking process.
2. Whisk the yolks until pale and thick; then gently incorporate the sugar syrup.
3. Allow to cool, then add the softened butter and the coffee extract.

COUVERTURE (TOPPING)

Chocolate	9 ounces
Heavy cream	¾ cup
Butter	1½ tablespoons

1. To make the *couverture* (topping), melt the chocolate in a double-boiler with the butter, and add the cream.
2. Cut the biscuit into three identical rectangles.
3. Assemble the cakes by layers, alternating biscuit, coffee cream, biscuit, ganache, biscuit, *couverture.*
4. Chill the cake before serving.

marquise au chocolat

CHOCOLATE MOUSSE CAKE
FOR 6 - REFRIGERATION TIME: 24 HOURS
COOKING TIME: 10 MINUTES

Savoiardi (ladyfingers)	24
Chocolate	14 ounces
Butter	⅓ cup
Egg yolks	4
Confectioners' sugar	½ cup
Chantilly cream (see page 456)	2 cups

1. Melt the chocolate with the butter in a double-boiler. Add the egg yolks and confectioners' sugar, allow to cool, and then incorporate the Chantilly cream.
2. Dip the ladyfingers in sugar syrup (made from equal parts sugar and water—see page 466, layered cake recipe) to which you can add an alcohol flavoring if you like (cognac, whiskey).
3. Line a terrine with parchment paper. Cover with the ladyfingers and fill with the chocolate mousse mixture.
4. Seal the terrine with plastic wrap and chill for 24 hours before eating.

COGNAC AND ARMAGNAC

Cognac, the alcohol of kings, is produced within a circumscribed area in the departments of Charente and Charente-Maritime. It results from the double distillation of fermented grape must, the unfermented grapes. Many grape varieties can be used to distil cognac—for example, Ugni Blanc, Folle Blanche, Colombard, Sémillon. Some cognacs are made exclusively from a single grape variety, which is often indicated on the label.

SIX APPELLATION REGIONS AROUND COGNAC

Grande Champagne, the premier cognac made from the best *eaux-de-vie* (fruit spirits)
Petite Champagne, made from excellent *eaux-de-vie*
Borderies, *eaux-de-vie* that are aged more quickly
Fins Bois, the largest cognac production area
Bons Bois, which is differentiated by its distinctive soil qualities
Bois ordinaires, area of production closest to the sea.

The age of a cognac is difficult to pinpoint; it corresponds to the age of the youngest *eau-de-vie* that goes into its composition. There are, however, a few indicators to act as a guide:

- ★★★ or VS—Very Special: the youngest *eau-de-vie* in its composition is at least two years old.
- VSOP or VO—Very Superior Old Pale or Very Old: the youngest *eau-de-vie* in its composition is at least four years old.
- XO Reserve or Napoleon—Extra Old: the youngest *eau-de-vie* in its composition is at least six years old.

The names of the vintages are English, as the export market to the United States represents 40 percent of cognac production.

Armagnac, for its part, is produced within an area that includes the departments of Gers, Landes, and Lot-et-Garonne. The varieties from which Armagnac is distilled are Ugni Blanc, Baco Blanc, Colombard, and Folle Blanche.

THREE APPELLATION REGIONS AROUND ARMAGNAC

Bas Armagnac, for *eaux-de-vie* of great quality and finesse, the most well regarded of which is *Grand bas Armagnac*
Armagnac-Ténarèze, more full-bodied
Haut Armagnac.

Its vinification and method of aging are almost identical to those of cognac, and the age of an Armagnac is calculated in the same way.

A FEW COCKTAILS

AMARETTO
1 tablespoon cognac
1 tablespoon Amaretto
¼ cup orange juice, grenadine

BRANDY
2 tablespoons cognac
1 tablespoon Cointreau
1 dash Angostura bitters

BIEN D'CHÉNOUS
(JUST LIKE AT HOME)
1½ tablespoons cognac
juice of half a lemon
⅓ to ½ cup Champagne, grenadine

PORT FLIP
1 tablespoon cognac
2 tablespoons red port
1 egg yolk, 1 teaspoon sugar

CORPSE REVIVER
1 tablespoon Armagnac
1 tablespoon Martini (vermouth)
1 tablespoon Calvados (apple brandy)

MARABOUT
1½ tablespoons Armagnac
1 tablespoon Malibu
⅓ to ½ cup pineapple juice

THE VALLOIS
2 tablespoons Armagnac
2 teaspoons *crème de cerise*
lemonade

MASCARA
1 tablespoon cognac
2 teaspoons pear brandy
1 tablespoon *crème de mûre*
Champagne

UN P'TIT CIGARE ?
A LITTLE CIGAR?

Mini Panatela
1/2-inch diameter
4 1/2 to 5 inches long

Demi-tasse
1/2 to 5/8-inch diameter
4 1/2 to 5 inches long

Panatela
1/2 to 5/8-inch diameter
over 5 inches long

Petit Corona
5/8-inch diameter
4 to 4 1/2 inches long

Corona
5/8-inch diameter
4 1/2 to 5 1/2 inches long

Corona Grande
5/8-inch diameter
over 6 inches long

Churchill
3/4-inch diameter
over 5 inches long

Robusto
over 3/4-inch diameter
4 1/2 to 5 inches long

Double Corona
over 3/4-inch diameter
over 5 inches long

APPENDIXES:
INDEXES/GLOSSARY

INDEX OF RECIPES

INDEX BY INGREDIENTS

GLOSSARY

A.O.C. (appellation d'origine contrôlée)
A French certification granted to agricultural products based on a number of criteria, the most crucial being geographical origin.

andouillettes Offal-based chitterling sausages, a regional French specialty (especially from Lyon).

bavette Also known as flank steak, a cheap cut of beef that can be cooked quickly like a minute steak.

blanquette A "white" stew; it is often finished by adding cream and sometimes egg yolks to the stew.

bouchon A type of bistro in Lyon.

boudin noir Blood sausage.

boudiou! A southern French version of *bon dieu!*, or "Good God!"

Bresse chicken A specially bred and reared chicken from Bresse in the Rhône-Alpes region of France, protected by an A.O.C. classification.

cagouilles Brown snails (*Helix aspersa*), also known as the garden snail or European brown snails.

calvados An apple brandy from the Normandy region.

cannelés A specialty of Bordeaux, sweet miniature batter pudding, with a base similar to a Yorkshire pudding.

cervelas (de Lyon) A pork sausage from Lyon, that often contains pistachios and truffles.

champignon de Paris A standard cultivated mushroom.

chapon Known as capon in English, a male chicken castrated and raised to encourage higher levels of fat.

charcuterie Referring to both the product and place it is sold and produced, it includes sausages, cured meats, pâtes, quenelles, and condiments sold in a type of delicatessen.

chiffonade A technique for preparing long, thin ribbons of herbs. The herbs are stacked, rolled tightly, then cut crosswise to produce long strips.

chinois A fine, conical sieve.

chouchen Breton mead.

clafoutis Fruit, often cherries, baked in a sweet, light batter.

coco de Paimpol A white bean from Brittany.

comté cheese A cow's-milk cheese unique to the French Comte region. Similar to a *Gruyère* cheese, it's often used in fondue. *Vieux* (old) *comté* cheese is aged for at least six months.

confit (duck) Duck *confit* is prepared by slow-cooking the duck and then preserving it in its own fat.

cornichons Small sour gherkins.

Crème de cassis Black-currant liqueur.

croûton Dry melba toasts.

escargots de Bourgogne Burgundy snails (*Helix pomatia*) that are classic *escargot* snails with the hard helix shell.

fines herbes Fines herbes, as they are commonly known in English as well, a collective term for parsley, chives, tarragon, and chervil.

fondant A glacé icing.

fromage blanc Known also as *fromage frais*, a fresh smooth cow's milk cheese known as quark in English.

herbes de Provence A Provençal herb mix that may contain thyme, marjoram, rosemary, oregano, and lavender.

jambon cru Literally "raw ham," this is the French equivalent of the Italian air-dried *prosciutto*.

jambon de Bayonne Ham from the Bayonne region.

magret Duck breast.

manchons The upper part of duck wings.

marc Refers to both the grape skins in winemaking and a pomace brandy made from these skins.

Mère Mère (mothers) A group of women in Lyon, originally cooks for the Lyon aristocracy, who started their own restaurants that became institutions of Lyon cuisine.

mignardises Miniature treats, like petits fours.

mistelle Grape juice in which fermentation has been stopped by the addition of alcohol. It is very sweet and used mainly as a base for aperitifs, particularly vermouth.

Morteau A strongly flavored, plump smoked sausage made from the Comtois pig of the mountainous Jura region.

pain d'épice A "spice bread," similar to gingerbread or honey cake, flavored with honey and various spices.

piment d'Espelette Basque chili powder or hot paprika.

quatre-épices A French spice mix, meaning "four spices," that usually consists of ground pepper (white, black, or both), cloves, nutmeg, and ginger or cinnamon.

quenelle A speciality of Lyon; a smooth oval-shaped dumpling (like fish balls in Asian cooking) made from fish or chicken and usually poached.

sabodet A rustic pig's-head sausage that is a speciality of the Lyon region.

salmi A rich, aromatic stew made with game or duck. The sauce may also be served with pasta.

sauce gribiche A sauce traditionally made with oil, vinegar, mustard, herbs, capers, cornichons, and eggs; the eggs are cooked, not raw.

saucisson de Lyon A specialty sausage of Lyon: a traditionally air-dried pork sausage, flavored with garlic and spices.

savora sauce A sauce made from 11 herbs, spices, mustard, and honey and served with cold meats, fish, and vegetables.

terroir A wine term also used to refer to factors (properties of soil, pasture, weather—the local ecological system) affecting food production associated with a specific geographic region.

Vieille Prune A brand of plum brandy, literally "Old Plum."

vin jaune A wine matured in a barrel under a film of yeast, known as the *voile* (veil).

vitelotte potatoes Purple dark-skinned potatoes having a sweet taste and suitable for frying and mashing.

VOLAILLES
POULTRY

GIBIER À GOGO
GAME A GO GO

POISSONS, COQUILLAGES
ET CRUSTACÉS
FISH, SHELLFISH AND CRUSTACEANS